Understanding Child Psychology

Christine Brain and Penny Mukherji

Published in 2005 by:
Nelson Thornes Ltd
Delta Place
27 Bath Road
CHELTENHAM
GL53 7TH
United Kingdom

05 06 07 08 09 / 10 9 8 7 6 5 4 3 2 1

A catalogue record for this book is available from the British Library

ISBN 0 7487 9084 5

Illustrations by Angela Lumley
Page make-up by Northern Phototypesetting Co. Ltd, Bolton
Printed in Great Britain by Scotprint

Contents

Acknowledgements

We would like to thank everyone at Nelson Thornes who has been involved in the publication of this book.

To Alex, Jenny, Doug and Sarah, my family support team and my mate, the unique Norm, who lets me be me - thank you.

Christine

The publishers are indebted to the following for permission to reproduce copyright material:

Page 17: Father and child – Photodisc 79 (NT); page 21: Twins – Corel 638 (NT); page 27: Mother and baby – Digital Vision PB (NT); page 31: Toddler eating cereal (CSM002566 RM) © copyright Ronnie Kaufman/CORBIS; page 35: Infant forming an attachment bond with a cloth mother surrogate – Harlow Primate Laboratory, University of Wisconsin, Madison USA; page 41: Mother, father and baby – Digital Vision PB (NT); page 42: Cheerful father carrying his kids (AXR002668 RM) © copyright Simon Marcus/CORBIS; page 45: Children's school at a Cambodian Orphanage (U2050830 RM) © copyright Bettman/CORBIS; page 65: Circus animal performing – Corel 640 (NT); page 79: Baby portrait (ADPC9C) © copyright Picture Partners/Alamy; page 98: Baby imitating gestures – Photodisc 79 (NT); page 101: Child communicating with parent using sign language, signing the word 'eat' (AGG8A5) © copyright Christina Kennedy/Alamy; page 132: Child caring for teddy – Corel 638 (NT); page 168: Image from the film 'Rainman' (RAI014BJ) © copyright United Artists/Kobal Collection

Introduction

THE PURPOSE OF THE BOOK

Understanding Child Psychology is for students of child development and particularly those following courses leading to vocational qualifications in childcare and education. It aims to provide theoretical explanations at a level suitable for those following a foundation degree course in early years – or at least to give a useful background to such studies. It focuses on the following courses:

- NVQ Level 2 in Early Years Care and Education (EYCE);
- CACHE Level 2 Certificate in Child Care and Education;
- Edexcel Level 2 BTEC First Diploma in Early Years;
- NVQ Level 3 in Early Years Care and Education;
- CACHE Level 3 Diploma in Child Care and Education (DCE);
- Edexcel Level 3 BTEC Nationals in Early Years;
- Advanced Diploma in Childcare and Education;
- The Foundation Degree in Early Years.

It presents all relevant aspects of child psychology in clear, accessible language so that the material is both interesting and understandable. Helpful features are included such as:

- introductory paragraphs to set the scene for each chapter;
- case studies for interest and to help illustrate the material;
- sections called 'think about it' to encourage reflection;
- sections called 'try this' to provide activities;
- reminders about 'good practice';
- sections called 'progress check' where questions test understanding;
- definitions of terms and a list of key terms;
- suggestions for 'further reading'.

WHAT IS COVERED?

Understanding Child Psychology covers a wide variety of issues within child psychology, ranging from suggestions about how children learn to the way in which attachments and friendships are formed. Topics include the development of cognitive (thinking) processes, language development, emotional development and factors such as stereotyping and labelling, which affect a child's development.

Development involves behaviour, emotions and thinking. This book focuses on all three and also provides a chapter looking at abnormal development and special needs for psychological development. The diagram below gives a very brief overview of some main topics in child psychology and how *Understanding Child Psychology* is designed to cover those topics.

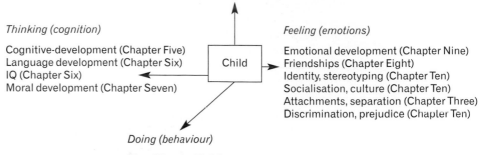

Biological bases and abnormal psychology

Biological bases for infant behaviour (Chapter Two)
Anxiety, dyslexia, managing behaviour, autism… (Chapter Eleven)

Thinking (cognition)

Cognitive-development (Chapter Five)
Language development (Chapter Six)
IQ (Chapter Six)
Moral development (Chapter Seven)

Child

Feeling (emotions)

Emotional development (Chapter Nine)
Friendships (Chapter Eight)
Identity, stereotyping (Chapter Ten)
Socialisation, culture (Chapter Ten)
Attachments, separation (Chapter Three)
Discrimination, prejudice (Chapter Ten)

Doing (behaviour)

Play (Chapter Eight)
Learning (Chapter Four)

What is involved in child psychology?

WHAT IS NOT INCLUDED IN THIS BOOK?

Understanding Child Psychology addresses issues within child psychology that are important in the study of child development when working in the field of childcare and education. The course that you follow will include other subject areas not covered here such as:

- biological processes;
- the development of physical skills;
- sociology;
- child health and safety;
- child education;
- professional knowledge and skills related to early years practice.

Nevertheless, you will find that a good knowledge of child psychology will enhance your understanding of all aspects of childcare and education.

Your course will emphasise the importance of taking a professional approach to everything that you do in your chosen field of work. To be 'professional' implies being competent, skilled and efficient, as well as being appropriately qualified, working responsibly, and conforming to a range of expectations. This is not easy to achieve and everything that you learn should help to guide you in your aim to become a good professional. Courses in childcare and education are vocational and entail learning through practical experience as well as theory. Although this book focuses on theory it also gives suggestions for practical activities for you to undertake in the workplace to help you relate theory to practice.

Linking child psychology with the early years curriculum

The curriculum for children from the age of 3 years until they finish reception in primary schools is called the Foundation Stage curriculum. The Foundation Stage, briefly, aims to:

- enhance the child's personal, social and emotional wellbeing;
- generate positive attitudes and dispositions to learning;
- provide opportunities to learn social skills;
- provide opportunities for development of language and communication skills;
- encourage and enable reading and writing skills;
- encourage and enable mathematical skills;
- encourage and enable knowledge and understanding of the world;

TRY THIS!

Look at a copy of Birth to Three Matters, the government curriculum framework for the under threes. In the same way in which child psychology underpins the aims of the Foundation Stage curriculum is identified here, see if you can identify ways in which knowledge of child psychology is relevant for this age group.

- encourage and enable physical development;
- encourage and enable creative development.

The child psychology topics in this book outline theory that directly or indirectly relates to these areas. For example, psychological influences on personal, social and emotional development and the acquisition of social and communication skills are looked at directly. How children learn is also considered, which will give you an insight into appropriate ways to help very young children acquire the concepts and skills outlined in the Foundation Stage curriculum.

STUDYING CHILD PSYCHOLOGY AND STUDYING CHILD DEVELOPMENT

Examples can help to show what this book does and does not cover. The book looks at the importance of stimulating children but does not really consider how to do this. The focus is on the psychological consequences of the lack of stimulation. Similarly, the importance of the adult as a role model is considered, as this affects children's learning (and their social and emotional development), however the physical layout of a setting and how it might encourage learning is not addressed as this is not directly about the psychological development of the child.

The environmental issues that students are specifically required to study in childcare courses, such as health and care issues, are not directly dealt with in this book.

IS THE TERMINOLOGY NECESSARY?

As you study child psychology you will come across new words and also words that you already know used in a new way. This new terminology can be confusing at first, but as you study psychology more you will realise that the terms are important and can act as a useful form of shorthand when discussing the subject with others. Terms such as 'social learning theory' have a lot of meaning once you have studied them. Consider the following conversation:

You may already know that they were saying that children model (imitate) what they see on television, so a programme with a lot of violence should not be shown until later. However, the two psychologists are saying a lot more than that. Even though the following ideas were not expressed, they would both know that if the murderers were male, boys would be more likely to imitate the behaviour, and that only some children would be likely to copy the behaviour. They would know that if the murderers are caught and punished, that might make the behaviour less likely to be copied, whereas if the violence were praised that would be worse. They would know that the reactions of adults watching with the children would also make a difference, and they would know more about the role of attending to what is happening, reproducing the behaviour, recalling it and having the motivation to copy it. In other words by mentioning social learning theory the first psychologist is signalling to the second one that all this (and more) is understood.

A good knowledge of the correct terminology is important whatever subject you are studying. As you read the text check at the end of each section that you fully understand the terminology used and use these terms in conversations with others and in your writing. The more you use the terminology of child psychology the easier it will become.

Throughout this book, whenever the word 'he' is used it also includes 'she', except where the context indicates that this is not the case.

What is child psychology?

INTRODUCTION

Chapter 1 introduces psychology, and in particular child psychology, mainly by focusing on various approaches to the subject. It looks at what researchers in psychology do, the relative advantages and disadvantages of their methods, and examines ethical issues within research. One section discusses quite complex theoretical issues that set the scene for later chapters, such as how much of what we are comes from our genes and how much from our environment, or whether we should look at ourselves as whole individuals or study ourselves in parts. This chapter contains a lot of background information about psychology itself. You should read it more than once and refer to it as you work through the other chapters because it will become clearer as your knowledge of psychology develops.

WHAT IS PSYCHOLOGY?

The introduction to this book should give you an idea of what psychology is. It is not easy to define but it has been called the science of mind and behaviour. It is the study of mental processes, of anything that leads to mental processes, and of actions that arise from mental processes. As our actions result from our thoughts and from reactions of things around us, both environmental and internal processes are studied under the heading 'psychology'. More specific issues about psychology are outlined below.

DEFINITIONS

Science – involves careful study, using control over all relevant aspects of what is being studied, so that something can reasonably confidently be claimed to cause something else.

Object permanence – it is claimed that very young babies do not know that objects exist once out of sight –in other words they do not have object permanence. Note that there is disagreement about the age at which a baby develops this ability.

Methods

Psychology is the study of mind and behaviour, often, but not always, using scientific methods. **Science** involves careful study, attempting to control all relevant aspects of what is being studied so that something can reasonably confidently be claimed to cause something else. Scientific methods involve looking at specific types of behaviour, or specific attitudes or opinions, and measuring responses in a way that can be repeated to check results. For example, it has been found that very young babies do not follow an object that they are looking at with their eyes once it goes out of sight. However, some studies suggest that, by around the age of 8 months, babies do 'look for' the object once it has been hidden. The type of behaviour that is measured is whether the baby 'looks for' the object or not, and the method involves interesting a baby in an object (say a teddy) and then hiding it under a blanket. This study can be done in a scientific way – for example, always following the same procedure, and making sure there are no other distractions. When babies 'look for' hidden objects they can be said to have **object permanence**. They know the objects exist (that is, that they are permanent) even when they are out of sight.

A baby looks at the toy monkey, but when it is hidden the baby looks confused. This baby does not have object permanence.

An important point about psychology is that our knowledge is always developing. It used to be thought that object permanence occurred at around 8 months, but now it is widely thought that babies have object permanence much sooner. This is explained more in Chapter 5, which looks at cognitive development.

CASE STUDY

When Kara was 5 months old her mother tested her for object permanence. First, her mother caught Kara's attention by showing her a favourite furry elephant toy. Kara reached for the toy. Then, while Kara was still watching, her mother put the elephant under a blanket. Kara could clearly see the object being hidden and its shape was still visible. However, she immediately stopped watching and made no attempt to reach out for it. By 8 months old, however, when her mother repeated the procedure, Kara kept watching the blanket and tried lifting the blanket to retrieve the toy. This was taken to mean that, at 8 months old, Kara realised that the object (the elephant) had permanence and would continued to exist even when she could not see it, though at 5 months old she had not understood this.

Less scientific methods involve a less structured means of studying a child. For example, a baby could be studied from a very young age, and its language development tracked from babbling through to use of words. This would be a case study, and interesting 'in-depth' data could be gathered from it.

TRY THIS!

If you have easy access to young babies from 3 to 12 months old (one baby will do), and if you feel confident enough, try directing their attention towards a particular toy and then try hiding the toy under a blanket. Do they look for the toy to reappear? Do they have object permanence? Note that you must have permission from parents to do this and should discuss it with your tutor too before carrying out the task.

CASE STUDY

In a private day nursery in London children's key workers record the developing language of the children in their care and share this with parents. It gives information that can be used when planning to meet the children's needs.

At 18 months, John was learning to name animals and it was recorded that he would copy an adult and say 'sheep' when he saw a picture of sheep in a book. A year later his key worker recorded him saying 'sheeps' when he looked at the same picture.

By saying 'sheeps' instead of 'sheep' John showed that he had learned the grammatical rule that, in English, plurals end in 's'. It was some time before his key worker noted that John had learned that there are exceptions to 'rules' and he began to use the word 'sheep' for more than one sheep.

As well as language development and object permanence, psychology covers many different areas of children's experiences when growing up. An examination of the contents page of this book will show you the areas covered. For example, more on language development, and how children develop language and add 's' to make words plural even when this is not appropriate, is found in Chapter 6.

You will learn more about methods of studying children in the chapters that follow, but some of the more useful ideas and terminology are briefly outlined here.

Primary and secondary data

When doing your own research within child psychology you will have to consider both **primary** and **secondary** data. Secondary data are gathered by others. Primary data are gathered by you. It is claimed that if one of a pair of identical twins has schizophrenia there is around a 50% chance that the other will get it too. This figure was obtained by considering many studies and averaging their results. The original researchers gathered primary data, but the 50% figure used in this book is an example of using secondary data – that is, the figure is used here but the data were not gathered firsthand. Data can include statistics from other publications such as *Social Trends*, and any information taken from other books or literature. These data are secondary data as you have not gathered them personally.

Informal and formal research

Research can be formal, where studies are planned and issues such as choosing an appropriate method are addressed carefully, or it can be informal. All of us observe and gather information informally most of the time. Even when doing informal research, you must be mindful of ethical issues. If you were carrying out a formal observation of children to see their level of language ability you would have specific issues to watch for, such as how many different words are used in a certain space of time. However, you might carry out informal research to look at language use, simply noting examples during a normal day, such as noticing that a particular child used very few words. That informal research might lead to a more formal study.

Gathering opinions, compared with collecting hard information

One way of discussing different types of data has been to divide them into two main types, **qualitative** data and **quantitative** data. Broadly, quantitative data involve quantity and number and tend to be 'harder' facts. For example, you can record how many times children play with toys traditionally associated with girls and compare this with the number of times they play with toys traditionally associated with boys. Of course, deciding what is a girl's toy and what is a boy's toy is quite difficult but, after that, the recording would be reasonably straightforward. Qualitative data, however, involve attitudes and opinions. For example, you could ask children which toys they preferred and record their answers. Then you could analyse their comments in terms of differences in preferences according to gender.

As long as you feel confident and can do this ethically, first spend 10 minutes recording what toys a child plays with and then spend a few minutes asking the child what he likes to play with. Compare your quantitative data (recording the toys) with your qualitative data (recording the conversation). There may be problems, for example, if the child only does one thing over the whole 10 minutes, but for the moment just make what decisions you can to overcome them. A section on ethics is found later in this chapter, so make sure that you understand how to undertake activities with children before doing this task. If in doubt, have a discussion with your tutor.

DEFINITION

Time sampling – choosing a regular fairly short time when each observation will be made – for example, every 2 minutes.

There is much debate as to whether qualitative or quantitative methods are most appropriate for use in early years' research. If you want to find out something about a particular child or group of children with whom you work then qualitative methods are often more appropriate. If, however, you want to discover something that advances our understanding about children in general then both methods have strengths and weaknesses. Often a research study uses both methods.

To participate or not to participate?

You can be a participant when observing – you can be part of the event that you are studying. For example, if you are telling a story to a group of children and observing their reactions then you are carrying out participant observation. Alternatively, you can sit somewhere away from a group of children and observe them as a non-participant observer while someone else reads them a story. Both of these methods have advantages and disadvantages.

When you participate you affect a situation and may not be able to record what is going on at the same time. However, you are also accepted and the children are more likely to behave naturally than if they think a non-participant observer is watching them. When you are not participating you are freer to record everything and can be more thorough.

Time and event sampling

When asked to observe children and record for 10 minutes what toys they are playing with, you may have had difficulty in doing the recording. For example, a child may just do one thing for 10 minutes. Instead of making one record, use **time sampling**. This is when you make a note of the activity every few minutes (decide a suitable time). Similarly you can sample specific events (event sampling) when observing. It is useful to choose one particular child (the target child) at a time.

Action research

Most of the methods discussed in this chapter are standard research methods that involve asking a question, gathering data to try to answer it and then drawing conclusions. For example, you might want to know which stage of language a child has reached so you observe him and count his words. Or you might want to know if there is a gender difference in play behaviour, so you watch children and ask their parents to find out if girls seem to play different games from boys. In both these examples the research ends once the answer is found.

Action research takes a different perspective as it focuses on making changes as well as finding out about things. There is a cycle of research. The idea is to evaluate something and find out what is working and what is not. This is just like other research and can take place by observation, interview, survey or other means. The difference is that an action plan is formulated to bring about some sort of improvement using information arising from the evaluation and data collection. This action plan is implemented for a specified time. Then the change is evaluated and the whole cycle starts again.

Some researchers are interested in theory within childcare, but there are many others who, having evaluated a situation, like to try to improve that situation for the children. Action research links in with policy changes too. For example, suppose that many researchers working separately find that daycare is much more successful if there are many staff members, if there is sufficient stimulation and if sessions are carefully planned to take a child's stage of development into account. Policy decisions may be made to encourage these aspects as a result of the research.

Of all the research methods, action research is the most useful tool for early years practitioners as it allows them to answer questions that are specific to their workplaces and it encourages them to reflect on their practice.

Summary of methods used in child psychology

There are many different methods used in the study of child psychology and if you were to undertake an extended research project you would need to study these methods in considerable depth. You will find suggestions for further reading about research methods at the end of this chapter.

The main research methods are now summarised briefly to enable you to understand terms that you will come across later on in the book.

Experiments

Experiments in psychology follow the scientific method and are studies in controlled settings focusing on one aspect of behaviour. This aspect is often varied. For example, helping behaviour can be studied when there is either one person or a group of people around to help. There would be two situations, one where one person accompanied a participant and another where there was a group accompanying the participant. All other aspects of behaviour, including the actual setting, would be kept the same. Some experiments take place in a participant's natural setting, and they are called field experiments. Experiments lead to quantitative data. The measures taken generate numbers, rather than, for example, opinions.

The *advantages* include the fact that you control what is happening, so you can draw quite firm conclusions. Controlling involves making clear decisions about all of the variables that might affect the outcome of the experiment and keeping them the same across the study. Then you can carry out the same experiment again and find the same results. If the same results are found, they are **reliable.**

The *disadvantages* include the fact that too many controls can make the situation unnatural so conclusions are not real – they may not occur outside of the artificial experimental situation. When this occurs, conclusions are said to lack **validity**.

Questionnaires

Questionnaires gather personal data by means of structured questions. For example they might ask about gender, age group and occupation. Then further questions try to uncover particular trends or attitudes. Some ask questions where the answers are fixed or 'closed'. An example of a closed question is one that requires a 'yes' or 'no' answer. Some questionnaires ask open questions too. Open questions allow for opinions to be given. An example of an open question is 'what do you think about . . .?' Closed questions give quantitative data – numbers and percentages can be generated from them (for example, recording how many people answered 'yes' and how many answered 'no'). Open questions give qualitative data and opinions and attitudes are recorded and summarised.

An *advantage* of this approach is that you can use set questions and obtain one-word answers, so you can compare participants' results easily and obtain clear data. For example percentages can be calculated.

A *disadvantage* is that participants may say only what they think you want them to say. In other words they might be influenced by the **demand characteristics** of the situation. Similarly, they may say what they think they ought to say, being influenced by **social desirability**.

Observations

Observation is not always as simple as it might seem because it is often necessary to use particular procedures otherwise it would be hard to make any sense of the data. There are participant observations, where the observer is part of the event with a role to play, and non-participant observations, where the observer is outside the event and simply watches. There are **overt** observations, where the participants know they are being watched, and **covert** observations, where they do not know they are being observed. Observations should be **naturalistic** where possible, in that they should take place in the individual's natural setting. This makes them more valid as the individual is more likely to be involved in natural behaviour. As with all methods, ethical issues are important. Knowing what to watch and how long for can also be an issue, so time and event sampling are useful. Time sampling involves observing for a particular period of time and at particular intervals – for example, for 1 minute every 5 minutes. Event sampling involves observing one event for a period of time and then changing to another one.

An *advantage* of the observation approach is that you can see real-life action and so obtain valid results, especially if the observation is secret. When an observation is secret, it is covert, and when it is known about it is called **overt**.

A *disadvantage* is that it is hard to record everything and so things are missed. It is also hard to decide how to do the recording. Time sampling (observing at regular intervals) can help but it can mean that things are missed.

Case studies

Case studies often involve a mixture of methods. They can be in-depth studies of one person, one event, or a small group. Many aspects of that person, event or group are examined to build a broad picture. Case studies can involve observations, interviews, questionnaires, or keeping diaries. It is desirable to use a variety of methods to help to obtain a clearer image of what is happening.

The *advantage* of case studies is that they gather a lot of data in depth and so are very true to life and thorough. They tend to involve following a particular person over a length of time. When a method reveals real-life data there is said to be validity.

A *disadvantage* of the case study is that it only covers one group or person, so it is not easy to say whether the findings apply to everyone. If they do not apply to everyone they are said not to be **generalisable**. If findings cannot be generalised to others then this may limit their usefulness in building a body of knowledge.

Interviews

Interviews involve asking people questions and can be structured (with set questions) or unstructured, where the interviewer has a topic to explore but is free to develop his own questions according to the responses of the person being interviewed. Semi-structured interviews can be useful. Here there are set questions, but the interviewer is still free to explore interesting topics and comments as they arise.

The *advantage* of this approach is that you can follow a person's thinking and explore issues to obtain in-depth data.

A *disadvantage* is that data can be hard to analyse if everyone has a different viewpoint. They can also be **subjective** as the researcher chooses what to explore and what to record.

> **DEFINITION**
>
> **Generalisable** – when results come from a sample that represents the main population, then they are generalisable and can be said to be true of the main population.

> **DEFINITION**
>
> **Subjective** – this refers to researchers' own views, which affect what they record and affect results. Objectivity is best because then results are more likely to be reliable and valid – but objectivity is quite hard to achieve.

✔ PROGRESS CHECK

1 Name two ways of studying children (methods)
2 Why would you choose to do a case study?
3 What are two problems about using questionnaires?
4 Give two examples of studies carried out in the field of child psychology

---

SOME GENERAL THEORETICAL ISSUES IN PSYCHOLOGY

There are general issues or themes that you will find recurring in psychological explanations for our thinking, feeling or actions. They are presented briefly here, as they will form a useful background to your studies. Whether you need to learn all the following information will depend on the level at which you are studying. If you are studying at Level 3 or over, then you should read carefully and learn the material. However, if you are studying at Level 2, then, although the following is of interest to you, you don't need all the official terms – read it for interest and background. If you find the terminology here offputting, refer back to the note on p. vii in the introduction. Remember that the ideas are more important than learning the terms at the moment.

Table 1.1   Examples of methods used in psychology

Scientific methods	Less scientific methods
Experiments – e.g. testing children to see if they have object permanence	Observations – e.g. observing children of different ages to identify different play stages
Questionnaires – e.g. asking people questions for examples, to look at racist attitudes	Case studies – e.g. following the progress of who was discovered having been very badly treated. Would she learn to speak?
	Interviews – e.g. asking children about their play, the rules and how they feel about rules

This section considers the following issues:

- Are characteristics born or learned?
- Is it better to study the whole person or to study people part by part?
- Do children develop continuously or in stages?
- The evolutionary approach.

Are we born with characteristics or are they learnt?

There is much debate about which human characteristics are learnt and which we are born with (in other words, which are **innate**). We can say that what is innate comes from our genes and what is learnt comes from our environment. Sometimes our genetic make up is called our nature, and environmental influence is called nurture, so this debate can be called the **nature/nurture** debate.

The interactionist view

It is unlikely that features of our brain and behaviour are either learnt or innate. It is more likely that there is an element of each. It is very hard to separate them. From conception a baby is already adapting to its environment. It is not as though the genetic blueprint develops and then 'meets' its environment. Both interact from the start. The idea that nature and nurture interact from the beginning is known as the **interactionist** view.

Studying the nature/nurture issue

Identical twins (called monozygotic, or 'MZ', twins) share all their genes, so if nature is responsible for a certain characteristic, if one of the twins has that characteristic the other twin is bound to have it too. This is because in genetic terms they are 100% alike, so if something comes from their genes then they are bound to share it. When a characteristic can occur in one and not in the other, then that characteristic is not 100% caused by genes.

To illustrate further, findings from a variety of studies have shown that if one identical twin has schizophrenia then there is an approximately 50% chance that the other twin will develop the condition. For non-identical twins, who only share half their genes, the chance that both twins will develop schizophrenia is 15% (Gottesman, 1991). These figures show that the development of schizophrenia is influenced by both genetic and environmental factors.

If twins who are 100% alike only share schizophrenia 50% of the time, then the other 50% (where one twin has it and the other does not) must be down to environmental or nurture factors. You would expect non-identical twins to have a far weaker genetic link, so the fact that non-identical twins share schizophrenia a lot less often (around 15% of the time) underlines the role of environmental factors in schizophrenia but also illustrates a genetic role in schizophrenia. However, even identical twins only share schizophrenia half of the time, which again shows the role of 'environmental' factors.

Think about as many members of your biological family as you can. Can you identify characteristics that seem to be genetic (because lots of your family members have that characteristic) and some that seem to be given by the environment? It is hard to say which characteristics are likely to be inherited and which come from environmental influences but it is an interesting to think about it. For example, eye colour is genetic, IQ might be and the accent you speak with is not.

CASE STUDY

Liam is 3 years old and has just entered nursery. He has great difficulty controlling his temper and will fly into rages. His mother tells his key worker that this is hardly surprising because his father has a fiery temper as well. The mother thinks that Liam's temper is inherited. What other explanation may there be?

DEFINITIONS

Holistic – refers to a way of studying that looks at people as a whole instead of looking at parts of them and their behaviour. It is now widely thought that an holistic approach to looking at an individual child is the best approach, rather than looking perhaps just at one aspect of their development. Compare with a reductionist approach.

Self-actualise – means achieve personal satisfaction in some way and to realise one's potential.

Reductionist – refers to a way of studying people that looks at parts of them and their behaviour rather than considering them as whole people. For example, you could use an EEG to look at brain processes whilst we sleep, and you could record sleep patterns by measuring the brain activity. This would not be looking at sleep as a whole though, because there could be other factors such as dreaming, or whether people feel refreshed when they awake. This contrasts with a holistic approach.

Studying the whole person or parts

Some approaches in psychology study the whole person and this is called taking an **holistic** approach. The humanistic approach (considered later in this chapter) takes an holistic view of people and focuses on how far they fulfil themselves (**self-actualise**). However, most approaches look at only part of the person at a time. When only parts are examined this is called taking a **reductionist** approach. For example, the biological approach might look at parts of the brain or stages of sleep rather than the whole picture, such as pressures of living that affect sleep. This is an important issue and some would say an holistic approach is better because whatever makes up the whole person can be missed when a reductionist approach is used. It is worth remembering, when looking at part of what makes a child's personality, for example, that the whole child is more than the parts. Children are not just the total of their height, gender, race, personality type, temperament and so on, but the way in which all these characteristics (and more) combine to make the whole person. You could study all of these characteristics separately and you might come up with quite a good idea of what that child is like but this would not be quite the same as studying the whole person (or so it is claimed).

In practice most early theorists in psychology took a reductionist approach, as do many current ones. It can be hard to look at ourselves as whole beings. When studying child psychology you will see how children develop cognitive processes (in the cognitive-developmental approach). At this stage you will not be considering their emotional development. However, later chapters (for example, Chapter 9) do take a more holistic view of the child. Examining part of what makes a child a person at one time is fine, and can give useful information, however it is one reason why psychology seems to have so many different unconnected theories. It is very important to see a child in an holistic sense – as a whole.

Do children develop in stages or continuously?

Another way in which theories differ is that some see a child's psychological development as continuous and some see it as occurring in stages. The learning theorists think that we learn continuously and continually, building on our knowledge as we go. However, cognitive-developmental theorists like Piaget suggest that children move through a series of stages. You will meet all these ideas in the chapters that follow, and more can be said then about the relative merits of stage theories and theories that propose that we develop continuously. Chapter 5 looks at discontinuity and continuity in more depth.

The evolution approach

Darwin (in the late nineteenth century) claimed that animals (including humans) have come to be as they are because their characteristics were useful enough to help them to survive. This is known as 'survival of the fittest'. This is not the 'fittest' in the sense of being physically fit but fittest in the sense of being the most suitable for the environment (what fits best). So characteristics that humans have, including children's abilities, have evolved because they are useful. This is a helpful explanation. For example, we can show that babies and mothers tend to bond and attach to one another. This would be a useful characteristic. If one mother bonded to her baby years ago, and one did not, you can imagine that the 'bonded' baby was more likely to survive. The 'bonding' mother's genes (with the bonding instinct) pass to the 'bonded' baby. Bonding is a useful (fit) characteristic and would have been likely to survive. This argument assumes that such characteristics are inborn (innate) because they would be passed on through genes. That baby survived and grew up to pass the genes on. The 'unbonded' baby did not survive so the 'unbonded' genes did not get passed on. This is an example of 'survival of the fittest' in action, and it demonstrates the use of **evolution theory** to produce an explanation in child psychology. Bowlby is a theorist who discusses bonding and attachment and starts with the idea that these are innate dispositions. The idea of bonding as an instinct is considered in Chapter 2 and Bowlby's theories are examined in Chapter 3.

✔ PROGRESS CHECK

Fill in the blanks in the paragraph below using the following words where appropriate: characteristics, Carl Rogers, reductionist, stages, evolve, innate, holistic.

We _____ through a process of survival of the fittest, so our _____ are likely to be those that help our survival. Instincts are, therefore, likely to be useful. For example, a baby attaches to its mother or caregiver, and that is likely to be an _____ characteristic, and a biological process. When studying biological processes, we are looking at parts of what make a whole person, and this is called a _____ approach. The humanistic approach suggested by those such as _____ takes a holistic view and looks at the person as a whole. Some approaches think that a child develops continuously, learning along the way, whereas other theories think that development is in _____. Piaget suggests that we develop in stages. Learning theorists think we develop continuously.

APPROACHES TO STUDYING MENTAL PROCESSES

Psychology is not really one field of study – it involves many different approaches or perspectives. For example, the humanistic approach has already been mentioned, and looks at how we all aim to self-actualise. The biological approach, which has also been mentioned, looks at our biological processes. One topic can be studied from more than one viewpoint – and viewpoints are called approaches or perspectives. Some of the main ones, which you need for your course and which are examined in this section, are:

- the learning approach;
- the cognitive approach;
- the cognitive developmental approach;
- the biological approach;

DEFINITIONS

Classical conditioning – refers to the process of association, where some response that naturally occurs following a certain stimulus (such as blinking naturally follows when someone blows on the eye) is associated with some other stimulus (such as the sound of a bell). Soon the second stimulus (sounding the bell) gives the response (blinking).

Operant conditioning – refers to learning mechanisms in which a) if something pleasant follows an action we are likely to do that action again, or b) if something unpleasant follows an action, we will avoid that action, or c) if something unpleasant follows an action, we stop doing it.

Imitation – is part of social learning theory and states that we learn through modelling on and copying people that are in some way important to us.

DEFINITION

Cognition – refers to processing the input that comes via our senses and then producing an output. Basically it means 'thinking'.

- the psychodynamic approach;
- the humanistic approach;
- the social approach.

The learning approach

The learning approach suggests that we are not born with any knowledge – we learn from our surroundings and environment. For example, if we naturally sneeze when there is dust, and we visit an aunt's dusty house fairly often, we may 'learn' to sneeze when with the aunt, even when not at the house. This is **classical conditioning**. Another type of learning is called **operant conditioning**. This is when, for example, we learn that a pleasant consequence (for example, a baby receives a smile from its mother) comes from a certain behaviour (the baby babbles 'mmm', 'mmm') and so we do it again (the baby learns to talk in this way). A third form of learning is **imitation**. This is when we learn from copying others around us. The learning approach is outlined in more detail in Chapter 4.

The cognitive approach

The cognitive approach looks at how we process information, from when it enters via our senses (hearing, sight, sound, touch, taste and smell) to the 'output' that results. The output is what a person does in response to receiving the information. This is similar to the way in which a computer works, with 'input', 'throughput' and 'output'. **Cognition** is thinking, and refers to this processing. It involves how we remember things, how we choose to attend to certain things, how we perceive, and how we use language – as well as other areas. For example, we can ask how we distinguish 'I scream' from 'ice cream' as we could argue that the sound input is the same. The cognitive approach is not used very much in this book as the focus is on cognitive development instead.

The cognitive-developmental approach

The cognitive-developmental approach looks at how we develop cognitive abilities, or thinking processes, through childhood. It has been suggested that the way children think is very different from the way adults think and that children pass through stages in the development of their thinking in much the same way as children pass through stages in learning to walk. For example, a very young child finds it hard to identify a photograph showing the viewpoint of another child – they identify the photograph showing what they themselves can see.

A young child (around 4 years old) sitting at position C would think that someone sitting at position A would see the large snow capped mountain in front, as the child sees it

DEFINITION

Egocentric – this refers to the fact that children cannot see the viewpoint of another person until they reach a certain age. They can only see things through their own processing and from their own point of view. Opinions on what the age is when a child decentres (stops being egocentric) vary, as studies have shown different results.

DEFINITIONS

Circadian rhythms – are bodily rhythms that happen in a 24-hour or daily cycle. One example is the sleep-wake cycle and another is our body temperature. If our circadian rhythms are disrupted, such as when we fly around the world across several time zones, or work shifts, then we can have difficulties such as jet lag.

Innate – refers to any characteristic that we are born with.

Imprinting – when ducks and similar animals hatch they follow the first moving object they see, which is usually the mother. This has survival value.

THINK ABOUT IT

Do you feel that a new-born baby has an instinct to attach and bond to its mother? Consider a premature baby who cannot be picked up. Would this mean that that baby does not attach? Consider the role of the father. Can a baby attach both to a father and a mother (or others such as siblings)? Does it mean a neglected baby never forms an attachment? These are some questions we look at in Chapter 3. Briefly, it is thought that babies do have a bonding instinct, that they can form multiple attachments, that attaching is a two-way process (they can't do it without feedback), and it is rare that a baby never attaches although, sadly, this can occur.

This is being **egocentric**. An older child, however, can pick out a view of what another can see. These sorts of findings suggest that there has been cognitive development (development of cognitive processing abilities). The cognitive-developmental approach is outlined in more detail in Chapter 5.

The biological approach

The biological approach is useful in many areas of psychology and focuses on our biological or physiological makeup and how it affects us. For example, we have inbuilt daily rhythms (**circadian rhythms**) and if they are disrupted, such as when we have too little sleep, we can have problems with normal functioning. According to some theories, one biological feature that we seem to be born with (called an **innate** feature) is a tendency to attach and bond to our main caregiver. Ducks and other similar animals appear to attach (imprint) upon the first moving object they see, which is usually their mother. This **imprinting** instinct has been said to be the same as a baby's bonding instinct. More on the biological approach including bonding is found in Chapter 2.

In early years care and education the biological approach has been useful in demonstrating the interaction between a child's environment and brain development and how vital it is for children to receive appropriate care and education in the first few years of life.

The psychodynamic approach

The psychodynamic approach, at first sight, will probably seem unusual to you and is not likely to be used much in the areas you are studying. It does, however, feature in the area of child psychology and will be returned to in Chapter 7, which looks at our gender and moral development. The psychodynamic approach suggests that things that happened to us in the past, especially relationships with our parents and significant adults around us, can have a lasting impact on the way that we act and feel when we are older and that we are often not aware (conscious) of these influences. **Freud** (1856–1939) is the main person in this approach as it arose from his theories. He suggested that our personalities consist of three 'forces'. There is what he called the id (the 'it'), which is the demanding instinctive part of our personality – the 'I want'. A newborn baby is all 'it'. Around the age of 3 years a child starts to develop the superego (the 'above I'), which consists of the conscience part of our personality. There is also the part that gives us the basis for what we think we should be like (our ego ideal). The superego is the 'you can't have' part of the personality that comes from rules that we learn from our parents and society. The third force is between the 'I want' id and the 'you can't have' superego, and is the ego (the 'I') that tries to satisfy these other two parts. The ego has to resolve conflicts between our demanding instincts (the id) and the demands of others (the superego). When the ego manages to balance things, we are well. However, imbalance can lead to problems.

As well as this explanation of personality, Freud suggested that we develop through five main stages. The baby is in the oral stage, with pleasure focused on the mouth. When approaching potty training the baby is in the anal stage. By around 3 years of age (when the superego is developing) the child enters the phallic stage. After about 5 years there is a latency stage when not much happens in terms of development, and the fifth stage occurs at puberty, and is the genital stage. Problems in any stage can cause sticking at that stage (fixation), which leads to difficulties in living.

There is a lot more to the psychodynamic approach, and this is found in Chapter 7, but hopefully this has given you a brief idea of how child psychology might use the psychodynamic approach to explain certain behaviours.

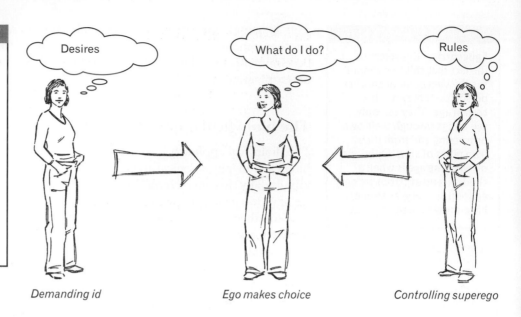

Demanding id   Ego makes choice   Controlling superego

The humanistic approach

The humanistic view looks at the whole person, as mentioned above. Carl Rogers is a person closely associated with the humanistic approach, whose 'followers' suggest that through life our goal is to fulfil ourselves (self-actualise). His approach is fairly modern in that many theories were developed in the first half of the twentieth century, whereas Rogers worked in the second half. We all have different ways of being fulfilled and need positive feedback from others to help us to find what these ways are, and to achieve them. When someone gives us positive feedback and no criticism, this is called giving **unconditional positive regard**. The modern emphasis on counselling is based on Rogers' views. The idea is that a counsellor has unconditional positive regard for the client. This is not easy. Imagine you are a counsellor and the client talks about something you strongly disapprove of (e.g. selling drugs, or paedophilia). You would have to either push your own feelings to the background or say that you cannot help and pass the client on to someone else. The point is that your empathy for the client must be unconditional – no strings attached and no judgements made. That person must feel able to tell you everything and anything. Only then can they talk about everything on their mind, and find out what their goal is. The humanistic approach is explained in more detail in Chapter 9.

The social approach

The social approach looks at how individuals and groups around us interact with us and affect us (and how we affect them). In early years care and education the influence of other people in forming a child's concepts about themselves and the world around them is recognised as being very important. Chapter 9 examines a social approach to topics such as the way in which children develop friendships and the origin and effects of prejudice.

Social constructivist approach

An approach that connects with the social approach is the social constructivist approach, which emphasises that children develop within a social and cultural system where they interact with others and things around them. They help to construct their own worlds as they are active in the process. Not only do social interactions affect the child, but children affect their surroundings too.

Cross-cultural studies

It could be claimed that there is a cross-cultural approach in psychology because so many studies do research in more than one culture in order to try to see which aspects of behaviour are innate and which come about through environmental influences and learning. The main point is that if a characteristic is found in many cultures then it is likely to be innate and biologically given because if it came from learning you would expect it to vary across cultures. If a characteristic is found mainly in one type of culture then it is thought that that characteristic is learnt because if it were biologically given it would be found in many cultures.

Table 1.2 Psychology – some approaches

Learning approach

- Sometimes called behaviourism
- To do with our actions in response to our environment
- Ignores our feelings and thoughts
- Focuses on our behaviour
- For example, we repeat actions that have had good consequences
- So a child repeats behaviour he or she is praised for

Cognitive approach

- To do with thinking processes such as language, perception, memory, and what we pay attention to
- Looks at brain processing
- For example, how a child might remember words better if they are presented in order or in a rhyming way

Cognitive developmental approach

- To do with thinking processes like the cognitive approach
- But this time concerned with how such processes develop from infancy (and earlier)
- A child may not use the same cognitive processing patterns as an adult
- For example, it is suggested that object permanence is only achieved by a certain age, and not before, so the older infant's cognitive processing has developed

Biological approach

- To do with our biological make up
- Looks at, for example, how the brain works
- Such as what parts of the brain are in use when we are using words compared with when we are understanding sentences
- Also looks at other biological processes such as stress or sleep patterns (and many others)
- For example, why is it important for a young child to have sufficient sleep?

Psychodynamic approach

- Looks at emotional development using a specific theoretical stance
- Focuses on the first 5 years of our lives and the effects of our experiences in those years
- Considers three main aspects to our personality: id (I want), superego (you can't have) and ego (decision maker)
- Has different views within the approach – e.g. we develop through psychosexual stages (Freud) or psychosocial ones (Erikson)

Social approach

- Looks at how we interact with society and how society affects us
- Considers issues like prejudice, obedience, and friendships
- For example, it seems children are affected by those around them (their peers) and will form **in groups** and **out groups**

Social contructivist approach

- Children have an inborn tendency to make sense of their world.
- This links with some cognitive developmental theories
- Social input is needed, for the child to develop and is the world that the child makes sense of
- This involves both an in built drive and environmental (social) input

Cross-cultural studies

- By looking at more than one culture we can see what features occur in the development of all children at a certain stage
- This would suggest that this is innate
- We can also see what is different between children in different cultures
- This would suggest that this is a learnt feature
- This is as much a method as an approach

✔ PROGRESS CHECK

Complete the diagram here by adding in two features of each approach

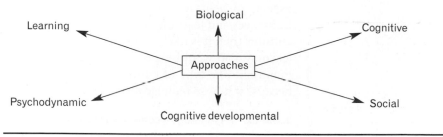

Some use the term SIMPLE to help them remember the main areas dealt with in child psychology. 'SIMPLE' stands for Social, Intellectual, Moral, Physical, Language and Emotional development. With the exception of physical development, these are the main areas of focus in this textbook.

WHAT ARE ETHICAL ISSUES?

Whilst studying child psychology you will look at many different theories about the way we develop and behave. You will also look at many different methods that are used to discover evidence to support or criticise these theories. You will also be carrying out practical research for yourself.

As part of your studies, and indeed throughout this book, you will be asked to relate theoretical issues to real life examples and to do a small amount of research yourself. This will make your studies more interesting and relevant, and will help you to learn and understand. You are encouraged to make links between what others have found (theory) to what you observe and discover (practice). However, you are not a psychologist and should take great care when 'using' others in your studies. Because studying people – and especially studying children, which is your area of interest – is such a sensitive area, there are **ethical guidelines**, produced by the British Psychological Society, that must be followed:

● Confidentiality – don't use a child's name when making your notes or handing in your work, and don't mention the name of your place of work, or anyone who works there. Do make sure that nobody involved can be identified.

● Consent – make sure that you have consent for what you are doing. This may be consent from your manager, from parents, from members of the public, and/or from children. Consent may be difficult to obtain. For example, a baby cannot really give permission. You need to make sure nobody will be upset – a baby can show lack of consent by turning away. It is not enough to obtain permission from the child, however. On the other hand, it is generally accepted that if people are in a public place where they would realise someone could watch them, then you would not necessarily have to go and ask permission.

● Right to withdraw – everyone has the right to stop taking part in your studies at any time and you must remind them of that on occasion through the study.

● Deceit – you may need to deceive your participants to an extent because if they know what the study is about it might affect how they behave, and hence the findings. For example, if you were observing children to see how gender affected behaviour and you let the children know that you expected the girls to spend more time in the book corner, then the girls might do that, having had it suggested to them. If you have to deceive participants then at least tell them everything you can. For example, you could tell them you are keeping something back for the sake of the study and that you will tell them everything at the end. Then make sure that you do tell them everything.

- Debrief – one way of making sure you are leaving people happy about what has been done is to talk to them about it afterwards and explain what it was about. This is debriefing them. At this stage ask them if they are happy for their results to be included in any report that is written or conclusions drawn.

- Competence – only work at the level at which you feel competent. For example, if studying a young child's language development and suspecting a particular difficulty, remember you must only comment about it to those who would have the competence to judge what to do – if anything. Remember health and safety advice too and work within safe limits.

- Respect – those taking part in a study are called participants as this reminds us that they are part of the study and must be respected at all times.

- Harm – do not do anything to harm anyone. You must leave your participant(s) in the same state (including mental state) as they were in before your study. Don't leave them worried or upset. For example, if you are interviewing parents about their children's progress in a nursery you should not leave them thinking that their children have a particular problem with their progress.

- Child protection issues. There is one exception where you may find that you need to break the guideline of confidentiality. Child protection issues should always be explored. However, don't do this on your own and don't talk to anyone outside the setting or outside the profession. Talk to a supervisor or some other suitable person and follow the guidelines for child protection issues. This does not mean that you break confidentiality to anyone else.

The CACHE statement of values

Many of you are on courses validated by the Council for Awards in Childcare and Education (CACHE). This body expects all students undertaking its courses to uphold its statement of values. Within this statement can be found expectations similar to those of the British Psychological Society (BPS), in that the welfare of children and their parents is vital. No action of yours should harm them in any way or compromise their right to confidentiality.

GOOD PRACTICE

Always remember not to 'use' people in your studies in the sense of including them for your own purposes rather than their own when doing so could be to your advantage but not to theirs. Obtain proper consent, tell them they can withdraw, do not do them any harm, make sure you feel comfortable with what you are doing, check with another adult before you do anything, and make sure nobody is identifiable in your notes or reports. Abide by the ethical guidelines

TRY THIS!

If you are on a CACHE course you will have a candidate handbook. You will find the statement of values in this. What are the similarities and differences between this and the BPS ethical guidelines?

If you are not on a CACHE course the statement of values can be found in candidate handbooks that are published on its website. www.cache.org.uk

TRY THIS!

Ask some adults who are either parents or carers or practitioners what they would feel about being participants in a study that observed them interacting with children. Ask them if you can record their comments about the idea. Then analyse the comments and link them to as many of the ethical guidelines outlined in this chapter as you can.

CASE STUDY

Jenny was in her local supermarket and she met an old school friend. Both of them still lived in the area and they spent some time catching up on what they had been doing since they last met. Jenny was working in a nearby nursery and enjoying it very much. Her friend said she had a neighbour whose children were at the nursery and those living nearby were very worried that the parents were abusing the children. Jenny immediately changed the conversation and talked about her recent holiday in Italy.

1 Why did Jenny change the conversation straight away?
2 Was Jenny right not to explore the issue further?
3 Should Jenny then report the matter to a superior at the nursery?

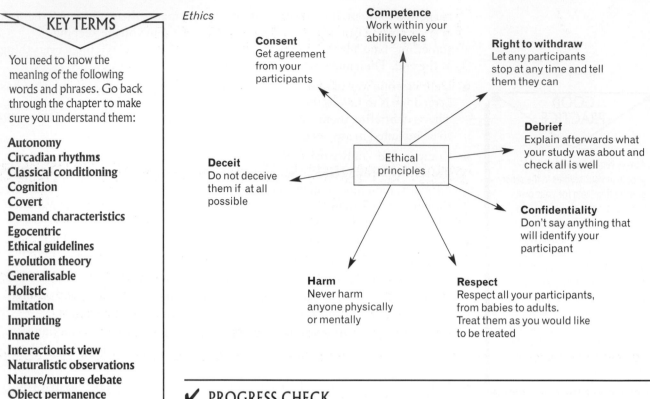

Ethics

Competence
Work within your
ability levels

Consent
Get agreement
from your
participants

Right to withdraw
Let any participants
stop at any time and tell
them they can

Debrief
Explain afterwards what
your study was about and
check all is well

Deceit
Do not deceive
them if at all
possible

Ethical
principles

Confidentiality
Don't say anything that
will identify your
participant

Harm
Never harm
anyone physically
or mentally

Respect
Respect all your participants,
from babies to adults.
Treat them as you would like
to be treated

KEY TERMS

You need to know the
meaning of the following
words and phrases. Go back
through the chapter to make
sure you understand them:

Autonomy
Circadian rhythms
Classical conditioning
Cognition
Covert
Demand characteristics
Egocentric
Ethical guidelines
Evolution theory
Generalisable
Holistic
Imitation
Imprinting
Innate
Interactionist view
Naturalistic observations
Nature/nurture debate
Object permanence
Operant conditioning
Overt
Primary data
Qualitative data
Quantitative data
Reliability
Reductionist
Science
Secondary data
Self-actualise
Social desirability
Subjective
Time sampling
Unconditional positive
  regard
Validity

KEY NAMES

Darwin
Freud
Gottesman
Piaget
Rogers

✔ PROGRESS CHECK

1 What does it mean to say you must give participants the right to withdraw?
2 What is the name of the society that regulates psychology in Britain and, amongst its other functions, produces ethical guidelines?
3 Why do you need to be competent when carrying out studies?
4 Give two ways in which confidentiality can be maintained

FURTHER READING

Davenport, G.C. (1994) *An Introduction to Child Development,* Collins Education, London.

Fawcett, M. (2003) *Learning Through Child Observation,* Jessica Kingsley, London.

Hobart, C. and Frankel, J. (2004) *A Practical Guide to Child Observation,* 3rd edn, Nelson Thornes Ltd, Cheltenham.

Biological bases for behaviour in the infant

INTRODUCTION

This chapter looks at babies' biological processes from conception to infancy. The aim is to provide some background information about the development of the use of the senses as well as to look at other tendencies such as bonding and forming attachments. Our interaction between our genetic makeup and our environment is also discussed, and the nature/nurture issue is revisited in a little more detail than in Chapter 1. Other issues include temperament, and how we seem to have genetic tendencies to behave in particular ways in certain situations. All these factors help to explain how a child develops.

INTRODUCTION

In 1834 Theodore Dwight said 'no child has ever been born destitute of an evil disposition – however sweet it appears'. In 1946 Benjamin Spock said 'your baby is born to be a reasonable friendly human being' (cited in Slater and Bremner, 2003).

Young children are surely as sweet as they seem!

Consider the different underlying opinions in these quotations. What do you believe current thinking is concerning the characteristics of new-born babies? Do you think, as John Locke suggested, that babies are born with their minds like a 'blank slate', which is subsequently modified by their experiences? Do you think some people are born evil? Probably you agree with our present views that babies come into the world with certain inherited, genetic characteristics and that then their experiences work with those characteristics to form the individual they 'become'. This view, to some extent, takes a position between the two quotations given above. It is not that every child has an evil disposition that must be beaten out. It is more likely that every child is born a reasonable friendly human being – however, we don't know that.

This chapter looks at biological factors that seem to be present in new-born infants.

Evolution theory

Chapter 1 briefly outlined some approaches to understanding child development. Evolution theory was one of these approaches. Recall how it is claimed that many of our characteristics are survival traits. One such trait seems to be bonding – a baby and caregiver bond together and form an attachment and the baby is more likely to be well taken care of and to survive. This trait is examined later in this chapter. Many of the characteristics outlined in this chapter could be viewed as useful for survival so you need to keep evolution theory in mind as you read.

Nature versus nurture

Another issue considered in Chapter 1 is the extent to which we are influenced by our nature (our inherited characteristics) and by 'nurture' (how our environment affects us). There is no easy answer to this problem. Much of what is known about biological factors is linked with nurture issues. For example, an infant's body weight at birth is affected by its environment even before birth, including such factors as whether the mother smokes. Only a very few characteristics appear to be totally biologically given. Keep this issue in mind as you read.

Bushnell *et al.* (1989) found that, within hours of birth, infants prefer to look at their mothers' faces, which must surely be an instinct as it is hard to see how that could be learnt. An infant also knows the direction of a sound at birth, but could this be learnt even whilst in the womb? One indication that it could be learnt is that babies may turn their heads towards their mothers' voice, but do not react to other voices.

GENES AND THE ENVIRONMENT

It is worth looking in more depth at the issue of which behaviours and characteristics can be said to be inherited and which appear to be learnt. In your course you will cover many aspects of childcare, and many of these will focus on learning and how environment affects development. Less attention is paid to those parts of a child's development that are biologically based. Biological aspects are important because they affect children's development and might affect childcare decisions, but in general, current thinking focuses on encouraging all round development and improving a child's learning and abilities. Given this current thinking it is important to understand, as far as possible, which of our characteristics are biologically given and which are caused by environmental factors. In this section background information is given about the very complex area of behavioural genetics. Table 2.1 briefly outlines three ways of explaining behaviour.

Table 2.1 Three ways of explaining how we acquire certain behaviours or characteristics

Cause of the behaviour or characteristic – different terms	Explanation of that cause
Nature / nativist / genetic	• Genes are passed on from father and mother • They have blueprints for certain characteristics • They prepare us for certain types of behaviour
Nurture / empiricist / environment / learning	• All children are affected by their environment • This can be family, school, media and so on • Cultural norms are instilled • Children learn to be what they are
Interactionist / nature and nurture	• Babies come into the world ready for certain abilities and not others – via their genes • From even before they are born they are affected by their environment (e.g. outside world and womb) • Genes and environment affect one another at all times

✔ PROGRESS CHECK

Complete the blanks in the text below using the following words where appropriate: nature, nurture, interactionist.

Children are born with certain characteristics that they inherit from their parents. These characteristics are likely to remain unchanged throughout their lives and are said to be the children's _____. These characteristics affect how the children interact with their environment and it is hard to see how far environment (or _____) affects the development of children. Its effect is likely to be considerable. Most researchers think that we are products of our genes and our environment. This is an _____ view.

The effects of environment

It is probably quite easy to see how babies' environments affect them and some of the issues are outlined here.

From the moment of conception the environment will have an effect on an individual. For instance the age and nutritional status of the mother will affect the health of the ovum; chemicals or radiation, all of which may damage the embryo, may adversely affect the father's sperm. Before birth babies are affected by the sounds they hear; they are nourished according to their mother's diet and they are affected by their mother's fitness and behaviours too. After birth babies are treated in particular ways and this will affect their development. One way to show this environmental effect is to study babies that are not looked after adequately. From birth babies are **socialised** – that is society in the form of parents, family, school, friends and other influences such as the media, affects children and shows them what is accepted and what the norms of that society are. Some babies are not socialised – they are **privated**. This issue of privation is discussed in Chapter 3 and shows how children need to engage with their world and with other people to develop 'normally'. Privation refers to the situation when children do not have anyone to care for them from the start. They do not form attachments, for example. If it is shown that privated children do not develop 'normally' then it can be assumed that children need to be cared for.

The environment affects children in many different ways, from developing language to being able to form relationships later in life. Chapter 3 looks at what happens if attachments are not formed. Chapter 4 examines how we learn through reinforcement by environmental factors – for example, how we repeat behaviour in response to a reward (a child works hard in school for a gold star, for instance). Chapter 6 looks at how we develop language and how we need someone to encourage us to do so. Indeed most chapters in this book at some time mention environmental influences, so by the end of your course you will be able to make a list of how we are influenced by our environment. If we did not believe that our environment had great importance in children's development we would probably not place such an emphasis on factors such as childcare. After all if the environment is not important then the type of childcare a child receives is not important either, which is contrary to current belief. So when considering the nature/nurture issue you are probably reasonably comfortable, even before you have done a lot of studying, in accepting that our environment does strongly affect what we become.

✔ PROGRESS CHECK

Define the terms 'sociability' and 'privated'. Then explain in your own words how evidence from privated children suggests environment has a strong effect on a child's development.

The effects of genes

Most people realise that children are very much affected by their experiences in the world but it is harder to be clear about genetic influences. One problem, of course, is that much is still be learnt about genes and their effects on us. A brief outline of how our genes affect us is given below.

The genotype – our genetic composition

> **DEFINITION**
>
> **Genotype** – the genetic make-up of the individual.

We all have a **genotype**. This is our genetic makeup. A great deal is now known about genes and their effects on us physically, however, there is not enough knowledge yet to be certain about the effects of genes on our behaviour. There might be specific areas of knowledge that are useful, such as where inherited conditions affect certain individuals, however, in general, in the field of behavioural genetics not enough is known to say that a specific genetic pattern will give a specific behaviour. This is certainly the case for intelligence, for example. There are no known genes that have definitely been shown to explain differences in intelligence between individuals. However, it is thought that such genes might well exist. Genes could affect our behaviour even though we don't know the full effect of our genetic makeup. So researchers study observable characteristics of individuals and compare them to see if a genetic basis for certain behaviours can be found.

The phenotype

> **DEFINITION**
>
> **Phenotype** – this is what is observable about an individual. Observable behaviour might show genetic makeup but will also include environmental effects.

The genotype cannot be observed and so cannot be measured in people. This means that it is difficult to study it directly. Or course research looks at genes in great depth but the genotype of individuals cannot be studied. What can be seen is the phenotype. The **phenotype** refers to people's observable characteristics, such as their intelligence level (there is some dispute whether this can be measured but it is a useful example here) or their levels of aggression. One difficulty is how far we can assume that the phenotype shows genetic influence and how far it shows environmental influence. Chapter 5 looks at cognitive (thinking) development. Cognition and problem solving are phenotypes in that they are observable and measurable characteristics of people. This idea of a phenotype is important when it comes to trying to see what comes from our genes and what is caused by environmental influences. Our phenotype shows individual differences because it emphasises people's genetic makeup as well as their personal experiences.

Twin and family studies

Some evidence for the effects of genes on our behaviour can be found, even if genes themselves cannot be shown directly to be responsible. Studies of twins can be very useful. Identical twins come from a single egg and are called **monozygotic (MZ) twins**. Non-identical or fraternal twins are not from the same egg and are called **dizygotic (DZ) twins**. Monozygotic (identical) twins share their genes completely. Dizygotic (non-identical) twins share half of their genes, as do brothers and sisters. Half of our genes come from our mother and half from our father, so we share half our genes with each parent too. Family members including MZ twins, DZ twins, parents and brothers and sisters share their environment too – usually. However, some family members, including sometimes MZ (identical) twins, are brought up separately in different environments.

If MZ twins share all their genes, similarities could be due to their genes. Admittedly they usually share their environment too. However, DZ (non-identical) twins also share their environment but only 50% of their genes. So if something is more common in MZ (identical) twins than in DZ (non-identical) twins it is likely to have a genetic cause.

MZ twins =   100% genetically similar and share environment
DZ twins =   50% genetically similar and share environment

So any difference between MZ and DZ twins is likely to be down to genetics.

Identical twins are monozygotic (MZ) and come from a single egg so share 100% of their genes

However, no two individuals can share their environment completely. Parents cannot really treat all their children the same. They may treat identical (MZ) twins more alike than they do other children, even non-identical twins; however, it is impossible to treat even MZ twins in absolutely the same way. Even MZ twins are not exactly alike in all characteristics – for example, there are often differences in temperament and there can be other differences such as in IQ. As they are not exactly alike, but have 100% similar genetic structure, this is evidence of environmental effects.

So from twin studies it can be seen that the environment and experiences affect development. It can also be seen that some characteristics have a genetic basis. One example of this was given in Chapter 1 where it was suggested that if one MZ (identical) twin develops schizophrenia, the other one has it in about 50% of the cases. In DZ (non-identical) twins if one develops schizophrenia, the other one has it in around 15% of the cases.

From the above statistics some conclusions about nature and nurture can be drawn. First, as it is not the case that in MZ (identical) twins if one has schizophrenia the other one always has it, then schizophrenia cannot be totally genetically given. Second, even in MZ (identical) twins, in half the cases only one has schizophrenia so there must be quite a strong environmental influence. Third, only in 15% of the cases do both DZ twins develop schizophrenia so there must be quite a large environmental role. However, fourth, in around half the cases both MZ (identical) twins do develop schizophrenia, so there is quite a large genetic influence involved. It can be concluded that there is some genetic basis for schizophrenia but that there is also a large environmental influence as to whether it develops or not. Probably some genes give a tendency to develop schizophrenia but there is some environmental trigger (or triggers) that dictate whether it is actually developed or not. This can be said for a number of other different behaviours and characteristics.

✔ PROGRESS CHECK

Sort the following statements into the two correct groups, one for MZ twins and one for DZ twins.

Headings	Statements
MZ twins	share 100% of their genes
	come from one egg
	come from two eggs
	are quite likely to share a characteristic that has a strong genetic component
DZ twins	are brought up in a very similar way indeed
	are brought up in the same environment but only a little more similarly than other brothers and sisters
	are always the same gender

Genes – types and influences

Each human cell has two copies of each chromosome. One copy comes from the mother and one from the father. Chromosomes are made of a genetic material (DNA), which is organised into genes. Genes dictate how proteins are synthesised and proteins are crucial to our survival. Human cells have 23 pairs of chromosomes except for sperm and egg cells. In order for reproduction to take place sperm cells don't have pairs of chromosomes and neither do egg cells. Both cells have only one copy of each chromosome, and when they join together at the moment of conception the fertilised egg cell then has a full complement of chromosomes (half from the mother and half from the father – egg and sperm). Twenty-two pairs of chromosomes are exactly the same for males and females, but one pair is different in each organism. That pair determines sex. Females have two large X-chromosomes and males have one X- and a smaller Y-chromosome.

Each gene has two copies, one maternal and one paternal and the copies are called alleles. Genetically given behaviours and characteristics rarely come from one gene. This is what makes the study of genetic influences difficult. Genetic effects can come from combined effects of various alleles (gene copies). An effect can occur within the two copies of the gene or can be between copies of genes. Alleles (gene copies) give a small effect, but when they are added together these effects can lead to a difference in the individual. For example, behaviour geneticists currently think that human intelligence relies on the effects of many genes, and small effects from many genes contribute to how intelligent someone might be. It is clear why this is hard to study and why no claims are yet made that there are specific genes for intelligence. Perhaps the main thing to note is that just because one gene is not found that links to something like intelligence it does not rule out a genetic effect. There are other ways in which genes can affect behaviour.

Gene and environment interactions

The main point to remember when thinking of how far behaviours or characteristics are influenced by genes or environment is to assume that most of the evidence points to both being involved most of the time. There are three different ways that genes and environment could interact and they are worth briefly considering.

There might be a passive link between genes and environment in that parents pass on their genes and also give children their environment. This environment acts on children and helps to shape them into what they become. This is passive as it does not give the child an active role – genes and environment act on the child. For example, social disadvantage is found to link to lower IQ, and social advantage to higher IQ. The child with high IQ might have inherited genes from their parents that gave them high IQ and might also have had a stimulating environment in that the parents read to the child a lot. So both their genes and their environment might have led to their higher IQ.

Another gene-environment link is called an evocative link. This means that something in the child might lead to certain responses from those around the child. For example, perhaps children with higher IQ do things that make their parents respond to them in a more stimulating manner. Perhaps a child asks to be taken to the library, for example.

A third link between genes and environment could be an active one. Children shape their own environments and are not really passive. For example, children with lower IQ might spend less time in activities that might stimulate them.

These three ways of looking at the interaction between genes and environment should help to show that children can actively affect their own experiences, even though they are passive to an extent as they cannot control all of their own environment any more than they can control their genes. In what follows in this textbook it is useful to remember this active role for the child. Some theories suggest that experiences shape the child (for example, behaviourism is outlined in Chapter 4). Some theories have quite a strong role for biological maturation (for example, Piaget's theory of cognitive-development outlined in Chapter 5). However, in most cases you will see that both our biology and our experiences have a clear role in shaping what we become.

Care in drawing conclusions

When studying the effect of genes on individual development it is important to say again that it is not known how genes directly influence behaviour. There can be a heritability estimate drawn from studies such as twin studies but this only suggests the proportion of some behaviour or characteristic that seems to come from genes. Similarly, there is an environmental estimate that suggests the proportion that comes from environmental influences. If it is said that genes help to cause a certain characteristic, for example intelligence, this does not mean that the underlying mechanisms are understood. It is just concluded that there is some genetic basis for such characteristics. It might also be said that environment is a cause in schizophrenia but this does not mean that the exact characteristics of the environment that would lead to the development of schizophrenia are understood. As IQ has been used as an example in this section, you might like to know that current thinking suggests that around 50%

of our general cognitive ability might have some genetic basis (Plomin and Neiderhiser, 1991). Much more research into this is needed, though. For example, it might be that for those with high IQ there is a high genetic influence but for those with low IQ the inherited factor seems low (Petrill *et al.,* 2001). So we might inherit a predisposition towards a high IQ (environment would affect this too) but we might not inherit a predisposition towards a low IQ. At least you can see that there is no easy answer to this sort of question. For your own studies perhaps it is best just to remember that there are possible genetic factors in many behaviours and characteristics but that we do not yet know enough about them.

Brain studies and the interaction between environment and genetic potential

Since the early 1980s there have been rapid developments in technology that have allowed us to gain more of an understanding of the development of the human brain. This has contributed to our understanding of the way biological factors and environmental factors affect children's development.

How does a baby's brain grow?

Research has shown us that babies are born with practically all their brain cells (**neurons**) in place but that the brain is by no means developed. The brain cells are only partially connected up and most of the connections older children and adults have are yet to be formed. These connections are called **synapses.**

Some brain cells are connected at birth and later on in this chapter you will find out that babies show instinctive, reflex behaviour, such as being able to suck. New-born babies also appear to have brain cells already connected (wired), which enable them to imitate gestures, such as sticking out their tongues.

At first there is a burst of synaptic growth, connecting brain cells. Later, many of these connections are pruned back if they are not used. The process of synaptic pruning appears to have a positive effect, allowing the connections that are left to become bigger and stronger.

Most brain growth occurs in the first 3 or 4 years of birth. There is a growing recognition that, although brains are genetically wired at birth, the complicated connections that allow us to develop fully are formed as a result of environmental input. David *et al.* (2003) summarise appropriate input as consisting of:

- warm, loving, appropriate interactions with parents and carers;
- a safe, nourishing and nurturing environment;
- opportunities to explore.

They also summarise what we know about the brain and the implications of this for our thinking about the genetics/environment debate:

- Brain development occurs as a result of a complex interweaving of genetic potential and experience. That is, you may have the genes that would potentially give you the ability to be a great athlete but you would also need training and good nutrition to enable you to achieve your potential.
- Early experience affects the way that the brain cells interconnect and this can have a lasting effect on the way that we think and behave as adults.
- Early interactions and relationships have a profound influence on the way the brain is 'wired'.
- At certain times there are sensitive periods during which particular kinds of learning occur best. This can be understood when you think about learning a second language. The earlier children are exposed to a second language the quicker they pick it up.
- The brain is at its most active in the early years. This level of activity reduces as we get older.

What follows in this chapter focuses on the biological development of infants.

PHYSICAL DEVELOPMENT – THE DEVELOPMENT OF MOVEMENT (MOTOR SKILLS)

In the first few years of life children's physical skills develop in a predictable way. That is, they are born unable to control their limbs or even hold their heads up and they gradually develop the ability to sit, turn over, stand and walk. At the same time as their **gross motor** skills develop babies also develop and refine the use of small muscle groups that allow them to use their fingers (**fine motor skills**), so by the end of the first year children can pick up very small objects. Such physical development does affect psychological development because being able to act on the world affects all other development. In Chapter 5 you will find that one theorist (Piaget) thought that the first stage of cognitive (thinking) development is the sensorimotor stage – that cognitive development starts from infants receiving sensory information and moving within their world. Emotional and social development are also affected by the child's actions.

At birth the infant's well-developed motor (movement) skills include sucking, looking, grasping, breathing and crying – and not much else. Note that these skills are needed for survival and so back the idea that we have evolved abilities that aid our survival, as suggested by evolution theory. However, an infant finds it hard to control movements. It is not until a few weeks old that the infant can lift his head when lying down.

Early studies have highlighted how motor skills develop. One interesting point about motor skills is that they almost always appear in the same order. First the infant can sit with support, then sit unaided, then crawl, stand and walk, and then climb. This suggests that there are biological maturational processes, which means that all infants develop as they grow and this is an inevitable process, biologically driven. Another important point is that, although motor skills (and perhaps cognitive or thinking skills, as you will see in Chapter 5) develop in sequence, the age at which they appear can vary quite a lot. Crawling can appear at any age from around 5 months to 11 or 12 months. Also, although the sequence remains the same, some babies skip stages – for example, some do not crawl but simply stand when ready.

It has been suggested (Gessell and Ames, 1940) that control over movement and muscles always goes from head to foot, in other words control over the head is first, then arms and body and finally legs. Similarly, control is always from the centre of the body to the outer limbs, so head and body are brought under control before elbows and wrists, knees and ankles. However, studies (McGraw, 1945) have shown that training can speed up the development of motor skills. For example, if one twin receives training in reaching out or climbing stairs and so on, then that twin develops motor skills more quickly than the other twin does. So although biological maturation may dictate the actual order of development, training and experience (as well as personal preference perhaps) can affect the timing of the development.

In summary, then, it appears that there is a biological sequence for developing motor skills (nature) but that environment can affect the timing of the ability (nurture). Motor skills that are needed for survival, such as crying for attention and sucking for food, appear at birth (but not all of them). Finally, there is the suggestion that temperament also matters, in that some babies skip stages such as crawling (and certain language stages, as will be explained in Chapter 6).

DEVELOPMENT BEFORE BIRTH

Touch

Senses develop in the same pattern for all mammals. Touch is the first sense to develop and by the age of about 8 weeks the foetus will move if the area around the lips is touched. If the fingers are touched at around 12 weeks of age the foetus will make grasping movements. Later the foetus will move towards touch, and this seems to be the start of the rooting reflex that helps a new-born baby to feed.

Taste and smell

It is hard to judge when a foetus starts to respond to taste and smell. It seems that all babies prefer sweet substances to bitter ones, before and after birth. Evidence for this is that if the amniotic fluid tastes sweet it will be swallowed more regularly than if it tastes bitter (Hepper, 1992). Exposure to alcohol in the womb also seems to increase swallowing by the foetus and might lead to a preference for alcohol later in life (Molin *et al.*, 1995).

Vision

There is not much visual stimulation in the womb and the dark environment might be needed for the visual system to develop (Fielder and Moseley, 2000). The visual system seems to start work mainly after birth when there is appropriate stimulation. However, by 30 weeks the foetus can distinguish light and dark and pick out patterns.

Sound

The foetus begins to respond to sounds by about the 24th week, although hearing is limited as parts of the system have yet to develop. Mainly low-frequency sounds are heard; sounds reaching the foetus would pass through liquid and so would have a low frequency. The mother's voice is the most noticeable sound and the most often heard (Abrams *et al.*, 1995). It has been shown that the baby's heartbeat is faster in response to sounds so it is assumed that sounds can be heard although what the foetus hears is less easy to discover. New-born babies prefer a filtered recording of the mother's voice to an unfiltered one and this suggests that the baby recognises the mother's voice in the womb, where sound would be filtered (Spence and Freeman, 1996).

ABILITIES AT BIRTH

A baby comes into the world with certain abilities or tendencies, as well as information from their senses that they acquired in the womb. Evolution has prepared the human baby to an extent. These abilities are sucking, crying, looking, grasping and breathing. Within hours of birth the baby recognises its mother's face – or at least the baby chooses to look at its mother's face when presented with two options, one the mother and one a stranger. The baby can also turn towards a sound and recognises its mother's voice and 'their' language. First specific abilities such as face and voice recognition will be looked at. Then babies' general abilities will be considered – including sucking and crying, and how such abilities can be seen to have survival value.

Perceptual abilities

Although a foetus develops a sense of smell and taste, and can hear sounds, the development of vision tends to occur more after birth, although the visual system is prepared for this. Infants cannot control their eyes very well, which means that visual development is slightly later than the development of other senses. However, infants can see larger scale objects. New-born babies do seem to be able to distinguish between shapes such as crosses and triangles. They also seem to be able to see shapes as whole, rather than just the lines that make up shapes. They can pick out face shapes too. Being able to select a particular face could be a survival instinct as the infant that can pick out the face of its carer is more likely to initiate bonding with that person. The importance of bonding and attachment is outlined later in this chapter as well as being the focus of Chapter 3.

Very young infants engage in 'conversations' with their caregivers

Face and voice recognition

Infants seem to prefer face shapes in general, although different studies suggest different timing for this preference to develop. There is a problem in testing these sorts of preferences: all that can be measured really are indirect responses such as how long babies look at something or their rate of sucking. Some studies show that even new-born babies prefer their own mother's face to another face, and older infants certainly do. This is very important for their social and emotional development and is a useful ability. It is quite interesting that infants, even new-born babies, will look longer at what adults would rate as being an attractive face than at a less attractive face, though the reason for this might be a bit hard to find. Perhaps what we think of as an attractive face is a regular one and one more like our general idea of what a face is, and that is why babies seem to prefer attractive faces – really they are simply identifying the more regular faces. Chapter 9 revisits this idea when showing how we 'prefer' attractive people.

A lot of research has been done on babies' recognition of their mother's voice. As outlined earlier a baby seems to respond to its mother's voice in the womb and can recognise it at birth. One study found that within 2 hours of birth infants moved more when their mother was speaking compared with when a stranger was speaking. Other studies use increased sucking to show preference rather than movement and also find that babies react more to their mothers' voices than to a stranger's voice. Within the first four days after birth babies seem to be able to discriminate and tell which is their maternal language as they respond more to that compared to a foreign language.

Reciprocal behaviour – imitating adults

There is evidence to suggest that infants copy the behaviour of adults. This could be a useful survival trait as it can assist the bonding process and can help to tie a mother to the baby, which in turn helps the baby's survival. Meltzoff and Moore (1977) have carried out studies showing babies copying adult behaviour such as sticking their tongues out and opening their mouths. The researchers used babies within a month of birth and also found the same behaviour in new-born babies in a later study. As babies seem to be able to imitate gestures, this suggests that their vision is sufficiently developed to enable this to happen.

Effect of handling and massage

Babies seem to respond to being cared for and it is thought that initial contact between mothers and their babies can produce a special bond. This is also likely to be true of contact between fathers and their babies but more research has been done on mothers and babies. At least, it used to be thought that special bonding takes place but new research has raised doubts about this and suggests that bonding can take place later. If a baby goat is removed from its mother immediately and returned after around 2 hours the mother will attack the baby. However, even 5 minutes with the mother first changes this behaviour and the mother will then welcome the baby on return. It was thought that this sort of process might apply to human babies too. A study was done in the 1970s that allowed some mothers more 'handling' time with their babies. It was found that these mothers seemed to be more interested in their babies, to look at them more and to be more responsive to them than the other mothers were (Klaus and Kennell, 1976). It is now thought that if a mother and baby cannot have this close contact they can still establish very strong emotional ties with their babies, so the 1970s findings are not thought to be absolutely right. However, there does seem to be some evidence that emotional ties do need to be formed and that some sort of bonding will take place. It is now thought that mothers and fathers form attachments to their babies in many different circumstances.

Temperament

It is widely thought that individuals have different temperaments and these are genetically given. **Temperament** refers to stable individual styles of responding to situations. Studies look at how active babies are, how easily they get upset, how intense their reactions are, how sociable they are and how characteristically they react to something new (Bates, 1994). Temperament is thought of as the core of someone's personality, although personality might incorporate learnt elements too. The main researchers studying temperament are Chess and Thomas (for example, Thomas and Chess, 1977). Studies found three main types of temperament and these are outlined in Table 2.2.

DEFINITIONS

Temperament – stable individual styles of responding to the environment, likely to be genetically given.

Sociability – refers to an innate tendency of babies to be social including giving social smiles and imitating the behaviour of adults paying them attention. This helps to bind the adult to the baby and helps to form a bond.

Table 2.2   Three types of temperament

Type of temperament	Description
Easy babies	Playful and adapt readily to new circumstances
Difficult babies	Irritable and either respond intensely to new situations or avoid them
Slow-to-warm-up babies	Mild responses and low in activity levels. Tend to withdraw from new situations but in a mild way

In general it is thought that temperament is genetically given. For example, twin studies have found that activity level, **sociability** and emotionality are very similar in identical twins but not in non-identical twins. Of course it is hard to claim that there are the three types of temperament as there are many different factors involved. Others have suggested five basic types (for example, Rothbart *et al.*, 1994).

It has been suggested that, in some circumstances, environmental effects might influence a baby's temperament at birth. For instance, mothers who have been very stressed during their pregnancy may have babies that are irritable and difficult to settle. Babies whose mothers have taken drugs such as crack cocaine during pregnancy have also been demonstrated to be irritable and difficult to settle. This raises doubts about what temperament is, and whether it is something stable or just depends on environmental circumstances.

Instincts with survival value – ethological approaches and evolution theory

Darwin (1809–1882) is the name linked to evolution theory. Basically when a gene is responsible for characteristics that give some sort of advantage to an organism, that organism is more likely to survive long enough to reproduce than an organism that does not have that gene. For instance it is suggested that when Britain became an industrialised nation and the buildings in towns became very dirty, some butterflies with genes for darker pigmentation were hard for predators to see against the sooty buildings of the cities. They were eaten less often than lighter butterflies, so more of the darker ones lived to reproduce. Gradually, over generations, one species changed colour completely. Genes give physical characteristics such as eye colour and body shape. They are also linked to certain behaviour patterns. Evolutionary theories of child development emphasise a genetic basis of behaviours and show how such behaviours have survival value. These theories are called **ethological approaches**.

Instincts – crying and sucking

It is fairly clear that both crying and sucking have survival value for babies. It is very hard to ignore crying infants and they use this piercing noise to make sure that they get what they need! Similarly, a baby that could not suck and did not have a rooting instinct would not survive.

Imprinting

One behaviour that is said to have an evolutionary basis, and to have survival value, is **imprinting**. Imprinting refers to the tendency of **precocial species** (those that can move around at birth, such as ducks, geese and sheep) to follow the first moving object that they see. The first moving object they see is usually the mother. Lorenz (1903–1989) is a main name in this area. Imprinting can be called an attachment between the young and their mother. This has survival value as the young are more protected, less likely to wander off, more likely to be fed and more likely to survive. Some ethologists (who study animals and humans in their natural environments) used to think that there is a **critical period** in which imprinting had to occur and if it did not happen then it would not occur at all. However, it is now thought that there is a **sensitive period** when this is more likely to happen but that it can still happen outside that time. It is not only imprinting that is thought to fit this sort of pattern. Language is also thought to have a critical period when it develops best but also a sensitive period when it can also happen but not quite so easily.

Attachment and bonding

Attachment is the subject of Chapter 3, so is only briefly touched upon here. However, there is a link to imprinting. In Chapter 3 it will be claimed that human bonding and attachment formation is like imprinting – it is a survival trait and usually happens within a particular period. Bowlby (1958), an important name in attachment theory, suggested that the need for comfort (from a mother or another) is a primary drive just as food and shelter are primary drives. Bowlby took an evolutionary viewpoint and saw attachment as a survival trait. After all, new-born babies cannot move as precocial animals can, so they have to keep their mothers near them by other means. The bonding instinct leads a mother to attend to their baby and leads their baby to respond to them. Remember it is suggested that very soon after birth the baby prefers its mother's face to another face. This bonding gives a secure attachment. This secure attachment is discussed more fully in Chapter 3, as it seems to have a huge impact on how a baby develops.

Geese imprint on the first moving object they see and this can be a human (here Lorenz shows this instinct). A baby's attachment to their caregiver may be an instinct like imprinting.

Social smiling and sociability

At first a baby tends to smile when asleep but this does not seem to be linked with any social activity. Babies smile when they are awake by the second week after birth – but, again, there seems to be no link to what is going on in the environment. Between the ages of about a month and two-and-a-half months the infant's smile does seem to be stimulated by the environment but not by anything specific in the environment – they smile indiscriminately. So even by this stage their smiles are not social smiles. For a smile to be a social smile it must relate to the smile of others and this happens from about the age of 3 months. The visual system works better by then, too, so in some way social smiling has to wait until the baby is able to perceive the environment sufficiently to detect smiles of others. Eye contact is an important part of social smiling.

As the baby starts to give social smiles, this affects the parents. Feelings for babies tend to change and a new emotional quality is involved in the relationship between babies and their carers. Fraiberg (e.g. 1974) studied blind infants and noted that social smiling did not develop at around 3 months old – and this is taken as evidence that social smiling is in response to seeing smiles of others. However, blind babies do develop social smiling. They smile later in response to sound and touch. It was noted that parents of blind babies seemed to touch them more and talk to them more when this was observed. This was used to train parents of blind babies, and social smiling occurred once more touching and sounds were introduced. It seems clear from these studies that social smiling comes from interactions with others and this underlines the fact that babies need stimulation for their development.

Evidence for social smiling suggests that a baby is born with a tendency to be sociable, and once the necessary sensory abilities are present, the baby can respond to others appropriately. The ability to imitate others is part of this sociability. Babies can also be seen to engage in turn-taking behaviour with their carers. For example, a mother might stick out her tongue, then a baby will follow suit, and this pattern can continue. Similarly a baby copies frowning or opening its mouth. There is a synchrony or patterning to this type of interaction called **interactional synchrony**. These processes – of social smiling, sociability and turn taking – all help in forming a bond between the infant and its caregiver(s). The importance of this bond and in the formation of secure attachments is discussed in Chapter 3.

DEFINITION

Interactional synchrony – the term for the turn taking that can be observed between babies and their care givers, including imitating smiles and copying behaviour.

Abilities of older babies

Babies develop abilities quickly. In fact it is quite hard to keep up with their learning. Of course it is difficult to give exact ages as different babies develop at different rates. However, there have been sufficient studies conducted on babies and children to be able to give approximate ages for the appearance of certain aspects of development. Here reaching and walking are given as examples.

Reaching

A study was carried out with four infants, following their progress from the age of 3 weeks to 1 year and looking at their reaching abilities (Thelen and Spencer, 1998). Infants need to be able to control head and shoulders before they can reach out. So it is quite a few weeks before the baby starts to reach. Then they need to develop grasping abilities before reaching becomes more purposeful, and they need to be able to control their fingers, which takes longer. Gaining fine motor skills (for example, picking up small objects) is important, not only because it gives babies control over their environment, but also because children develop thoughts (cognitions) about the world around them by being able to manipulate objects.

As babies develop they interact more and more with their environment

Infant walking

Babies' interactions with their world are important for their learning. A child that can crawl can explore more, and a child that can walk can explore even further. Infants are top heavy (with heavy heads) and have weak legs, so they cannot walk until the centre of gravity has shifted down and until they gain more strength in their legs. So it is not until around 12 to 14 months that babies begin to walk. The age at which a child learns to walk also depends on opportunities for practice and the encouragement of those around them as well as their developing cognitive skills, which are needed to guide such a complicated sequence of actions.

SUMMARY

Remember the above information when continuing with the other chapters in this book. Use your understanding of how a baby develops visual abilities to make sense of the studies outlined (for example, in Chapter 5). Throughout the study of child psychology you will come across the issue of how far an ability, characteristic or behaviour is genetically given and how far it is affected by experience and environmental influence (the nature/nurture debate). On these occasions remember what you have read about how genes can affect development and how they are likely to set someone up to develop certain tendencies – even if environmental triggers are then required before that tendency develops into actual behaviour.

KEY TERMS

You need to know the meaning of the following words and phrases. Go back through the chapter to make sure you understand them:

Critical period
Dizygotic (DZ) twins
Ethological approaches
Fine motor skills
Genotype
Gross motor skills
Imprinting
Interactional synchrony
Monozygotic (MZ) twins
Neuron
Phenotype
Precocial species
Privation
Sensitive period
Sociability
Socialised
Synapse
Temperament

KEY NAMES

Darwin
Locke
Lorenz
Piaget
Plomin

FURTHER READING

David, T., Goouch, K., Powell, S. and Abbott, L. (2003) *Birth to Three Matters: A Review of the Literature Compiled to Inform the Framework to Support Children in their Earliest Years,* DfES, Nottingham.

This book is particularly recommended for students on higher level courses.

Gopnik, A., Meltzoff, A. and Kuhl, P. (1999) *How Babies Think,* London: Weidenfield & Nicolson.

This book is essential reading for students studying higher level courses.

www.zerotothree.org/brainwonders

A very useful, easy to understand site, that looks at Early brain development and has a section especially for early years practitioners.

Karmiloff-Smith, A. (1995) *Baby It's You,* Ebury Press, London.

An easy read, recommended for all students.

Attachments

INTRODUCTION

This chapter presents a fairly detailed examination of how infants and their caregivers interact, particularly in the very early years. Privation, which means the infant has no attachment, is examined and found to have profound effects on the developing child. Daycare is addressed in some depth, because there are important conclusions to be drawn from studies about what makes good-quality daycare. Deprivation, including long-term deprivation, is also studied, to see how its effects may be minimised. Attachment types and parenting styles are considered, to try to draw some conclusions about how parenting styles can affect attachment. Multiple attachments are examined, and the role of fathers.

This chapter looks more closely at issues raised in Chapter 2, in particular those issues that relate to how infants and caregivers form attachments to one another. Attachment theory is at the heart of child development. It is becoming increasingly clear that it is not only the children's emotional wellbeing that depends on how securely attached they are but all other aspects of development as well. When there are no attachments, or poor attachments, it is thought that this affects the child's development negatively. These claims are examined in this chapter and, as is usual in these sorts of areas, it is hard to draw precise conclusions. One difficulty is that there are many variables affecting a child's development, so pinpointing or blaming one particular issue such as attachments for problems is not straightforward. Questions asked in this chapter include:

- Does the baby only attach to one person?
- Is that person always the natural mother?
- Are there different types of attachment (for different babies)?
- What role do fathers play?
- Can there be multiple attachments for each child?
- Are there different caring styles?
- Do caring styles link to attachment types?
- What is separation anxiety?
- What is stranger fear?
- What are effects of privation?
- What are the effects of deprivation?

So that you are ready for what follows, here are some brief answers to the above questions. Then read on and decide whether you agree with these answers. Remember to be critical of the studies and to keep asking questions. Where were they carried out? Who was asked? Do the findings apply to all cultures? Have the findings been replicated? This chapter offers criticisms where it is appropriate but you can make your own mind up of course.

The suggested answers to the above questions are:

- Does the baby only attach to one person? *No, the baby can form multiple attachments including to mother, father, brothers, sisters, aunts, grandparents and key people in the nursery.*

- Is that person always the natural mother? *No, but there is usually one main caregiver*

- Are there different types of attachment (for different babies)? *Yes there are different attachment types. They may come from different parenting styles.*

- What role do fathers play? *In this culture fathers tend to have a special role to do with playing and giving attention rather than caring (although of course this varies). Their role can be equally important to the child.*

- Can there be multiple attachments for each child? *Yes there can and they can have different quality and value.*

- Are there different caring styles? *Yes there are different caring styles and they tend to link to different attachment types – and can differ between cultures.*

- Do caring styles link to attachment types? *Yes, this does seem to happen as has been outlined above.*

- What is separation anxiety? *Securely attached children will normally show separation anxiety when they are separated from someone they are attached to. They feel insecure and cry when separated. This seems to be part of normal development.*

- What is stranger fear? *Like separation anxiety, stranger fear is part of a secure attachment – a baby prefers its attachment figure and turns away from strangers. This seems to be part of normal development.*

- What are the effects of privation? *Privation is when a child has no attachment figure and this seems to have severe consequences – although with excellent quality care later these severe effects can perhaps be overcome.*

- What are the effects of deprivation? *Short term deprivation can be very distressing for children but can be overcome if the child is prepared – for example if they know the person they stay with. Long-term deprivation is even more distressing and can lead to severe long-term consequences. However, it depends on factors such as age of the child. For example, can they form new attachments? It also depends on whether another attachment figure is still in the picture. So this is not straightforward.*

Attachment and bonding

Bonding was discussed in Chapter 2. It seems to be a survival trait with a biological foundation. Babies appear to need to bond with a **significant person** and they rely on that bond to build a **safe base** from which they can explore their world. **Attachment** refers to the two-way process where the baby and main caregiver bond and come to rely on one another.

Bowlby's views on attachment

Bowlby is an important name in this area of research. He prepared a report to the World Health Organisation (1952) about the importance of attachment. He considered it to be a primary drive and a survival instinct. At the time of his work the main caregiver was usually the mother and it was concluded, therefore, that babies need their mothers' continual presence. This is an important conclusion from a political viewpoint as at the time it was useful to encourage mothers to remain at home to look after their children. This period was immediately after World War Two. During the war many women had come out of the home to take up jobs so that men could be released to fight. When the men returned from the war they needed to take up their jobs once again. It is widely thought that Bowlby's report went a long way to giving evidence needed to the government for them to encourage this reorganisation of roles. Bowlby's original ideas were outlined in 1958, but he went on to develop his work after that time. He was influenced by Freudian views as well as by biological ideas such as imprinting.

Bowlby originally thought that the attachment that babies formed for their main carer was instinctive – that babies produce a range of instinctive behaviours such as crying and smiling and that these behaviours trigger instinctive 'mothering behaviour' in the adults that have the main parenting role. This communication between baby and adult is the beginning of the process of attachment. Later, in 1969, Bowlby modified his theory to suggest that the process was not entirely instinctive and that environmental factors also play a part in the development of attachment. For example, the attachment process can be adversely affected if there is something wrong with the baby or if the mother is depressed. Whether the behaviour is instinctive or is influenced by environmental factors, Bowlby still thought that attachment is an important part of an infant's development.

Evidence that attachment is a primary drive

Harlow and others carried out experiments in the 1950s and 1960s (e.g. 1959) using rhesus monkeys, which have many similarities to humans. In one experiment the researchers separated baby monkeys from their mothers. Then they offered them two alternative 'mothers'. One was a model of a wire 'mother' that gave milk but no comfort. The other was the same model but wrapped in soft cloth to provide comfort but no food. These two 'mothers' were both in a cage with the monkeys. The baby monkeys fed from the wire 'mother'. However, they cuddled up to the cloth 'mother' and, when researchers made sounds to frighten the monkeys deliberately, the monkeys ran to the cloth 'mother'. Harlow and his colleagues concluded from this and other studies that the monkeys needed contact comfort to satisfy a primary need. The food itself was not enough. The findings of this study have been used to suggest that human babies also need contact comfort as well as food.

The Harlows showed that young rhesus monkeys 'attached' to the cloth mother and seemed to seek out comfort

DEFINITIONS

Monotropy – a baby's need to form an attachment with a single significant person. This is not necessarily the mother.

Stranger fear – babies cling to their mothers when a stranger approaches, and bury their heads in their mothers' (or main caregivers') shoulders, turning away from the stranger. They are showing stranger fear, which might be a survival instinct.

Separation anxiety rather like stranger fear, but in an older child. As children start to crawl and move away, they check frequently to make sure their attachment figure is still there. They show separation anxiety if the attachment figure goes away – even for a short while.

Bowlby built on the evidence of studies such as Harlow's and concluded that human infants need a single person with whom to form an attachment. That person was needed to provide contact comfort and a safe base, for example, when the infant was frightened. This idea is called **monotropy**. It should be noted here that the significant person with whom a child forms such a bond does not have to be the mother but it usually was at the time Bowlby was developing this theory.

There are two types of infant behaviour that you should be able to watch for and that give evidence for attachment: first, **stranger fear**, and, second, **separation**

anxiety. Bowlby thought that attachments developed in phases. The first is the pre-attachment phase (0–2 months) where babies' responses to those they know and to strangers do not differ. (Note that it is now thought that babies can almost immediately recognise their mother's voice and face, so perhaps Bowlby was not right about this.) In the second phase (2–7 months) babies start to recognise their main caregiver and to develop attachments. From 7 months babies start to show anxiety when strangers approach (stranger fear). As children grow older they will start to feel more comfortable away from their caregiver for longer and longer periods, although they will still show separation anxiety. The final phase is at around 2 years old as children develop more independence and less separation anxiety. It is as if infants from 7 or 8 months are linked to their attachment figures by a rubber band that can stretch as they move away but can still draw them back as needed. Table 3.1 summarises Bowlby's three phases of attachment.

Table 3.1   Bowlby's three phases of attachment

Attachment phase	Description
The first phase: 0–2 months	Babies do not recognise things sufficiently to form an attachment. They are just as happy with anyone – no special attachments have formed.
The second phase: 2–7 months	Babies start to attach to their main caregiver and by the end of this phase, they attach firmly, as shown by stranger fear.
The final phase: 2 years old	Separation anxiety comes towards an end as attached children have confidence to explore their world.

Stranger fear

Infants of around 6 months old are expected to show **stranger fear** if they are securely attached. Typically babies who show stranger fear cling to their mothers (or attachment figure) and turn away from the stranger. This can be very awkward if the 'stranger' is a grandparent whom the baby rarely sees but it should be seen as evidence of a strong attachment and is considered normal (at least in our society). It might be of more concern if a baby of that age was willing to go to anyone – although, again, each case must be viewed individually and sweeping generalisations should be avoided. Indeed stranger fear could be seen as having survival value. Babies that cling to their main caregiver would perhaps be better

Babies who show stranger fear usually cling to their mothers (or attachment figure) and turn away from the stranger

protected than babies who would happily to go to anyone. Individuals showing this behaviour would be more likely to live to adulthood, passing on the gene that controls this behaviour to future generations.

Separation anxiety

Separation anxiety is similar to stranger fear although it appears when the child is slightly older. Bowlby's last attachment phase is at about the age of 2 years, when the child feels secure enough to move away from their attachment figure. This is when separation anxiety can be found if the attachment figure is not there for the child to refer back to for reassurance.

Types of attachments

Ainsworth, a student of Bowlby carried out studies that examined how secure attachments are. She developed the idea of different types of attachments and wondered if attachment types differed between cultures. If all cultures show the same attachment types this would suggest that they are innate and instinctive. If there are different attachment types in different cultures this would suggest that such types are learnt and influenced by environment. There is also the question of whether some types of attachment are better for the child than others, irrespective of cultural differences. Ainsworth suggested that there are different attachment types and carried out studies in different cultures when developing her theories. She worked for a time in Uganda and she observed infant-mother interactions, focusing on Bowlby's ideas. She noticed how different infants had different attachment behaviours. Then she worked in Baltimore and watched American children, again noting variation in attachment patterns, and she became interested in these differences.

The strange situation procedure

One of Ainsworth's most important contributions was the method that she used for studying attachment types. She wanted an experimental method that would enable her to compare different kinds of attachment. She devised what is called the 'strange situation procedure'. The infant and mother are placed into a strange situation and their reactions are observed. The focus is on stranger fear. Ainsworth expected to find this if a child was securely attached. Separation anxiety is also important and Ainsworth chose to study children between 1 and 2 years of age. If a mother and child are observed in the home then the child will be less distressed when the mother leaves than if the child is not in familiar surroundings. So, in order to instigate anxiety, Ainsworth decided to carry out her observations in a laboratory situation (a strange situation) away from the home. If the situation and procedure are kept the same for all the infant-mother pairs then different types of attachment can be compared.

The procedure involves the mother, the child, and an unfamiliar woman who is the stranger. A room is set up with toys for the child to play with, and two chairs, one for the stranger and one for the mother. Observation is possible from a different room, so that the researchers are not involved in the situation. Table 3.2 outlines the strange situation procedure.

The mother and baby interactions during the strange situation procedure are judged according to what happens. The most important aspects are the infant's reactions during the two reunions, when the mother comes back into the room and tries to settle the baby. Ainsworth *et al.* (1978) formed a coding system to categorise the mother/child behaviours so that they could summarise their findings into types of attachments. They found four categories of behaviour that they could record. One category considered whether the baby tried to come near to the mother; one was whether the baby held on to the mother; one was whether the baby resisted the mother's attempts to calm it, and the final category involved whether the baby avoided the mother altogether. These four categories are summarised in Table 3.3.

Table 3.2   An outline of the strange situation procedure

Timing	Strange situation procedure
Start	Mother and baby enter the room
3 minutes	Mother and baby stay alone, with baby playing
3 minutes	Stranger enters, sits, talks to mother, tries to play with baby
*Up to 3 minutes	Mother leaves stranger and baby alone
3 minutes	Mother returns, stranger leaves, mother settles baby and withdraws to her chair (reunion)
*Up to 3 minutes	Mother leaves baby alone
*Up to 3 minutes	Stranger returns, tries to settle baby, withdraws to her chair
3 minutes	Mother returns, stranger leaves, mother settles baby and withdraws to her chair (reunion)

*if mother feels baby is too upset then this is less than 3 minutes

Table 3.3   Behaviour that was coded by researchers to test for attachment type (Ainsworth et al., 1978)

Behaviour	Description
Proximity seeking	The baby tried to get near the mother
Contact maintenance	The baby held on to the mother in some way, to maintain contact
Resistance	The baby resisted the mother's attempts to calm them
Avoidance	The baby avoided the mother altogether

By using the four categories the researchers found three types of attachment. They found Type A children, who showed an insecure-avoidant attachment type, Type B children, who showed a secure attachment type, and Type C children, who showed an insecure-resistant attachment type. In 1990 Main and Solomon added another category to Ainsworth's three types. They called this Type D, as there were infants who did not match any of the three categories. Table 3.4 summarises the three initial attachment types and the fourth one that was added later.

Table 3.4   Three main attachment types, and a fourth that was added later

Attachment type	Description
Securely attached (Type B)	This seems to be the right balance between seeking comfort and exploring the environment. Children explore appropriately until the caregiver leaves, then they seek comfort when the caregiver returns, until comfortable to explore again. They are not always distressed when the caregiver leaves but they are quick to respond when the caregiver returns, being ready to approach and interact with her immediately.
Insecure-avoidant (Type A)	Children avoid seeking comfort from the caregiver when she returns. They remains focused on playing. They don't seek out the caregiver and will even avoid eye contact with the caregiver on their return. These children treat the caregiver and the stranger in a similar way.
Insecure-resistant (Type C)	The child is very focused on the caregiver and avoids playing. When the caregiver is present the child even focuses on the caregiver rather than playing. The baby becomes very upset when the caregiver leaves and is hard to comfort when the caregiver returns. When the caregiver returns the child might push them away and resist comfort.
Insecure-disorganised (Type D)	Children are disorientated during the procedure and have no clear strategy for coping. They might seek comfort and resist at the same time, for example. There is the suggestion that such children have been frightened by their caregivers or have seen their caregivers in a fearful state.

Findings from studies using the strange situation procedure suggest that in Britain and America around two-thirds of infants are securely attached, around 20% are insecure-avoidant, and 10% are insecure-resistant. There are few insecure-disorganised as that type is only found in special situations, not in samples from the general population. The above summary of Ainsworth's three main attachment types suggests strongly that the securely attached infant is developing appropriately. This is what, in our culture, we perceive as being correct attachment behaviour. We expect babies to be able to play happily, we expect them to show stranger fear and to seek comfort from their caregiver when faced with a strange situation. Harlow's monkeys followed a similar pattern and clung to the soft cloth 'mother' as outlined earlier, so this is taken as evidence for this being appropriate behaviour.

Cross-cultural studies

Studies carried out in other countries show the same attachment types but they find that they occur in different proportions, so it seems as if there are typical patterns but that some cultures show more of one pattern than another. British and US cultures tend to show more secure attachments and it is considered that this is the 'right' pattern. However, there is evidence that other cultures have different expectations so show different patterns, and we should not, therefore, assume that there is something 'wrong' with children from these cultures because they show different attachment patterns. Table 3.5 gives some results of studies done in other cultures.

Table 3.5   Findings of cross-cultural studies using the strange situation procedure

Study	Findings
Grossman *et al.* (1981) in Germany	Only 35% were securely attached (compared with around 66% in the USA). An insecure-avoidant attachment pattern was shown by 52%.
Sagi *et al.* (1985) in Israel	More infants were insecure-resistant.
Miyake *et al.* (1985) in Japan	More infants were insecure-resistant. There were no insecure-avoidant infants.

The three cross-cultural studies listed in Table 3.5 show that there may be the same attachment types overall but different proportions in different countries. However, as Miyake *et al.* found no insecure-avoidant types in Japan it may be that the same types do not exist across all cultures. If the same types had been found then this would suggest that genetic factors influence these types.

Researchers began to wonder why children showed differences in attachment behaviour and suggested that these differences were due to the different ways that their attachment figure had interacted with them (parenting style). The findings that there are cross-cultural differences in the proportions of children who are securely attached suggests that there may be different child-rearing styles in different cultures. If there are differences does this mean that attachment is not instinctive? Or is attachment instinctive but the type of attachment affected by cultural differences?

From cross-cultural studies such as these it has been concluded that attachment between caregiver and child is instinctive but that child-rearing styles affect how this attachment works. For example, German mothers do seem to emphasise independence in their children more quickly than American and British mothers. The researchers found that the children of German mothers who did not enforce independence early (within the first year) were not more insecure-avoidant than the children of American mothers. So it is likely that enforcing early independence leads to insecure-avoidant children, and this is part of German culture. The researchers carrying out studies in Japan found that Japanese mothers tended to keep in much closer bodily contact with their babies both at night (when they slept with them) and during the day (when they carried them around in slings). So it is possible that the strange situation when used in the research caused Japanese infants much more distress than American babies because of what they were used to. This additional distress may have led to them being given more 'insecure-resistant' labels. So the conclusion is that differences in child-rearing styles lead to differences in attachment types.

Note that this is a case of using an experimental technique – the strange situation test – so the findings may tell us less about attachment types than about the use of a procedure in different cultures. This shows how important it is to look at cultural differences when drawing conclusions because tests that are devised in a Western culture might not be suitable in a different culture.

Overall, the conclusions from cross-cultural studies tend to show that in all cultures an attachment is formed between the infant and their caregiver but that different child-rearing practices – perhaps resulting from different child-rearing needs – give different proportions of the different attachment types.

✔ PROGRESS CHECK

Using what you have learnt in this chapter so far, answer the following questions:

1 Which researcher built on Freud's ideas?
2 Which researcher worked with Bowlby?
3 Which researchers, who studied monkeys, gave Bowlby evidence for infants needing contact comfort as well as food?
4 Which three groups of researchers carried out three cross-cultural studies, other than Ainsworth?

Multiple attachments

Bowlby, and later Ainsworth, concentrated mainly on the idea that infants form a special attachment with their main caregiver – usually their mother. Most people, however, would say that babies have more than one person with whom they feel comfortable and safe. Babies tend to have two parents, grandparents, and possibly brothers and sisters. Researchers have studied the idea that babies can have more than one attachment figure – they can have multiple attachments. Schaffer and Emerson (1964) suggested that multiple attachments are formed, including with the father, grandparents and peers. Others in the infant's life might not all help in taking care of the infant but might interact with them in different ways, including playing with them. These different interactions still have value and still mean that an attachment is formed. Schaffer and Emerson's (1964) study that suggests that infants form multiple attachments.

Schaffer and Emerson's (1964) study

Schaffer and Emerson chose a sample of families with new born-babies and made visits to the family homes during the babies' first year and another visit when the children were 18 months old. They made visits every 4 weeks and measured attachments. They watched the amount of protest the baby showed when separated from a familiar person and they asked mothers whether the baby cried when left alone. At about 7 months they found that 29% of the babies had formed more than one attachment and in 10% of cases the baby had formed five or more attachments. By 10 months 59% had formed more than one attachment and by 18 months 87% had formed more than one attachment. It was usually the case, though, that there was only one particularly strong attachment – that is, they found a main attachment figure. Half the 18-month-old children formed their main attachment with their mother, with nearly a third having their main attachment with their father; 75% were attached to their father by the age of eighteen months, even if he was not their main attachment figure.

An infant showing multiple attachments

DEFINITIONS

Temperament – people's emotional reactivity or characteristic way of interacting with their environment. Individuals can be highly emotional or emotionally unreactive; they can be active, restless or placid; they can be very responsive to others or avoid social situations.

Parenting types

Ainsworth *et al.* (1974) studied how mothers interacted with their babies. A baby tends to focus on emotions, such as fear, pain, happiness and discomfort. The way caregivers respond to babies' needs, via their emotional cues, seems to have a strong effect on the babies' development. The strange situation measures a baby's emotional responses to a caregiver when they return after a short separation, and the researchers thought that the way in which a mother or caregiver responded to the baby's emotional needs from the start was likely to dictate the sort of attachment that baby and mother had. It was suggested that sensitive, responsive mothering led to a more securely attached infant. Mothers who ignored or rejected their infants' emotional cues tended to have babies with insecure-avoidant attachment types. When attachment type was insecure-resistant, this linked to inconsistent patterns of response to the baby's emotional cues. As the researchers seemed to be able to link parenting style to attachment type this tends to reinforce the idea that these different types exist. It also reinforces the idea that parenting style links to attachment type. This is not quite the same as saying that parenting style causes the attachment type as there are other issues that are involved as well, such as the **temperament** of the baby (see Chapter 2). It might be hard to be consistent in parenting style if babies are inconsistent in the cues they give. It must be hard to be sensitive and responsive all the time to a baby that cries a great deal, and much easier to act in that way to a relaxed baby.

It seems logical to say that sensitive mothering will lead to a more secure attachment. However, there have been studies that have not found a link between parenting style and attachment pattern (for example, Rosen and Rothbaum, 1993). Again it should be mentioned that emotional interactions such as attachment formation are not easy to study and there are so many factors involved. These include mothering style, whether there are multiple attachments, temperaments of both child and caregiver, and the situation itself – it is a very hard area to study.

The father's role

Much of the research given above on attachments has focused on the mother and main caregiver. This can be the father but most of the earlier research has looked at mother–infant interactions. It might be said that fathers have become more involved in the caring role in any case, and so should be studied. However, most studies in the 1980s and 1990s have found that stereotypes still apply and the mother in a family spends much more time caring for the children, with the father taking the role of playing with them. Studies do show that where fathers are the main caregivers they are just as successful in that role, it is just that this is not the usual situation. In general it is concluded that fathers who interact with their children often do tend to feel closer to their children, and that this is true across different cultures (Ishi-Kuntz, 1994).

In general some conclusions about the role of the father can be drawn. Fathers give a role model for their families. Children who are brought up without fathers do not seem to do as well as those with fathers, even when financial difficulties are taken into account (Snarey, 1994). For example, where there is a father who gives financial support and visits often, the children still seem not to do so well as families with a father present (for example, King, 1994). It is thought that fathers help to show their children how men behave. This can be linked to the idea of social learning theory and how we learn by modelling on others, as will be outlined in Chapter 4. It seems that the father's role in the family is a special one.

Children enjoy father's role as playmate

Using relationships with caregivers as models for later relationships

Bowlby was not only interested in attachments for the sake of the young child – though he believed that strong attachments were needed for 'normal' development – but he also thought that the strength of an early attachment affected the later development of the young adult. Bowlby (1980) built on his idea that a secure attachment is the foundation of successful child development and claimed that children's relationships with their caregiver in the early years gave them an **internal working model** of how a relationship should work. Babies form internal working models from other relationships too and in this way learn how to interact with others as an adult. Children who have sensitive and loving support have a model of themselves as good and worthwhile and are more self-confident. However, insecurely attached children, who show resistant and avoidant behaviour, have a model that expects others to be resistant, avoidant and inconsistent. Bowlby suggested that in some cases very poor or non-existent attachments can lead to severe difficulties in adulthood and his ideas are explored below when **privation** (having no attachment) and **deprivation** (which looks at broken attachments) are considered. Note, too, that if adults' relationships are affected by their own attachment pattern, then this in turn is likely to affect how they attach to their own children, and a cycle might develop in this way. Will it be harder for adults who had insecure attachments when they were young to form a secure attachment with their own infants? Some research does suggest that attachment types and attitudes to attachments are the same through families for at least three generations (Benoit and Parker, 1994), which supports the idea that forming internal working models guides our interactions with others.

This link between attachments and emotional development has been explored. It is rather simplistic to say that an attachment type can be easily recognised and then it can be seen that this type governs a person's later development. For example, it is said that an insecure-avoidant attachment type is recognised by seeing that a child is not so distressed when their caregiver returns after a short separation. However, the measure of distress here was observed behaviour. It has been found (Spangler and Grossman, 1993) that if the measure of distress is a physiological one, in other words if biological measures are taken, then the child is as distressed, or even more distressed, than a securely attached child. So it seems that the children are still distressed but that they hide their emotions. These sorts of findings show how studying emotional responses such as attachments is not easy. It seems that certain types of parenting style do affect attachment and that secure attachments seem to lead to a more secure and self-confident child. However, there are factors here that are hard to measure and it is important to measure the complexity of human emotions and how they affect a child's development. Chapter 9 of this textbook focuses on emotional development and explores these issues in more depth.

Bowlby's ideas link to other theories

Bowlby did not follow Piaget's ideas but this is an example of how the different theories in psychology do not contradict each other but simply take a different approach to the same questions. Bowlby did work within a psychoanalytic framework and Freud's ideas can be seen within Bowlby's theories. For example, there is the importance of the early years in shaping the adult – which Bowlby, following Freud, underlined. There is the importance of the early relationship between infants and their caregivers, which again Bowlby believed in, following Freud's ideas. Bowlby's idea that babies, in the very first months, focus on their own emotions and how their needs are met (including attachment needs) follows Freud's view of the demanding id, which is the initial part of the personality, and Freud's view that the baby is driven by the id. Freud's ideas are outlined in more depth in Chapter 7.

Intervening to improve attachments?

If it is found that a secure attachment leads to a more self-confident and secure individual, then should there be intervention to help insecurely attached children, so that they can develop internal working models that help them progress in a self-confident and secure way? A group of 100 mothers who were not wealthy had a low socioeconomic status and who had come from Mexico to America, were considered at risk and were chosen to undertake a programme to help to improve their attachments (Lieberman *et al.*, 1991). Sixty-three per cent of the young children were classified as either insecure-avoidant or insecure-resistant. They were divided into two groups: one group (the experimental group) received 'therapy' and one group (the control group) did not. The securely attached children formed another control group. The therapy consisted of a therapist who visited the experimental group (half of the insecurely attached children) and spent time with the mother. The therapist listened to the mother's concerns and helped her to understand her child's needs. For example, a mother might see a child who is getting into everything as being naughty, but the therapist can help to point out that the child is just too young to know any different. The results were that after 2 years there was no difference between the experimental group and the securely attached children (one of

TRY THIS!

If you have studied cognitive development, link the idea of the child building internal working models with Piaget's idea of how we build schemas from our experiences and then use these schemas to make sense of our world. Chapter 5 looks at cognitive development.

the control groups). However, the other control group, the half of the insecurely attached children who did not have therapy, remained insecurely attached. This study suggests that intervention can change attachment type, which strongly indicates that there are environmental reasons for the attachment types that form, and that it is not only the temperament of the child or mother that gives this pattern.

Early years practitioners are increasingly working with parents who seem to have difficulties in relating to their children appropriately.

CASE STUDY

Tracy and her daughter, Susan, were referred to a social services family centre. The family's health visitor had observed that Susan, aged 18 months, was small for her age and fretful, with poor language development. The health visitor noticed that Tracy often ignored Susan's approaches to her and wondered if Tracy's behaviour was adversely affecting Susan's development.

Tracy agreed to attend the centre on a regular basis where she joined in a mother and toddler group supervised by experienced early years practitioners. When her key worker had built up a good relationship with Tracy, Tracy agreed to undergo some more intensive work. This involved the practitioner making video recordings of Tracy playing with Susan and discussing the videos with her.

Tracy was gently shown how she often failed to notice Susan making an approach to her. For instance Susan might come up to Tracy and try to start a game with her. On other occasions when Susan was deeply involved in playing on her own, Tracy sometimes forcibly interrupted this to try to engage Susan in an activity that was adult directed. The upshot of all this is that there was a mismatch between what Susan wanted and what Tracy wanted. Tracy was not being at all responsive to Susan's needs.

After several sessions where the practitioner and Tracy discussed the videos it was noted that Tracy was becoming more responsive to Susan and the mother/child relationship was much more satisfying for them both.

PRIVATION AND DEPRIVATION

Privation occurs when a child has had no opportunity to form an attachment. Deprivation occurs when an attachment bond is broken. Although it is interesting to focus on attachments to see what good comes from them, another interesting way to study them is to see what happens when they are not formed or when they are broken. This is partly because a lot can be learnt from things that go wrong, and partly because researchers in psychology are interested in knowledge not only for its own sake but also to use it to improve things. Child psychologists want to improve children's experiences and their life chances.

Privation and deprivation – definitions

Deprivation refers to the loss of an attachment figure. Attached children are separated from their main caregivers and are deprived of that relationship. This can be short-term separation or long-term separation. Short-term separation can occur, for example, if an attachment figure is in hospital for a short period. You could say that a child attending a daycare facility also involves short-term deprivation, and this is discussed later in this chapter. Long-term separation can occur, for example, when there is a divorce and a child is separated from one parent, or perhaps on the death of a parent. Deprivation caused by short-term and long-term separation is discussed later in this chapter.

THINK ABOUT IT

Make a quick list of all the things you think a privated child would not be able to do. Remember that a privated child has had no bonding experience and no attachment figure. Then make another list of how you think a well-attached child would be affected by short-term deprivation. How do you think a child would react to such a separation, both on being separated and on the return of the caregiver? This exercise will help you to see the difference between privation and deprivation.

Privation is different from deprivation in that a privated child has not had an attachment figure in the first place. There is no separation as the child has not experienced bonding and attachment. This is, of course, a rare occurrence.

'Normal' development – and socialisation

Much research has focused on the effects of privation and deprivation on children. This is because we make the assumption that children are **socialised** – that is they grow up normally when surrounded by (and influenced by) others. As has been shown in Chapter 2, babies come into the world prepared to interact with others. For example, they start to recognise voices early on, and they enjoy turn taking, and so start learning in that way. From that early start bonding takes place and attachments with caregivers occurs. It is now recognised that children are programmed to learn and develop best in a social situation. This is as true for older children who learn from their peers and the adults around them as it is for very small infants, whose development in all areas is promoted by the special relationships they have with their attachment figures. Those closest to us are often referred to as **significant others** as it tends to be those who are significant in our lives who affect us more. This has already been explored when looking at attachments, multiple attachments and the role of the father.

When children are deprived of the influence of others, in particular significant others, then their development might well be profoundly affected. This is even more likely to be the case if they are privated. So the study of privation and deprivation is seen as very important and is outlined in some depth here.

Children in a Cambodian orphanage – a more stimulating environment is likely to lead to 'better' development

What are the effects of privation and are they reversible?

Privation is difficult to study because it does not happen very often. First some of the research on privation will be investigated, and then the question of whether the effects of privation can be reversed will be examined.

The therapist monkeys – Harlow's privated monkeys were helped

Harlow's studies with rhesus monkeys have been outlined earlier in this chapter. One of Harlow's procedures was to deprive monkeys of their mothers and to see if they then preferred a wire 'mother' that fed them or a cloth 'mother' where they could get comfort. As outlined earlier, the monkeys ran to the cloth 'mother' as a safe base and this was taken as evidence that comfort is an innate need. The monkeys themselves (including those in other studies that Harlow did, using other situations) then found it very hard to make normal relationships when they were older and they also became 'bad' mothers themselves. So we can say that the monkeys were privated and did not form normal attachments. Privation appears to lead to problems in later life in humans as well, such as problems forming relationships and problems in forming attachments with one's own children. The monkeys also showed a lot of aggression and it is thought that this, too, was a result of privation.

It is important to ask whether those early experiences could be reversed and whether such monkeys could then develop normal attachments themselves. This is important because if the effects of privation are not reversible then, as a society, we need to take note of this as it means that privated children are going to have problems throughout their lives. However, if the effects are found to be reversible, and we know how to reverse them, then we should be able to take steps to improve such children's lives.

Suomi and Harlow (1972) tried to overcome the social and emotional damage to the monkeys. The monkeys had experienced 6 months of isolation and the researchers tried to overcome this by pairing the monkeys with 'normally reared' monkeys. They had already tried using what they called 'therapist' (normal) monkeys of the same age but this did not work because the isolated monkeys were then overwhelmed. So this time the researchers used younger monkeys. The isolated monkeys were 6 months old and the therapist monkeys were 3 months old. There were four monkeys that had been isolated and four therapist monkeys. The therapy involved one-to-one sessions (with one isolated and one therapist monkey) and group sessions too. The 'therapy' (letting the monkeys mix) took place for 6 hours a week and it was found that after 6 months' therapy the isolated monkeys had overcome their problems. These findings suggest that the effects of privation can be overcome, at least in rhesus monkeys – perhaps depending on issues such as the age of the infant monkey and the length of time of privation.

Although the above findings are widely used to show, first, the effects of privation and, second, that it might be overcome, there are criticisms of the studies. For a start, monkeys, not babies, were studied so there should be some caution in drawing firm conclusions about humans from these animal studies. However, humans and rhesus monkeys have a lot of genes in common and there are many similarities, including their 'child rearing' habits, so perhaps results of studies on monkeys can be generalised – which means that the findings might be said to be true for humans too. It would not be possible to carry out such studies with humans. This is often given as a justification of doing animal studies – although you might not agree.

A study of humans

Skeels, in the 1930s, carried out a study of human babies, similar to the study of monkeys outlined above, to see if therapist monkeys could help. Of course, Skeels did not intervene with the human babies. He did not isolate them for the first 6 months of their birth and then see if such isolation could be overcome. That would not be ethical. However, he did find a group of children that had been privated (with no attachment formed). He found an overcrowded and understaffed orphanage and arranged that half of the children would be sent to another institution. He found a residential school for women aged from 18 to 50 years old who had learning disabilities and sent half the orphanage children there. The children from the orphanage could relate to the women, who cared for them on a one-to-one basis, giving the children a much more enriched environment than they had in the orphanage. The adults, whilst having learning disabilities, were intellectually superior to the children in the orphanage. Thirteen children from the orphanage were sent to the school. Their average age was nineteen months and their average

THINK ABOUT IT

Do you have concerns about using animals for experimentation? There are a number of arguments for and against this idea and you should weigh them all up before coming to your own conclusions. The arguments are presented in Table 3.6

IQ was 64. Note that normal IQ should be 100 and scores below 70 indicate a learning disability. The average IQ of the orphanage children who stayed behind was 87 so Skeels chose the children with the lowest IQ to try to give them help. On the face of it this is an ethical thing to do, but the other children were not helped, which is regrettable.

Table 3.6   Some arguments for and against the use of animals in psychological research

For the use of animals	Against the use of animals
• We cannot do similar studies on humans (unethical)	• Just because we have power does not mean we should use it.
• We owe it to our species to find the answers	• It is 'speciesist' to favour our own species
• The costs (in terms of harm to animals) are worth the benefits (for humans)	• We should not cause others harm including animals
• What we learn can help animals too (e.g. caging and conditions)	• In practical terms perhaps we cannot generalise the findings to humans in any case (humans and animals are different), so there is no point
• In practical terms there are advantages in using animals (e.g. easier to handle, reproduce more quickly)	

Using animals within careful guidelines

There are strict guidelines to be followed including:

• Adequate caging and care of all animals

• No unnecessary pain and suffering

• Qualified staff available at all times

• Medical care required when appropriate including surgical procedures, use of anaesthetics

• Home Office licence required

• Premises visited and vetted by officials

• No use of endangered species unless for their own safety and care

• Care of not upsetting the habitat of animals in the wild when studying them

• Knowledge of the species to treat them as fairly as possible

Cost benefit analysis

The generally accepted view is that animals can be used in studies but that there must be a careful balancing of the costs and the benefits to show that such studies are worthwhile.

• The cost in terms of suffering must be as low as possible

• The benefits in terms of help to humans and / or animals must be high enough

• The research must be of good quality so that the findings are sound (to make it worthwhile)

After 18 months in the new institution the orphanage children's average IQ was up by 29 points. In the school the children spent time with the brighter women there, and the attendants looked after them too. The women and attendants became fond of the children and often played with them. In response to this attention the children seemed to do better. Skeels even followed the children as they grew, to see if any improvements were long term ones. He found that they were. Eleven of the 13 children were adopted and their average IQ, about two-and-a-half years later, was 101. The other two children were reinstitutionalised though and lost the gains they made. The 12 who had stayed in the orphanage all the time actually had a lower average IQ, of 66, when studied two-and-a-half years later.

Skeels, in 1966, went back to see the children as adults, and found huge differences in the two groups. The experimental group, who had gone to the school and had then been adopted, showed no deficits. There were also very striking differences between the occupations of the adopted group compared with the group that stayed in the orphanage. The experimental group did much better. The study was criticised – IQ is not measured successfully at 19 months, for example – but the differences were so great that the findings of this study are generally accepted and it is concluded that the effects of early privation can be overcome, with special care.

Koluchova's study

Another study of humans strongly suggests that the effects of privation can be overcome with good quality care. Jarmila Koluchova (1972, 1976) carried out a case study of twins in what was then Czechoslovakia. The mother of the identical twins, who were born in 1960, died when they were very young. Then, when they were about one-and-a-half years old, their father remarried. The stepmother took an active dislike to them and did not give them any care. They spent most of their time together shut in a room without adequate food, exercise or light. They could not visit other parts of the house, where the rest of the family lived, and they were rarely visited. When they were around 6 years old they were found and at that time they were in a very bad state both physically and mentally. They could not use language, for example, and were very undernourished. They were frightened of anything new and could not recognise photographs of objects. They were below the developmental level for their age. At first they went to a children's home and did quite well, because of the attention they received. They were well cared for and in a non-threatening environment. At the age of 8 years, however, their IQ was tested and was well below normal for their age. However, with additional care and attention they flourished and their IQ became normal by the age of 14 years. It was concluded that very special care would enable the effects of privation to be reversed.

The case of Genie

One case study (Curtis, 1977) showed a young girl who had suffered extreme privation. She had spent 11 or more years of her life tied either to a potty during the day or to her sleeping bag at night. Nobody spoke to her at all. Her father did feed her and tie her in at night but did not speak to her. She was found at the age of 13 and was very small for her age. She rarely made any sound and was not toilet trained. She could not walk normally either. Psychologists then tested her – indeed she went to live with various psychologists and their families over a period of years. They found that she was quite perceptive and could solve problems, although she rarely spoke. Despite being looked after and taught, Genie (not her real name) did not develop normal language and did not develop normal social behaviour, although she did improve and she did become attached to various people. The funding ran out – the psychologists had looked after her as if she was a research project – and then she went to live in a home (after being reunited with her mother, but her mother could not cope).

The study of Genie shows that early privation cannot always be overcome. However, this study is slightly different from the others outlined above, and these differences might explain why the effects of privation were not reversible. Genie was not found until she was around 13 years old, which is older than Koluchova's twins were when they were found. Also Genie may have had deficits from the start. It was thought that the twins were normal at birth but it was not known whether this was the case with Genie.

Conclusions – the effects of privation are reversible to an extent

It does seem that with additional attention and care the effects of privation can be reversed. Harlow's six-month old monkeys improved when they were able to socialise with other monkeys. Skeels found that very young children – from 19 months – improved when they were cared for and played with. Koluchova found that the twins improved after the age of 6 years with extra quality care.

However, note that the twins did have each other and there would have been some sort of attachment formed between them. This could have been enough to give them some form of model for later relationships. Moreover, the children that Skeels studied, and Harlow's monkeys, were very young. The study of Genie, who was alone up to the age of 13, suggested that the effects of privation are not reversible, so the fact that the twins had each other may have been significant. However, Genie was older when found, and may have had other developmental difficulties, so no firm conclusion can be drawn. Perhaps up until a certain age the effects of privation are more easily reversible (the age of 3 years has been suggested). After that it is much harder. Perhaps it also depends on other circumstances, such as there being someone else to attach to.

More recently the long-term effects of early privation have been studied in infants and children who were kept in extreme conditions in orphanages in countries such as Romania, Albania and China. Because of extreme social and political circumstances large numbers of children were given up at birth by parents who were unable to care for them. In many orphanages the children's physical needs were just about met, but there were too few carers to give one-to-one attention, so their psychological needs were neglected. Many of these children were adopted by families in the UK, the US and Canada.

It was thought that once children were in a normal, loving family, the effects of early privation would be reversed. Research has shown that the children improved in all aspects of development compared to children who had not been adopted but the majority of children continued to show pervasive effects into their late childhood and adolescence. It is now generally recognised that unless children are adopted at the age of a few months old, the effects of privation are unlikely to be completely reversed.

The effects of short-term deprivation

Almost all children must suffer short-term deprivation – some form of separation from their attachment figure. Bowlby outlined three stages that children might go through when deprived of their attachment figure. First, there would be distress as expected. Then there would be a stage of despair, when the child is extremely upset. Finally, disattachment or detachment would be found. In this final stage children might seem to have overcome their acute distress but in fact they are, though outwardly more calm, inwardly even more affected and likely to suffer in the long term.

Temporary (short-term) separation

Rutter (1976) carried out a well-known study to see whether infants who had been in hospital early in their lives had any long-term consequences from the experience. He studied 100 10-year olds to see whether those that had been hospitalised seemed to be affected by this early separation from their caregiver. Rutter found that one stay in hospital that lasted less than a week and took place before the age of 5 years did not produce any emotional or behavioural disturbances later in life (at least not by the age of 10 years). He did find, though, that if children were in hospital repeatedly then this did lead to problems later in childhood. However, the illnesses themselves could have caused problems. Moreover, it is possible that families with greater levels of social and economic disadvantage might have more problems with illnesses. So the problems Rutter found in children who had had repeated hospital stays might have come from difficult family circumstances rather than from the separation due to the hospital stay.

Planning for short-term deprivation

Studies carried out by James and Joyce Robertson in the 1950s and 1960s, (e.g. 1968) suggested that short-term deprivation would have less severe effects if it were planned for. The idea is that if short-term deprivation causes problems because an attachment is broken then perhaps if steps are taken to minimise the disruption then there will be fewer problems. James Robertson was convinced that the practice then of not keeping the mother and child together when a hospital stay separated them was wrong.

Until the 1970s it was common practice to admit children into hospital without offering parents the chance to stay with their children. Parents were expected to leave the children at the ward door and could only visit them once a week.

TRY THIS!

Ask older members of your family, or older acquaintances if they experienced periods of separation through hospitalisation. Can they remember how they felt? Knowing what you do about separation, what do you expect happens to young children when they are hospitalised without the comfort of their attachment figure?

In the 1960s James Robertson filmed a 2-year-old girl throughout her hospital stay. She was admitted for a relatively short time – under a week – but in this short time Robertson showed that she passed through the typical stages of separation of protest, despair and detachment. This film was shown to doctors and nurses who were, at first, angry that the care of children was criticised. They had presumed that because children were quiet they had settled into the ward and were happy. Robertson showed them that many children were, in fact, disintegrating emotionally. Later studies showed that children suffered long-term ill effects from hospitalisation even after they returned home.

Gradually there was a realisation that it is important that parents are allowed to stay with young children when they are admitted into hospital and this is common practice now.

Robertson filmed other children aged between 17 and 29 months to show their reactions to different kinds of separation. One child, John, was 17 months old and stayed in a residential nursery when his mother was having a second child in hospital. John showed distress at first, which then changed to despair and finally detachment. When the mother collected John he ignored her and would not allow her to comfort him. John also showed long-term effects, although of course there was then another baby in the household so this might have had an effect on John too. The Robertsons, upset by what they found, then tried fostering children whilst their mothers were in hospital. They fostered (separately) four children who stayed with them for between 10 and 27 days. They found that the younger ones coped well although the two older children did have some problems. None of the four, however, had the problems that John had, so it was concluded that short-term separation can cause problems for the child, but that fostering and better attention and care can go some way to making the situation better. Planning for the situation and arranging proper care can make a difference. The four children that were fostered by the Robertsons were introduced to them with their mothers there, for example, and there was some planning involved.

The effects of daycare

Placing an attached child in a daycare facility disrupts the attachment between the child and the caregiver. As has been outlined above, this attachment is of great importance to the child, so such a disruption is likely to cause distress and difficulties. However, children might gain a lot socially from experiencing daycare. They will learn to interact with others, both adults and peers, and this can be a useful grounding for future development. Are the effects of daycare desirable? This question has been researched and findings vary.

One problem with studying daycare is that institutions and types of daycare vary quite a lot, so what can be said about one type of daycare might not apply to another. Since the mid-1990s great improvements have been made to the monitoring of daycare facilities and the training of staff. Legislation has meant that daycare facilities have to be monitored and inspected, for example, and the need for more trained staff has meant that more training courses have been set up, with a greater focus on having trained staff in all facilities. Daycare for children can include private nurseries, maintained nurseries, playgroups, and childminders. Some daycare is full time and many choose part-time daycare. Moreover, even if daycare for children is not set up formally, very often grandparents and others are involved in caring for children on a regular basis. With all this variety – of type of provision, staffing preferences and individual choices of how to run the facility – it is hard to draw precise conclusions about the effects of daycare on the child.

Some studies carried out from the late 1970s, when daycare became a focus of interest, tended to find that the effects of short-term deprivation caused by leaving a child in a daycare facility were detrimental to the child. However, some studies found that there were advantages to this type of care. In America in 1993 (US

Bureau of Census) it was found that more than 40% of mothers with children under 6 years old were working, In many countries women work, including in Japan (even though in Japan mothers have traditionally stayed at home), so there was widespread use of daycare.

Many of the late 1970s studies looked at daycare in universities, as such places were readily available for study, and these involved high quality daycare for families that were quite well off. Few adverse effects were found in these studies (Belsky and Steinberg, 1978), however, with such a selected sample, this might be expected. It could be concluded, then, that high-quality daycare does not adversely affect the child.

However, when children in more typical settings were studied, it was found that children who spent more than 20 hours a week without their mothers caring for them in the first year of their life were more likely to have less secure attachments with their mothers (Belsky, 1988). There are some criticisms of the findings. For example, the 'strange situation test' was used and children who have spent time in daycare might be more used to separation and so react differently, seeming less securely attached. Remember that it was suggested earlier that children who seem less securely attached might simply be hiding their distress. Children who have experienced daycare might be more likely to hide their distress (although in itself this is an interesting finding and tends to suggest that daycare is not a good thing).

In America standards were introduced in terms of child ratios, group size and teacher training and these standards were based on what high-quality care should include. This followed a study (Howes *et al.*, 1992), which showed that facilities not meeting these standards had fewer children who showed a secure attachment and fewer who were competent with their peers. Table 3.7 shows some examples of what high-quality care should include, according to studies.

Daycare provision can differ tremendously so should be thoroughly investigated – it can be a great source of stimulation for a child

Howes (1990) found that children in lower quality daycare were less considerate and less able to focus on a task than those who were in low-quality daycare but had come from high quality daycare. Those in high-quality daycare did better at school when judged in terms of popularity, attractiveness, leadership qualities and assertiveness (Field, 1991b). This positive aspect to daycare is emphasised by a study that showed that children from low-income families displayed better cognitive development at about 5 years old when they had been in daycare than those from low income families who had not (Caughy *et al.*, 1994). This finding has to be balanced with others that found some link between daycare in early years and problems adjusting at primary school (Bates *et al.*, 1994). As mentioned above, there is some evidence that daycare can advantage some children and that high-quality daycare can be a benefit, however, there is also evidence to show that such short term deprivation is not beneficial. The study carried out by Howes (1990), outlined in Box 3.1, emphasises the complex issues involved and helps us to draw some conclusions about whether daycare is good for a child or not (and whether such a sweeping claim that it is good or bad is possible).

Table 3.7   Facilities that high quality day care should include according to studies

Examples of what seems to give high quality day care

An individual child gets on better in a small group, including 18 or fewer children of the same age or older

The most effective teachers were those with the highest education level and who had the most training in child development

Where staff had conversations with the child at an appropriate level, children developed language more effectively – and better trained staff were more likely to interact in this way with children

---

Box 3.1. Howes' (1990) study of daycare

Howes looked at the ages at which children entered daycare, the quality of the care and their family characteristics. It was found that all these were important variables in whether daycare affected children's later interactions with their peers. A child was more likely to have later problems with peers at school if they entered low quality daycare before the age of 1 year. These children were easily distracted in school, did not concentrate on tasks well and were less considerate of others. Children enrolled in high-quality daycare, however, did not have such behaviour problems at school, even if they were less than 1 year old. Families using low-quality daycare when the baby was less than a year old tended to have complex problems and less access to social support.

Many of the studies undertaken on the effects of daycare were undertaken in the US. In the UK there was a corresponding interest in the effects of group childcare. The Effective Provision of Pre-school Education (EPPE) Project, an ongoing longitudinal project, has generally found that pre-school education has developmental advantages for children from the age of 2 years old.

The age of the child attending group care is an important factor in most of the studies undertaken both in the UK and the US. Younger children are more likely to suffer ill effects due to being separated from their main attachment figure. Melhuish (2004) summarised findings from a number of studies looking at children from 0 to 3 who attend childcare provision and found that the main effect was on language development. High-quality care was seen to facilitate children's language development whereas poor quality care was found to have an adverse effect on language development.

Melhuish (2004) outlined the key messages from research, suggesting that quality care is identified by:

- 'Well trained staff that are committed to their work with children
- Facilities that are safe and sanitary and accessible to parents
- Ratios and group sizes that allow staff to interact appropriately with children
- Supervision that maintains consistency
- Staff development that ensures continuity, stability and improving quality
- Provision of appropriate learning opportunities for children.'

THINK ABOUT IT

Read through the section on quality daycare. Think about the early years facility you know best. How do you think the provision rates when judged against the quality criteria that have been identified?

What do you consider to be the barriers preventing the establishment and maintenance of 'quality?'

TRY THIS!

In order to make the separation of infants from their attachment figures easier, most nurseries have settling-in policies/procedures. If you attend a nursery, look at the settling-in procedure. If possible observe a child during this settling-in process. What attachment behaviour did you notice when the child separated from his main attachment figure? Was the settling in procedure effective? Do you think changes need to be made?

DEFINITION

Transactional model – the way in which interactions between a child and family can lead to certain types of behaviour and if perceptions are different between the individuals, then behaviour can change. Transactions involve both sets of people and how they see each other affects their behaviour with one another.

The key person approach to quality

One of the factors that is often mentioned when looking at quality daycare is the need for sufficient members of staff to be able to interact appropriately with the children. In the UK it is generally accepted that the key person approach is the most appropriate way of providing for quality care, especially for the under threes.

In the key person approach children and their families are allocated a member of staff whose aim is to establish and maintain a reciprocal attachment relationship with the child. The nursery's policies, procedures and routines are structured in such a way that the key person is given the support and opportunity to be the main care giver for the child from the moment the child enters the nursery in the morning to the moment he leaves. Key people are not there to be substitute mothers or to usurp the main attachment figure in the child's life but there is a recognition that, without a warm, reciprocal, responsive relationship with an attachment figure in the nursery, children will fail to thrive and their all-round development will be adversely affected.

It is clear that there is no straightforward answer to the question of whether daycare is good for a child. There are many factors that affect how successful daycare is and these include the family circumstances, the age of the child and the quality of the daycare provision. Although Howes did not look at the temperament of the child, that too is likely to be a factor. It seems that when a family is under stress, using daycare can add to difficulties with the infant–adult attachment and can make infants more vulnerable when they become adults. The conclusion could be that families need more support to look after the child themselves, or that daycare needs to be of high quality – or some combination of these sorts of solutions.

Transactional models of development

The above discussion about daycare, and the observation that there are many factors that affect whether daycare adversely affects a child or not, suggest that a good way of looking at child development is to consider more than one factor at a time. Instead of just looking at how a child's temperament affects an attachment, or how a parenting style can affect an attachment, perhaps it is better to try to look at the whole process – or at least at more than one factor. A **transactional model** tries to do this – it tries to see the child and family as interacting with each other and affecting one another. A child might be seen as having a particular temperament, perhaps being 'difficult', and then the family treats the child as 'difficult'. When the child is older he is likely to see himself in that way too. However, if that 'difficult' temperament is seen as 'artistic' perhaps, or as something positive, this can change the whole outcome.

Thomas and Chess (1984) studied these sorts of issues and found that the way a temperament is perceived can affect later development – with negative perceptions leading to negative behaviour. Given a social identity as a talented child and one worth working with, a 'difficult' child can change quite considerably. This might help to explain how when a child is labelled in some way – for example, as mildly autistic perhaps – then the family report finding the behaviour much easier to deal with. Presumably the behaviour stays the same but transactions (interactions) are different between the family and the child because perceptions are different. Perhaps there is less blame laid on the child, or more understanding brings more acceptance. These are interesting issues and link with the discussions of labelling and self-fulfilling prophecy which are found in Chapter 9.

The effects of long-term deprivation

The previous section investigated what may happen if children are separated from their main attachment figures for short lengths of time. This section looks at what happens if children are separated for longer periods, undergoing long-term deprivation.

Bowlby thought that long-term deprivation would lead to disattachment and when this stage was reached it might seem that the child has settled. However, in fact it is a serious situation as their internal working model would not longer include attachments, and this could lead to difficulties with relationships when the child is older. Bowlby drew some of these conclusions from his own study of 44 juvenile thieves.

Bowlby's 'thieves' study

Bowlby worked in a child guidance clinic in the 1930s and whilst there he observed a number of adolescents. He chose 44 of them for study. These 44 had all been convicted for stealing. He noted that around 40% of them had been separated from their mothers for around 6 months before they were 5 years old. Of these, 14 were diagnosed as having **affectionless psychopathy**. Affectionless psychopathy is a condition where they had no compassion for their victims and felt no guilt for their crime. Bowlby wondered whether the separation from their mothers (**maternal deprivation**) had led to the delinquency (the stealing) and to the affectionless psychopathy. Bowlby thought that there was a very strong case for saying that maternal separation had led to the delinquency – and not only to affectionless psychopathy but also to social maladjustment and emotional disturbance, which he also found in the adolescents who had had the early separation.

Note that only 40% of the juvenile thieves had had the early period of separation, and only 14 of those separated showed affectionless psychopathy. This suggests that we cannot say that only maternal separation causes problems. It might, however, be that it is an important factor in leading to such maladjustment.

One criticism that has been made of studies such as this, which show that maternal deprivation can lead to problems as severe as affectionless psychopathy, is that factors other than maternal deprivation might have contributed to the problems. In most cases there has also been institutional upbringing, which tends to suggest lack of stimulation as well as the lack of an attachment figure. It has been said (for example, by Rutter) that it is this lack of stimulation and other similar factors that have led to the later problems rather than the maternal deprivation itself.

A study reinforcing Bowlby's claims

Goldfarb (1943) carried out a study of two groups of 15 teenagers. All had been in an institution. One group had been fostered before they were one year old and the other group had spent at least the first three-and-a-half years of their lives in an understaffed institution where they were understimulated. The two groups were similar in age, contained similar numbers of each gender, and were similar in terms of the social background of their families. The question was how far had the lack of stimulation affected the non-fostered group and how far had the fostering affected the other group. Those who had stayed in the institution had a lower IQ score, were more dependent on adults and had more temper tantrums. They found it hard to make friends, too. However, those who were fostered earlier might have had characteristics that led to them being chosen for fostering. At the age of between 10 years and 14 the group was revisited and tests showed that the average IQ of the group that stayed in the institution was 72 compared with an average IQ of 95 for the fostered group. The fostered group was also socially more mature and better able to form relationships.

Does early separation lead to later problems?

Goldfarb's study reinforces Bowlby's claim that early deprivation leads to later problems. Note, however, that the studies of privation outlined earlier did suggest that very special care can lead to an improvement and can help to reverse the effects of problems in early attachment and development. There is also the criticism by Rutter and others that the maternal deprivation experienced by the children was not the only problem. The children in the studies tended to live in institutions

KEY TERMS

You need to know the meaning of the following words and phrases. Go back through the chapter to make sure you understand them:

Affectionless psychopathy
Attachment
Bonding
Deprivation
Internal working model
Maternal deprivation
Monotropy
Privation
Safe base
Separation anxiety
Significant others
Socialisation
Stranger fear
Temperament
Transactional model

KEY NAMES

Ainsworth
Bowlby
Curtiss
Harlow
Koluchova
Robertson and Robertson
Rutter
Schaffer and Emerson
Skeels

where there was a lack of stimulation so they were deprived in other ways as well as being deprived of maternal care. Overall, however, it can at least be concluded from all the above that a secure attachment is preferable to separation, deprivation or privation.

CONCLUSIONS ABOUT ATTACHMENTS

It has been shown above that privation leads to serious consequences but it might be possible to overcome them to an extent by very special care if a child is very young when helped. Short-term separation can cause problems too but, again, can be less of a problem if planned for and if substitute care is good. Daycare can be a good thing if it is of high quality, depending on family circumstances. However, daycare can be a form of separation with all the problems that this seems to bring. Separation from an attachment figure does cause distress, if not later despair and detachment, but it seems that children can form multiple attachments and separation can be less of a problem if there is good substitute care.

FURTHER READING

David, T., Goouch, K., Powell,S. and Abbott, L. (2003) *Birth to Three Matters: A Review of the Literature Compiled to Inform the Framework to Support Children in their Earliest Years,* Dfes, Nottingham, Chapter 3.
This book is particularly recommended for students on higher level courses.
Elfer, P., Goldschmied, E. and Selleck, D. (2003) *Key Persons in the Nursery* David Fulton, London. An excellent book for all students which puts attachment theory into a practical context.
Goldschmied, E. and Jackson, S. (2004) *People Under Three. Young Children in Daycare,* 2nd edn, Routledge, London.
This book is suitable for students studying at Level 3 and above. Chapter 3 is particularly recommended.
Gopnik, A., Meltzoff, A. and Kuhl, P. (1999) *How Babies Think,* Weidenfield & Nicolson, London. This book is essential reading for students studying higher level courses. Chapter 2 is particularly recommended for this topic.
Karen, R. (1998) *Becoming Attached. First Relationships and How They Shape Our Capacity to Love,* Oxford University Press, Oxford.
An easy to read text that is appropriate for students studying on higher level courses.
Karmiloff-Smith, A. (1995) *Baby It's You,* Ebury Press, London.
An easy read, recommended for all students.
Melhuish, E. (2004) *Child Benefits The Importance of Investing in Quality Childcare,* Daycare Trust, London. Facing The Future policy paper no. 9, www.daycaretrust.org.uk.
An easy read, recommended for students studying at Level 3 and above.

Learning theories

INTRODUCTION

This chapter looks at seven different theories of learning. There are many different ways of looking at how a child learns. Two important theories are presented first – classical and operant conditioning – and both of these treat the child as a **passive** learner receiving information. Classical conditioning explains how we learn to link reflexive behaviour (such as fear, pleasure, and sneezing) to various things in the environment, and this can explain phobias. Operant conditioning explains how much of our voluntary behaviour (such as tidying a room, using table manners, and doing homework) is conditioned by means of either rewards or punishment, so our behaviour is largely shaped in this way. There are three 'smaller' theories of learning linked to these two. One-trial learning is when we just have to have one bad experience (such as eating 'bad' food) and we learn not to repeat it. Latent learning is when we learn accidentally when doing something else (such as learning the names of streets even though we don't really notice them when we walk by). Insight learning suggests that perhaps we are not as passive as the above theories suggest. Perhaps we sit and think about problems and then solve them – we learn from previous experience. Finally, two other fairly important theories are considered, which you will find useful when explaining a child's learning. Social learning theory states that children learn through observation and imitate certain behaviour that they see. From this theory comes the idea that violence on TV can lead to violence in real life. This is perhaps rather simplistic, if basically true. The final theory is called 'social constructionism'. This theory holds that nobody learns in a vacuum. There are social and cultural influences that help to shape what we learn, we are influenced by many factors in our environment, and we actively construct our own world by interacting with others and within our society. At the end of the chapter there is a brief summary of the theories and some comparisons between them are made. If we have a good understanding of theories of learning this can help us plan appropriate programmes for the children in our care and can help us reflect on our practice.

There are many different approaches in psychology to the ways in which humans develop. The biological approach focuses on our physiological make up and, amongst other issues, considers the effects of our genes. The psychodynamic approach, like the biological approach, also assumes the existence of instincts and inner forces that drive us. Both the cognitive and cognitive-developmental approaches accept a role for innate factors. However, learning theories specifically focus on behaviour, without reference to genes, instincts or biological factors. That is what makes learning theories different. Basically, learning theories focus only on behaviour and not on emotions or thoughts. John Locke (1632–1704) was a philosopher who suggested we are all born as a 'blank slate', ready to be written on and shaped by our environment. As you see there is little room here for any inborn capabilities or temperament. There are different theories of learning, and they are described below.

CLASSICAL CONDITIONING – LEARNING BY ASSOCIATION

In the early twentieth century **Pavlov**, studying biological processes, observed that dogs salivated when a laboratory assistant was around. Pavlov was measuring the salivation of the dogs whilst doing a different study. He realised that the dogs salivated when food was brought in. The laboratory assistant brought in the food. So Pavlov concluded that the dogs had somehow associated the laboratory assistant with the food and had learnt to link the salivation response with the assistant, even when food was not present. The process of learning to associate a response with a new stimulus is called classical conditioning.

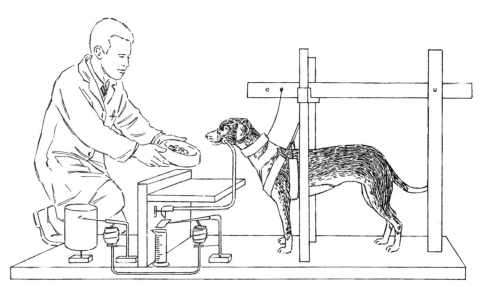

Shows apparatus used by Pavlov. A tube to the salivary glands measures salivation

The response that is classically conditioned is always a reflexive response and, although other responses to stimuli can be learnt this would be by means of different processes. So you need to think only about innate, instinctive responses when identifying cases of classical conditioning. Consider any natural response to any naturally occurring stimulus and you should be able to say how any other stimulus could come to produce that response. Some examples follow to help to illustrate the processes involved in classical conditioning.

Terminology in classical conditioning

It is useful to learn the terms used when explaining classical conditioning because explaining how different behaviours can arise through classical conditioning is then clearer. You may find it easier to use Diagram 4.1 at the same time as you read the following explanation:

- The innate instinctive response is called the unconditioned response (UCR) because it is unconditioned and occurs naturally, for example salivation.
- The stimulus that always produces the response is called the unconditioned stimulus (UCS) because no conditioning has to take place but the stimulus always produces the unconditioned response – for example food produces salivation.

- When a neutral stimulus (one that would not produce a reflexive response) is introduced it is the conditional stimulus (CS) because it will be used to produce the response. In the example given above, the laboratory assistant is the conditional stimulus.

- Finally, when the response (such as salivation) appears following the conditional stimulus (for example, the laboratory assistant) it becomes a conditioned response (CR).

Food (UCS) ⟶ Salivation (UCR)

Food (UCS) + Assistant (CS) ⟶ Salivation (UCR)

Assistant (CS) ⟶ Salivation (CR)

Diagram 4.1 Diagram showing the process of classical conditioning (dogs salivate on sight of an assistant)

✔ PROGRESS CHECK

Consider how you would condition a dog to salivate to the sound of a bell. Draw a diagram like Diagram 4.1 and substitute a bell for the assistant as the conditional stimulus.

An example of classical conditioning in humans

The above example shows how dogs can be classically conditioned. It is claimed that people can learn through classical conditioning too. An example is given in Chapter 1, p. 10, and another is outlined here. Phobias are said to come about through classical conditioning. For example, if we hear an unexpected loud bang we may startle; the noise frightens us and we jump. If, at the same time as hearing the bang, we also see a red car, the next time we see a red car we may feel fear, or even jump.

The Little Albert study

A study was conducted (Watson and Rayner, 1920) to see if learning could occur through the mechanisms of classical conditioning. The researchers used an 11-month-old boy they called Albert. He was in an institution whilst his mother worked there, and he was available for the study, although his mother seems not to have known all the details. Watson and Rayner found that Albert liked a pet white rat (a real one). He was also fairly placid and did not startle easily. However, when they banged a hammer loudly on to a metal rod, Little Albert was startled. Watson and Rayner decided to make the loud noise when Albert played with the rat, to see if he would associate fear with the rat, and he did. The process is outlined in Diagram 4.2.

Loud noise (UCS) ⟶ Startle response – fear (UCR)

Loud noise (UCS) + pet rat (CS) ⟶ Startle response – fear (UCR)

Pet rat (CS) ⟶ Startle response – fear (CR)

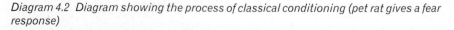

Diagram 4.2 Diagram showing the process of classical conditioning (pet rat gives a fear response)

So you can see that responses like phobias can occur from stimuli that seem odd. In Chapter 1 an example of this was outlined: children might come to sneeze every time they meet a particular aunt if they visit her dusty house frequently.

TRY THIS!

Use your knowledge of classical conditioning and the terms UCS, UCR, CS and CR, draw a diagram showing the processes outlined in Chapter 1, p. 10, where a child develops a sneeze when he sees his aunt. See p. 73 for an answer.

DEFINITION

Generalisation – this occurs when an animal or person responds to something similar to the stimulus that they first associated with their reflexive response.

DEFINITION

Discrimination – this is when an animal or person responds only to the stimulus that they first associated with their reflexive response, and not to any similar stimuli.

TRY THIS!

Talk to some friends and family and make a list of their possible fears. Make sure you do not upset them of course, or bring to mind a real phobia and so make them anxious. They may want to talk about it but check carefully first. Then sort your list into fears that could have come about through evolution, and those that are unlikely to have done (such as a fear of buttons). You should find that your list of 'understandable' fears is longest and this is evidence that fears are at least to an extent inherited. This is the concept of **preparedness** – we are prepared by our genetic make up to fear certain things more than others do.

DEFINITION

Preparedness – this is the term meaning that we are prepared through evolution to have certain phobias and not others. Snakes, spiders and heights seem to be natural phobias – they would have survival value.

Other mechanisms within classical conditioning

Phobias can be learnt through classical conditioning, just as Little Albert learnt a fear of his pet rat. He then developed a fear of other white furry objects and seemed to transfer his fear of the rat on to similar objects. There are other mechanisms, like transference (generalisation), which are involved in classical conditioning. Some of these are outlined here.

Responding to very similar stimuli

Generalisation refers to our tendency to respond not only to the conditional stimulus (a bell) but also to very similar stimuli (for example, a different tone of bell). So we could be conditioned to have a fear of a pet white rat, as Little Albert was, and then generalise that fear to other white furry objects like a Father Christmas beard. Little Albert did indeed generalise his fears to such objects.

Learning to respond only to a particular stimulus

The opposite of generalisation is when we **discriminate**. This means we learn to respond only to a particular stimulus (for example, a particular tone of bell). So we may develop a phobia of flying from a particular airport because of a bad experience but this fear may not generalise to flights from other airports. We may discriminate, which is another way of saying that we can tell the difference.

✔ PROGRESS CHECK

Babies can be startled by the noise that their parents' cars make. Being strapped into their car seats may set off conditioned fear reactions. Some babies may show fear when they are strapped into any car seat, whereas some babies will only cry when strapped into the car seat in their parents' car.

1 If they cry whenever being strapped in any car seat, what is this an example of?
2 If they only cry in response to a particular car seat, what is this an example of?
3 How could this fear develop as the child grows?

Prepared for certain fears

Some fears are reasonably harmless, and some are understandable. It is fairly understandable to fear flying as we are not in control and it is a fairly unusual experience for most people. A fear of heights is quite understandable because if we fell we would be seriously injured. Such a fear is usually quite harmless. Spiders and snakes can be harmful (in some parts of the world at least) so a phobia of spiders and snakes is also quite understandable. However, electric plugs can be harmful but we don't usually fear them. One explanation why some fears are more common than others is that humans have evolved to fear some things. For example, those humans who feared heights were presumably more likely to survive and pass on their genes, so, through the idea of survival of the fittest (see Chapter 1, p. 9), a fear of heights could have been passed on by means of genes (inherited). Note that a fear is only really a phobia when it interferes with normal functioning. If you are afraid of spiders, as long as you cope well with the fear, this is not a phobia.

Removing a conditioned response

It is said that Watson and Rayner, when giving Little Albert the fear of rats and other white furry objects, did not take the fear away afterwards. This is a strong ethical criticism of their study, although it is claimed that they would have removed the fear if Little Albert's mother had not taken him away from the study. However, their work inspired another study by another researcher, this time using a little boy who was called Peter. Peter did have a phobia and this researcher used the principles of classical conditioning to remove the phobia – a much more ethical study with a strong practical basis. Classical conditioning can be used to remove problematic (**maladaptive**) responses.

DEFINITIONS

Maladaptive – a response that is not desirable.

Aversive therapy – this is used to cure various problems such as smoking and drinking. Classical conditioning principles are used.

GOOD PRACTICE

Remember the need to look after your participants. This is your responsibility although it can be shared by making sure someone else always knows your intentions regarding any research, whether formal or informal. What can seem very harmless to you, such as the questions you are going to ask about fears, can be very threatening to someone else. Good practice requires that you always remember this. Practise putting yourself in your participant's position.

DEFINITION

Systematic desensitisation – a form of therapy used for problems such as phobias. A preferred response (relaxation) gradually replaces the fear, and the phobia is extinguished.

DEFINITION

Extinguished – this is the term for when an association is removed and the person or animal no longer gives the response to the stimulus.

Consider the example of **aversive therapy**, which uses classical conditioning principles to deter people from some unwanted habit or addiction. For example, alcoholics can be treated using such a therapy. Whisky would give pleasure. An emetic drug makes a person sick. If the whisky is paired with the emetic drug, then people should develop a 'feel sick' response to the whisky. This can work, although there are probably other factors at work too.

Emetic drug (UCS) ⟶ Unpleasant sick feeling (UCR)

Emetic drug (UCS) + whisky (CS) ⟶ Unpleasant sick feeling (UCR)

Whisky (CS) ⟶ Unpleasant sick feeling (CR)

Diagram 4.3 An example of aversive therapy for alcoholism

So classical conditioning can be used to reverse unwanted conditioning. Note that it would be important to give people soft drinks as well, when they are not affected by the drug, so that they do not associate sickness with all drinking.

Phobias can be 'cured' in a similar way. **Systematic desensitisation** is a way of 'curing' phobias. The individual is taught deep muscle relaxation, which is more than just simple relaxation and involves concentration. Then the therapist and the individual build up a series of steps leading up to presenting the phobic object. For example, for a phobia of spiders, the first step might be a picture, the next step a real small spider some distance away, the next step a larger spider nearer, and so on. For each step individuals have to call on their relaxation skills so that the relaxation response replaces the fear response until gradually (systematically) they learn to relax to the actual object (they are desensitised). The idea behind systematic desensitisation is that two conflicting emotions cannot be felt at once, so the fear and the relaxation are incompatible. The relaxation will have to replace the fear if it can be achieved. This, of course, is the hard part.

Another way of 'curing' phobias is flooding. In flooding people are faced with their most feared object straight away – for example, they might be put in amongst a lot of snakes! The idea is that their fear (and all the emotions involved!) cannot be maintained as energy levels would fall. As that happens they will think they are calming down and the fear response (to snakes in this example) would cease (be **extinguished**).

CASE STUDY

Jane, an 8-year-old girl, was frightened of trains ever since she had had a fall when running up a train corridor just when the train braked suddenly. Although this would not always lead to a phobia, in Jane's case it developed into one. Jane's mother could no longer take her on a train although she needed to travel long distances to visit her own mother who was ill. Jane's mother took her to a therapist who asked if Jane could be left with him for the day to try to cure the fear. The therapist took Jane on a train ride and made her stay on the train until she had calmed down. This took some time and was very distressing for Jane, but was successful.

1 What was the technique that the therapist used called?

2 Why was it successful?

3 Do you think this was an ethical thing to do?

THINK ABOUT IT

Think about how advertising works. For example, let's say the sight of a beautiful woman is arousing for a man, and gives pleasure. Those advertising cars use this idea. They pair an image of the car with an image of a beautiful woman (using still or moving pictures) and through the principles of classical conditioning the car should give the feelings of pleasure. In advertisements a 'hunky' man may be linked to products to encourage women to buy, using the same principles.

TRY THIS!

Using the diagram format for classical conditioning draw up the diagram that shows how a car can give rise to pleasure feelings when paired with an image of a hunky footballer. An answer is given on p. 73.

TRY THIS!

Make a list of three things you do when getting ready in the mornings and three things you do when getting ready to go to bed at night. For example, cleaning your teeth, or folding your clothes. Then make brief notes on how these behaviours could have come about. Could you have learnt them all by being rewarded for doing them when you were a child? Could they be innate behaviours? It is unlikely that they are innate, and this is what Skinner meant when he said that much (if not all) of what we do is through conditioning process and learning.

It is possible that a conditioned response would cease in any case after a certain length of time, as the unconditioned stimulus stops being paired with the conditional stimulus. It is, therefore, possible that Little Albert did not go through life with a phobia.

✔ PROGRESS CHECK

1 Write a short paragraph explaining how a child could be 'cured' of her fear of dogs using the principles of systematic desensitisation.
2 Can classical conditioning be used to explain all learning? If not, outline what associations can be explained using classical conditioning

OPERANT CONDITIONING – LEARNING BY REINFORCEMENT

In classical conditioning an automatic response such as salivation or fear becomes associated with a new stimulus. Operant conditioning describes ways in which any behaviour, not just automatic responses, can be learned. The basic principle of operant conditioning is that any behaviour that is rewarded (reinforced) will tend to be repeated. Processes of operant conditioning are outlined below.

B. F. Skinner (1904–90) is an important name in operant conditioning. In 1913 **Watson** discussed the idea that all behaviour could be controlled and he used the word 'behaviourism' to describe this type of learning theory. Skinner built on Watson's ideas and suggested that all behaviour was learnt from the environment. He did not focus on any innate processes or characteristics.

Chapter 1 examined the 'nature versus nurture' debate – the debate about how much of our behaviour and individual characteristics results from genetic/biological influence and how much is learned. Skinner was on the 'nurture' side of the debate, considering that all learning is as a result of environmental influence.

Basic mechanisms of operant conditioning

Operant conditioning involves principles different from classical conditioning principles, such as rewards and punishments, as well as other principles to do with the timing of when, for example, rewards might work best. These principles are outlined below.

Encouraging required behaviour by giving rewards

If you want to encourage children to help to tidy their bedroom you probably reward them. For example, you could say that after the bedroom was tidy you would all go to the playground to play, or you could say that the child could only have sweets if the bedroom was tidy. This is assuming that the child enjoys going to the playground and enjoys sweets. Operant conditioning involves choosing a desired reward and then using that to condition certain behaviour. The idea is that the behaviour is carried out for the reward, and the reward reinforces the likelihood that the behaviour will occur again.

DEFINITION

Positive reinforcement – occurs when a desired reward is given for required behaviour, so that behaviour is learnt.

Reinforcing by reward is called **positive reinforcement**, because a positive reward is given and brings about the required behaviour. This type of reinforcement is used in nurseries and children can be rewarded in many ways, for example by praising (for example, praising a painting they have done) or by reading a story. Schools might use a star system. Positive reinforcement is a successful technique as the desired behaviour is exhibited and the individual gets a positive reward because of it. This means there is no negative experience so the behaviour is likely to be repeated. There are some issues about frequency of rewards, however, and these are considered later in this section.

In 1991 Robert Slavin looked at several research studies designed to investigate the effect of using positive reinforcement to improve children's behaviour. He concluded that positive reinforcement works best if:

- you decide what behaviour you want from the children and reinforce it when it occurs;
- you tell children what behaviour you want;
- you tell children why you are praising them when they show the behaviour you want.

Experiments have also shown that the timing of reinforcement is important. A small reinforcement given immediately after the desired behaviour is generally more effective than a larger reinforcement given later. For instance a quiet word of praise at the time that you notice a child behaving well is more effective than a treat given at the end of the day.

Negative reinforcement

Negative reinforcement is a situation when something unpleasant stops. Originally this was demonstrated when rats learned to press levers to stop getting an electric shock. The removal of the shock was rewarding.

If children are not enjoying playing in the sand because other children are using the toys then they will move to another task. They are reinforced for moving when they are able to enjoy playing with toys involved in the new task. They have not been given a reward for moving to the new task but they are rewarded nonetheless because they have avoided something unpleasant. This sort of conditioning can be seen in many different aspects of life. If a cinema is always noisy during a film you would go to find another cinema, and if that one were quieter you would choose it. You would be rewarded by the move in the sense that you no longer had the noise – you have avoided something unpleasant. This is **negative reinforcement** because something is not given (as in positive reinforcement) but is taken away. Although behaviour in order to remove something unwanted can be learnt quite well, this is possibly not quite as good as giving a reward, as that is a more positive experience.

TRY THIS!

Consider a childcare setting with which you are familiar with and note down five types of reward. Note down first the reward and then the behaviour that is being conditioned.

DEFINITION

Negative reinforcement – occurs when a behaviour is learnt in response to the removal of an undesired stimulus. We do things to get away from something we don't like, and this can be successful learning.

✔ PROGRESS CHECK

Here are two examples of conditioned behaviour. One is an example of the use of positive reinforcement and the other is an example of the use of negative reinforcement.

1 A childminder knows that the children in her care (age 3 and 4) are looking forward to a cooking session but she wants them to complete something else first. She tells the children that they will do cooking afterwards.

2 A child tries to play with three others who are playing together in a playhouse outdoors. They are not involving her, however, and push her away. She moves over to join a group who is listening to a story read by a practitioner.

Undesired behaviour is discouraged by punishment

There is another way to condition a required response, and that is to administer **punishment** for undesired behaviour. This means giving punishment for the wrong or undesired response. The problem here is that, although this might stop undesired behaviour, it is not likely to condition required behaviour, so it is not a very successful procedure.

Problems with the use of punishment

The use of punishment to obtain desired behaviour is not usually recommended. If children experience someone punishing them, they could model that behaviour another time and could become aggressive. Social learning theory explains this, and is covered later in this chapter. Moreover, the child receives attention from the punisher. That attention can itself be reinforcing if it is the only attention the child receives. So punishment can actually reinforce undesired behaviour. Research undertaken by Bates in 1987 seems to indicate that the effects of punishment are only temporary and that punishment produces aggression. In general, then, punishment is not seen as a successful method to choose when trying to achieve desired behaviour.

Learning theorists who do support the use of punishment agree that it should only be used as a last resort when:

* positive reinforcement methods have been tried and have failed;
* punishment is part of a carefully controlled plan;
* the method of punishment is consistent and never used out of frustration.

In childcare situations punishment in the form of removing a treat or a privilege may be appropriate in some circumstances but physical punishment or the use of humiliation is never appropriate on scientific or moral grounds.

Table 4.1   Mechanisms of operant conditioning

Mechanisms	Description	Example
Positive reinforcement	Responds because a desired reward is given	Normally very active children listen patiently to a story and are then allowed to choose their own activities
Negative reinforcement	Responds because an undesired stimulus is removed	A child tidies away some toys to stop its mother being cross with it
Punishment	Stops a behaviour because an undesired stimulus is given	A child stops asking for sweets in response to a smack

✔ PROGRESS CHECK

Imagine that you are to give a short presentation to a small group of parents about how to manage undesirable behaviour.

1 What would you say about the use of punishment? Would you advise it? If not, why not?

2 What would you advise as the best mechanisms to use when suggesting using operant conditioning?

3 Why is it important that in positive reinforcement the reward given is something that is desired? What would the effect be if the reward were not actually desired?

CASE STUDY

Surinda's father writes using his right hand but he plays 'left-handed' golf. His writing is very poor and he is not good at it. Surinda prefers her left hand for writing. Her father explains to her that he thinks he is left handed too but when he was at school he was reprimanded for using his left hand and was forced to use his right hand. This sort of practice is not found so much today as it once was. Surinda's father has struggled to remain right handed because he was rewarded for using his right hand when writing and punished for using his left hand. Surinda, who was not reprimanded for using her left hand, continues to do so. This shows the power of a reward and punishment regime and shows operant conditioning in action. Actually another learning theory, social learning theory, can also help to account for characteristics such as the hand we use when writing.

TRY THIS!

Go back to the previous 'Try This!' section and see if you can classify the rewards into primary and secondary reinforcers.

Primary and secondary reinforcement

Rewards (reinforcers) can be described as being either primary or secondary. Primary reinforcers involve meeting a basic need such as the need for food, warmth or a cuddle.

However, many rewards are secondary ones, which can be used to obtain primary rewards. Money is a secondary reinforcer.

The adult says the child has been good and gives them some money. The child happily thinks they can go to the shop to buy sweets.

Using operant conditioning principles in practice (and therapy)

Operant conditioning principles are used as therapy and to change behaviour for an agreed reason.

Shaping behaviour using operant conditioning principles

DEFINITION

Shaping – this is the term for gradually achieving the learning of required behaviour by reinforcing in small steps until the behaviour is arrived at.

Like the principles of classical conditioning, mechanisms of operant conditioning can be put to good use, for example in **shaping** behaviour. You would normally want to reinforce more than a single action. A parent could want a room tidied and could offer a particular reward but usually the required behaviour is more complex than one action. In that case such behaviour must be shaped. This really just means that the whole behaviour would be broken down into stages and each stage

'Shaping' is used when training animals

reinforced separately. For example, if a child is disruptive in a nursery it is unlikely that a desired behaviour, such as sitting still through a whole story, will be achieved in one go, so such behaviour would not occur and could not be positively reinforced. Children would need to be rewarded for sitting calmly for a very short time. Once that was achieved, they could be rewarded for sitting quietly for slightly longer, maybe with one practitioner talking to them. In this way behaviour could be shaped until the required behaviour was achieved.

Using shaping behaviour as treatment/therapy

Shaping using principles of positive reinforcement is found in schools for children with special needs, one particular example being children with autism. Autism takes many forms but can often mean that a child does not talk. This is by no means always the case, and some autistic children talk very well. Autism is discussed further in Chapter 10. Consider an autistic child who is not talking. The first task would be to encourage the child to make noises. This could be done by music therapy, by singing with the child and rewarding any sounds at all. Rewards could be smiles, praise and laughter – something that the child enjoys. This is by no means an easy process but it can lead to the child making noises more readily. Once this is achieved, a therapist could gradually start rewarding particular sounds – sounds that are like words or letters. With a lot of patience and a great deal of positive reinforcement it is possible to shape speech sounds in this way. It is likely that there would be more to it, such as parents being involved in the process, and sounds being modelled too (modelling is explained later in this chapter, when looking at social learning theory). The main process here involves operant conditioning but other factors are probably also involved.

CASE STUDY

Although Ted was 3 years old he hardly spoke a word. His parents thought it was because his older sister did all the talking for him but when she went to school he still did not develop language properly. After checks had suggested that there was no physical difficulty that would prevent Ted from talking, Ted was referred to a speech therapist who helped his parents to encourage him to talk. At first they used pictures and praised Ted whenever he made a sound in response to the pictures. Gradually they waited longer until Ted's sounds were closer to the word that matched the picture. With plenty of praise, smiles and encouragement, and working with Ted whilst his sister was at school, Ted quite quickly started naming objects, first from the pictures, and then objects around him. He quickly progressed to two-word phrases and on to a language pattern to match his age. It seemed that there had been nothing to prevent his language from developing normally.

1   What operant conditioning mechanism was used with Ted?
2   Give two important parts of the therapy and explain them.

✔ PROGRESS CHECK

Here are four examples of learning. Two show learning using operant conditioning principles and two show learning using classical conditioning principles. Identify which is which, and then write a short explanation.

1   Sam does well in class and is rewarded with a gold star. He rushes home excitedly to tell his parents.
2   When Anne was very young she was badly frightened by a large snake in a zoo and now she is afraid of going to any zoo or wild life park.
3   An advertisement shows a hunky footballer driving a new car.
4   Sarah does not like the noise at playgroup and won't go, even for a short time. When she is taken to a quieter nursery, however, she stays happily all day.

SOCIAL LEARNING THEORY

So far in this chapter we have looked at explanations about how behaviour is learned through the processes of classical conditioning and operant conditioning.

It has been found that there are other ways in which we can learn. For example, social learning theorists introduced the idea that we can also learn by imitation and that our thoughts also have a part to play. Before looking at social learning, there are three other forms of learning that are worth mentioning, though they don't have such a large place in learning theories.

Three more types of learning

In this section we will investigate:

- one-trial learning;
- learning by accident – latent learning;
- problem solving by insight – insight learning.

One-trial learning

One-trial learning is when an association is so strong on one occasion that learning takes place immediately. This is a very strong form of learning. This type of learning is linked to classical conditioning and reflexes. For example, you may once have eaten something that made you ill. That tends to only happen once and you won't try that type of food again. This is a form of one-trial learning.

CASE STUDY

Sue fed her baby food that she liquidised herself. Once, by mistake, she included some chicken that was not fresh and this made the baby ill. Afterwards the baby refused all food with that particular taste. Sue had to work hard to persuade the baby to take food off a spoon at all for a little while.

1　What type of learning is shown here?
2　What is the term used that explains why the baby then at first refused food off a spoon altogether, not just food with that particular taste? Think back to the features of classical conditioning.

Learning by accident

Learning by accident whilst doing other things is called **latent learning**. It is hard to demonstrate. Latent learning has been shown in experiments with rats.

Rats can be taught to negotiate a maze to find food and it can be demonstrated that they learn all about the maze, not just the route they need to get the food. This is shown because when their learnt route is blocked, they can still use the next shortest route, which they therefore must have learnt 'by accident', as they were not rewarded for that learning. These findings have been used to suggest that we learn as we go, and not just because we are rewarded. This might be a survival trait. It might have been useful for us to learn without being rewarded for doing so, as that learning might come in handy later. This type of 'accidental learning' is latent learning.

Problem solving by insight

Animals have been used to show another form of learning too. This is **insight learning**, which suggests that we might sit and think about something before doing it. One study (Köhler, 1925) had a chimpanzee in a cage with a banana just out of reach above the chimp. Assuming the chimpanzee wants the banana, how

TRY THIS!

If you can, observe a young baby who is mobile. Remember ethical issues and good practice when observing. Watch the baby and look out for insight learning. Note down when the baby seems to be thinking about something and then when an action follows that thinking time. You should see insight learning in practice. You may see toddlers using a combination of furniture and other objects to reach something they want. You may also observe babies of about 8 months pulling a cloth towards them so that they can reach a toy on the cloth.

THINK ABOUT IT

Note that, in this chapter, studies using animals are used to show types of learning that humans are said to use. There is an assumption that humans are sufficiently like other animals so that we can take findings from other species (dogs, rats, chimps, and so on) and say that such processes also apply to us. You could query this assumption, although it is generally accepted. If we did not agree with evolution theory, which claims that animals (including humans) have evolved certain characteristics because they are useful for survival, then we might not have thought of using animals to learn about humans. If we believed that humans were completely separate from animals, then we would not have found out quite so much. You can decide whether you are happy to go along with the idea that we are enough like other animals that animal studies can help. Most people think we are.

will it work out how to reach it? The chimpanzee clearly looked at the banana and wanted it. However, it did nothing straight away and did not thrash around trying to reach the banana all the time. What it did after a little while was to get a stick that was in the corner of the cage, and it used it to knock the banana down. Clearly it had learnt that a stick can have that use and it put that learning to good use. Humans might do that too. They solve problems without being rewarded every step of the way.

Principles of social learning theory

One-trial learning, latent learning and insight learning are all ways of learning, other than classical and operant conditioning. However, there is one other important learning theory, which is now outlined. This theory starts to link to other approaches in psychology and hopefully, you will find this theory easy to understand as it is common sense.

Modelling, imitation and copying

Social learning theory really rather simply shows that we learn by modelling on and imitating others. There is a bit more to it than that, as we don't usually copy just anyone, but only people that mean something to us, or who we look up to. For example, children quickly pick up habits of their parents as if imitating them. This behaviour is not necessarily reinforced – they seem to just do it.

Social learning theory focuses on the idea of identification and tries to obtain scientific evidence for this process and more information about how it takes place and who is involved. Social learning theorists do not deny that conditioning is a way of learning too – they agree with the principles of behaviourism. However, they focus on other processes as well, such as imitation and modelling, and tend to look more at the learning of moral and social behaviour, rather than the learning of all behaviour.

Children learn by modelling on and imitating others

Observational learning – factors involved in whether we imitate or not

A important name in social learning theory is **Bandura** (1925–), who studied **observational learning**. One of Bandura's studies is outlined briefly below so that you can see where the evidence for his ideas comes from. Observational learning involves modelling and imitation. There is no planning involved – behaviour is simply observed and repeated. However, it does not seem to be the case that just any observed behaviour is copied. There are other factors involved such as whether children watch that behaviour being rewarded (in which case they might copy it) or punished (in which case they probably won't copy it). Similarly the gender and age of the model might be important – for example, boys tend to copy male models, and we tend to copy models we see in some way as similar to ourselves. Boys are more likely to imitate aggressive models than girls are, perhaps suggesting that boys think it is more appropriate to be aggressive (in our culture) than girls do. Children are more likely to imitate behaviour when they are motivated to do so – reinforcement is motivational. We can be motivated by rewards, and here you can see that Bandura draws on other learning theories such as operant conditioning principles. It seems, then, that cognitive (thinking) processes are involved. The child seems to decide in some way whether to imitate or not, and motivation comes from within the child. This learning theory does not treat the child as **passively** receiving learning, but as actively relating to the situation and making decisions (even if not consciously).

Using our thought processes in learning – active learning

The other theories outlined so far in this chapter have not emphasised the individual in the learning process: they view learning as something that happens to individuals. They don't actively learn. Social learning theory does begin to look at cognitive (thought) processes. The thought processes that we use during observational learning are:

● Attention – observers need to pay attention to what is important so that they observe properly.

● Remembering – observers then have to record the information in their memory. Young children might find this a bit difficult. Theories of cognitive development suggest that young children have to mature in order to achieve certain cognitive (thinking) abilities, so they might find it hard to remember the 'right' processes when observing.

● Organising the memory – those with a good and organised memory might learn better from observing.

● Motivation – the consequences of the observed behaviour (whether it is rewarded or punished, for example) can affect whether it is imitated. The child must be motivated to imitate the behaviour.

● Physical ability – it must be possible for the observer to carry out the behaviour physically.

✔ PROGRESS CHECK

Why do young footballers like Wayne Rooney quickly get contracts to do advertisements? Use your knowledge of social learning theory principles to write a paragraph on why advertisers so often choose well-known figures to promote their products. If you can (and this is not easy) use principles of classical conditioning too, as these can also explain why advertisers do this.

DEFINITION

Control group – in an experimental study there should be one group to which nothing is done. This is called the 'control group'. It is used so that the group involved in what is being done can be compared with the control group to see the effect of what is being done. Without the control group there can be no way of knowing what would 'normally' happen.

A study demonstrating social learning theory in action

Bandura and his co-workers did various studies, first to show that modelling takes place and then to look in more depth at who is imitated and under what conditions. An important study is Bandura, Ross and Ross (1961).

What was done

Thirty-six boys and 36 girls (around 4 years old) watched aggressive and non-aggressive adult models. There was one male and one female model. There was a third group of children (a **control group**) who watched neither aggressive nor non-aggressive models. The models (adults) were 'aggressive' by hitting a Bobo doll (a doll that is quite tall and can be hit and bounces back). The behaviour of the children (after watching the models) was then observed and rated for aggression (whether they hit the doll). The researchers thought that:

- the boys would copy aggression more;
- those (boys and girls) watching a non-aggressive model would be even less aggressive (they would imitate 'nice' behaviour);
- boys and girls would each copy models of their own gender more than models of the other gender

The results

It was found that:

- children who watched non-aggressive models and those in the control group (who watched neither aggressive nor non-aggressive models) showed practically no aggressive behaviour;
- those who watched aggressive models (hitting the doll) did show aggressive behaviour (they hit the doll too);
- the aggressive acts were directly like the acts they had watched (including some verbal comments);
- boys were more physically aggressive, when aggressive at all;
- both boys and girls were verbally aggressive (when aggressive at all);
- the aggressive male model was imitated more that the aggressive female model.

What conclusions were drawn?

It was concluded that:

- watching non-aggression (nice behaviour) tends to lead to more non-aggression;
- watching aggressive behaviour (especially specific acts) tends to mean that behaviour is fairly precisely reproduced;
- it is not just boys who imitate aggression, but they tend to be both physically and verbally aggressive, whereas girls tend to be verbally aggressive;
- watching violence on TV could lead to such violence being acted out in real life by children (maybe especially boys?) (however, other studies have shown that this can depend on who is watching the violence on TV with the child, as they would be a model too and if they react calmly then the child would probably react calmly too);
- male models tend to be imitated more than female models. Is this to do with power in our culture?

Do children imitate violence on TV and in computer games?

The findings of Bandura, Ross and Ross's (1961) study tend to suggest that children will imitate anything they see on TV and also on videos, DVDs and in computer games. There are complex issues involved and a direct link between a film and a violent act has not been proved (though many believe this to be the case).

- In 1982 a report by the National Institute of Mental Health claimed that violence in TV programmes does lead to aggression in children.

- In 1985 the American Psychological Association (APA) informed broadcasters of the dangers. They said that, by watching violent TV children might:
  - be desensitised (become used to it);
  - be more afraid;
  - be more aggressive to others.

- Eron (1971) did a longitudinal study (followed children through their childhood to their teens) which showed that children who watched a lot of TV violence when young, showed more aggression when teenagers.

- In 1992 Huston *et al.* did a study that showed how, after watching violent cartoons, children were more likely to hit out, disobey rules and leave tasks unfinished.

- In 1992 the APA published another report showing the harmful effects of violence on television.

- Studies tend to suggest that parents watching with their children can affect a child's response to violence on television by their own reactions. They can also affect the situation by monitoring the number of hours of such television a child watches and they can explore non-violent solutions and discuss programmes with their children.

- There have been quite a few reports in the media of incidents and accidents where there have been clear similarities between what has happened and something that has been shown on television. These incidents have been used as evidence to prove a link between violence on the media and violence (or accidents) in real life. However, such a link, even if it has common sense appeal, is far from being evidence.

- Studies tend to suggest that if good and moral behaviour is modelled on TV then there is more likely to be positive behaviour shown in real life. This adds to the evidence that suggests that social learning theory is correct in predicting that we imitate what we see (in certain conditions).

CASE STUDY

Charlton and others carried out a study of St Helena. St Helena is an island where there was no television but then it was agreed that television would be introduced. Researchers were able to study the children on the island before and after the introduction of television and were then able to draw some conclusions about the effects of this change. This sort of study is not usually possible as you need to find a naturally occurring situation like this. When it is possible, however, it is very useful and interesting. One problem, though, is that there could be other changes, not just the addition of television, so it is hard to draw hard-and-fast conclusions from such studies. Basically it was concluded that television itself did not lead to more violence as other factors such as norms on the island and family life patterns seemed to have more effect.

LEARNING WITHIN A CULTURE, WITH SOCIAL RULES

From the relative simplicity of classical conditioning, through the more complex processes of operant conditioning to the idea of imitation with cognitive processes involved, learning has been shown to occur in quite a few different ways. These are summarised in Table 4.2 (overleaf).

There is one more theory that you need to read about. This is a theory that is used quite a lot to explain behaviour. It could be said to be a reasonably new theory, and it is fair to say that it is currently 'in fashion'. This theory states quite simply that learning does not take place in a laboratory, but within a social and cultural setting. This social and cultural setting sets the scene for any learning that takes place. This can be by rewarding desired behaviour (for example, queuing in English culture or taking shoes off in someone's home in another culture), focusing on certain aspects of our development (such as developing thinking in our culture or emotions in another), or imitating relevant models (like Britney Spears). There are two ways of looking at this. We can say that we are constructed by our culture and society and cannot stand away from that as separate individuals who have undertaken separate learning (**social constructionism**). In this way of looking at things the child is rather passive. Or we can say that as children we actively construct our world in a social and cultural setting and we are not undertaking learning as separate individuals outside of any social influences (**social constructivism**).

Social learning theory emphasises the impact of role models on a child's development and this links in quite clearly with social constructionism. Role models, TV programmes and all other forms of media are ways in which social and cultural influences are transmitted to the child, and they are also very much part of a child's environment. Until recently the term 'teacher' was seen as unproblematic – but then it was seen as suggesting a passive learner being given knowledge (sometimes called 'jug and mug' as if knowledge is being poured into a container). A more modern view is that a 'teacher' is a 'facilitator' and this emphasises the active role of the child and also acknowledges the importance of interaction between the child and its environment (including social and cultural influences). Social constructivism is a widely accepted theory now, and teachers do try to facilitate learning rather than give knowledge.

DEFINITIONS

Social constructionism – the view that we all learn and develop within a social and cultural context, and not separately. So it is important to take such a context into account when considering our behaviour. We cannot grow up outside cultural influences and we need to take note of them when considering our development.

Social constructivism – like social constructionism, this view focuses on the influence of society and culture on our development, and emphasises that the child is an active participant in the process too. It is not that we learn and develop passively, with forces acting on us but we are active in our development, as are those around us.

TRY THIS!

Watch an adult/child interaction and note down any areas where you think cultural aspects or habits are relevant. For example, is the child being shown how to write letters or numbers? If so, presumably 'our' alphabet is being used. Then comment on the influence of culture on a child's learning.

✔ PROGRESS CHECK

1 Why do you think the theory that claims that we cannot escape from our society and culture and all our learning and development takes place within a setting is called 'social constructionism'?

2 Explain how the following examples of a child's behaviour come from a particular social context: a young girl vacuuming the floor with a toy vacuum cleaner; a three year old trying to write his name; a four year old using a toy telephone to phone his mother; a three year old pretending to read a book.

COMPARING THE DIFFERENT LEARNING THEORIES

Children probably learn in all the ways outlined above. Table 4.2 suggests ways to compare the different theories and is a useful summary.

Table 4.2 **Comparing seven theories of learning**

Theory	Summary	Comparison points
Classical conditioning	Association of neutral stimulus in the environment (e.g. bell) with natural response/reflex (e.g. drooling).	• Conditions involuntary reflexes • Stimulus has to happen first, to be conditioned • Generalisation or discrimination can occur • Phobias and what gives us pleasure can be learnt in this way (for example) • Treats responses as mechanistic (no conscious thought)
Operant conditioning	Shaping to obtain required behaviour by means of reinforcements (or punishment). Behaviour follows reward or promise of reward, or behaviour ceases in response to punishment.	• Stimulus comes afterwards in the form of reward or punishment • Responses are voluntary, not reflexes • In theory any behaviour can be conditioned • Treats behaviour as mechanistic (no conscious thought)
One-trial learning	One experience is sometimes enough for very strong learning to take place. Follows classical conditioning principles (association is with reflex, e.g. feeling sick).	• Follows classical conditioning principles and reflexes are conditioned • Could have a survival value (be an innate tendency) • Mechanistic, not under our control
Latent learning	Learning can be accidental – which is not specifically shaped or reinforced. During a normal course of action we can learn without realising it. This learning may not always be obvious.	• Mechanistic and not under our control • Presumably involves cognitive (thinking) processes, which are not emphasised in all forms of learning • Can explain why some behaviour appears without reinforcement
Insight learning	We sit and think before acting and problem solving takes place. We work things out and learn from experience to apply this to other situations.	• Involves cognitive (thinking) processes and so we are more actively involved in the process • We might solve problems as a natural thing, rather than being reinforced by the solutions being pleasant • Not so mechanistic and makes the individual active not passive
Social learning	We learn by imitating those around us and using them as models. These are particular people (role models) and we copy in certain situations.	• Agrees that classical and operant conditioning are processes in learning • Adds that we imitate and use observational learning – which suggests that cognitive (thinking) processes are involved too • Can explain behaviour such as copying pop stars • Suggests that others are important figures and should be careful what they do around children (including the media)
Social constructionism and social constructivism	Our learning is within a social and cultural context and will inevitably be affected by that.	• We are active in shaping our own development, but we are strongly affected by cultural and social factors such as rules and habits. • We are active to an extent but passively shaped by our environment too, so this is a mechanistic view.

Summarising the learning theories outlined here

In summary:

- It seems that we have reflexive responses such as fear and pleasure and these can be associated with all sorts of different stimuli without us being aware of it.

- It appears that a lot of our behaviour is in response to desired rewards and that the promise of a reward will extract desired behaviour. Smiles and encouragement are rewards for most people.

- Some of our behaviour is an avoidant response. The reward is to avoid something unpleasant rather than getting an actual reward.

- We also learn not to do things because we are punished for doing them. This is not a very successful form of learning, partly because we are not learning what we *should* do.

- Alongside all the above learning we also learn by copying those around us. We observe and then imitate people who are important to us (parents, brothers, sisters, teachers and friends) as well as those we identify with (such as media figures).

- Some learning happens without us realising it (such as learning about our physical environment).

- Learning is not always mechanistic (that is, it does not always just happen *to* us). We can actively use previous learning to solve new problems, and cognitive (thinking) processes are involved.

- We are actively constructing our own worlds as we develop, too – again the importance of cognition (thinking) is seen.

- We develop within a social and cultural context rather than in a laboratory. What we learn is dictated by such a context and we cannot separate ourselves from our environment – which is a physical, social, and cultural environment.

THINK ABOUT IT

How far do you think we should use social and cultural aspects to guide a child's learning? Would you choose the child's own culture and for each individual emphasise that? Or would you choose all the cultures represented in your setting and address them all on different occasions so that all children had experience of all the different cultures? What effect would these sorts of decisions have on the child's development? Who has the right to make decisions like this?

WORKING WITH CHILDREN AND THEIR LEARNING

The above theories can be practically applied to an extent. Sometimes we learn from the theories what not to do, and sometimes we learn what to do. Ideas about how to apply theories in a practical and useful way have been given throughout this chapter – for example, how to 'cure' phobias or to manage behaviour. However, what is useful can differ between cultures and people can disagree over what children should or should not learn. As soon as we start to shape a child's learning we can be said to be interfering – or it could be said that that is in fact the practitioner's job.

ANSWERS TO 'TRY THIS!' PROBLEMS

Here is the answer to the problem in the first 'Try This!' section, which was on p. 59.

Try This! – answer

Dust (UCS) ⟶ Sneeze (UCR)

Dust (UCS) + Aunt (CS) ⟶ Sneeze (UCR)

Aunt (CS) ⟶ Sneeze (CR)

Here is the answer to the problem in the 'Try This!' section on p. 61.

Try This! – answer

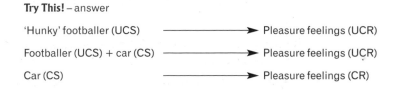

'Hunky' footballer (UCS) ⟶ Pleasure feelings (UCR)

Footballer (UCS) + car (CS) ⟶ Pleasure feelings (UCR)

Car (CS) ⟶ Pleasure feelings (CR)

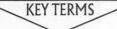

KEY TERMS

You need to know the meaning of the following words and phrases. Go back through the chapter to make sure you understand them:

Aversive therapy
Control group
Discrimination
Extinguished
Generalisation
Insight learning
Latent learning
Maladaptive
Negative reinforcement
Observational learning
One-trial learning
Passive
Positive reinforcement
Preparedness
Punishment
Shaping
Social constructionism
Social constructivism
Systematic desensitisation

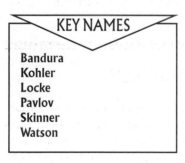

KEY NAMES

Bandura
Kohler
Locke
Pavlov
Skinner
Watson

FURTHER READING

Jarvis, M. and Chandler, E. (2001) *Angles on Child Psychology,* Nelson Thornes Ltd, Cheltenham.

An accessible text designed for those studying at Levels 3 and 4.

Lee, V. and Das Gupta, P. (1998) *Children's Cognitive and Language Developemnt,* Blackwell, Oxford in association with the Open University.

This book is useful for students studying at Levels 3 and 4. Chapter 1 is particularly recommended.

Mukherji, P. (2001) *Understanding Children's Challenging Behaviour,* Nelson Thornes Ltd, Cheltenham.

This is an easy read for students and practitioners studying at all levels.

Chapters 2, 4 and 5 are all relevant and give practical suggestions for managing children's behaviour using the principles outlined in this chapter.

Cognitive development

INTRODUCTION

Children's social and emotional development are important – as is learning – but much attention has also been given to cognitive development because it seems so central to how we structure early years care and education practice. It seems, historically, that cognitive (thinking) development was studied before social and emotional development, which also emphasises the importance placed on this area of development. This chapter begins by outlining one important theory, that of Piaget, in some depth. Children are seen to develop their thinking in stages according to their age. They are not little adults – they have their own (limited) capabilities. Other theories are then examined, the two main ones being those of Bruner and Vygotsky. These two theories did begin to look at social development and to link how children develop socially with their cognitive (thinking) development. It is seen that children do not develop in a vacuum without any social interactions but that those interactions can affect their cognitive (thinking) developing – interacting with others can help understanding. Educational practice has been informed by cognitive developmental theories and examples of how this has occurred are given at the end of this chapter.

THINK ABOUT IT

Think about a time when you have seen something in a shop without knowing what it is for, so you don't know what it is. This might be a garlic press, for example, or something in an electrical store. When you discover that it is a garlic press or a new style of doorbell, you experience 'seeing' it differently. You might, for example, mentally see the piece of garlic in the holder ready to be pressed.

If you try this next time you are shopping you should share a little of what a young child experiences as it learns to 'see' things for what they are. This is an example of cognitive processing.

WHAT IS COGNITIVE DEVELOPMENT?

Cognitive development refers to the development of thinking processes. You can substitute the word 'thinking' for the term 'cognitive'. 'Thinking' covers memory, concentration, curiosity, imagination and understanding. It looks at how we attend to some things and not others, and how we see, hear, taste, touch and smell. For example, we do not 'see' everything that comes into our brain via our eyes. We see something or someone as a particular object or type of person rather than simply seeing all we view. That is we don't see a flat square piece of wood on top of four straight pieces running to the floor on all four corners, we see it 'as' a table. All this brain processing involves thinking, and how we develop our thinking (cognitive development) is an important area studied under the wider heading of child psychology.

Some questions asked within the cognitive-developmental approach

Refer back to Chapter 1 (p. 10) where the main approaches within psychology are outlined, and reread the material on the cognitive-developmental approach as this will refresh your memory ready for this chapter.

Cognitive-developmental psychologists ask questions such as:

- Do children think in the same way as adults?
- Are babies born with structures that lead to certain thinking patterns?
- Are we born with the capacity to develop and extend our cognitive (thinking) abilities through childhood to adulthood?

TRY THIS!

Before finding out what different theorists say about how children develop, carry out this task. Make a list of all you know about young babies and their psychological (or indeed physical) development. At the end of this chapter (on p. 94) you will find a summary of the sorts of things you might have assumed. Remember that such assumptions are behind much of what we think and what we think we know. Often your assumptions will be correct but you should find that what you learn from this book will change them. The theories outlined in this book are almost certain to be built on and to be amended during the course of your lifetime. There is not much about knowledge within child psychology that is certain, and this is worth bearing in mind. What you read about here is what we think at the moment.

- Are patterns of cognitive development that are found through studies in one culture (such as Western culture) also found in all cultures? (In other words do they appear to be innate?)
- What cognitive abilities do newly born babies have?
- Can knowledge of how cognitive abilities develop inform and improve educational procedures to enhance a child's learning?

Brief questions and answers

These questions and answers will signpost what follows in this chapter.

- Do children think in the same way as adults? *No, they don't. They have to 'mature' to be able to achieve adult thinking abilities.*
- Are babies born with structures that lead to certain thinking patterns? *Yes they are. Newly born babies must have the necessary processing ability even though so many cognitive abilities develop as the child develops (and development requires interaction with the environment).*
- Are we born with the capacity to develop and extend our cognitive (thinking) abilities through childhood to adulthood? *Yes, there seem to be maturational processes at work alongside of our interactions with the environment, and some cognitive abilities seem only to appear with time. However, some theorists believe that the development of such abilities can be speeded up with guidance.*
- Are patterns of cognitive development that are found through studies in one culture (such as Western culture) also found in all cultures? (In other words do they appear to be innate?) *Yes, studies do tend to find that patterns of cognitive development (together with approximate ages when these patterns develop) are similar across cultures, so are probably innate.*
- What cognitive abilities do newly born babies have? *Newly born babies seem to be able to recognise voices and faces. They have reflexes such as sucking but also processes to do with building ideas in their minds so that they can begin to learn, and to understand and build knowledge.*
- Can knowledge of how cognitive abilities develop inform and improve educational procedures to enhance a child's learning? *Yes, understanding both of young children's abilities and their limitations (they are not miniature adults) has helped in planning a suitable curriculum as well as in providing suitable activities and methods of learning.*

PIAGET'S THEORY OF COGNITIVE DEVELOPMENT

Probably the most influential figure, the 'founder' of the cognitive-developmental approach, is **Piaget** (1896–1980). This chapter looks at Piaget's views, and then considers other theorists in the light of Piaget's initial assertions about how we develop thinking. If you have already studied some child psychology you will realise that one single answer to the question of how a child develops thinking is not likely to be found. As is usually the case in psychology, different theories are offered. These theories rarely actually contradict one another. Rather they look at slightly different areas and issues, or they build on one another to add in new aspects. First Piaget's theory is looked at, followed by those of Vygotsky, and **Bruner** (1915–).

THINK ABOUT IT

Think back to the arguments outlined in Chapter 1 (or read them now) about whether characteristics come from our nature (what we are born with) or nurture (what influences us from the outside world). Piaget thought that we are born with some abilities such as the ability to build knowledge and to mature in certain ways (how we learn). He also thought that we are influenced by our surroundings (what we learn). So, as with many theories in psychology, his theory incorporates both our nature and our nurture, and takes a **constructivist** approach.

The building blocks of a child's thinking processes

Think about a newly born baby. In Chapter 4 we saw that Locke believed that a baby is born a 'blank slate', in other words without any knowledge. It is accepted that babies' environment, including interactions with others, will play a large role in shaping the person. Chapter 4 shows how shaping behaviour takes place using rewards and punishments, and also shows how we model on those around us. However, in Chapter 2, it was shown that a baby comes into the world prepared in many different ways to develop into the adult they will become. It seems clear that if a baby did not have certain capabilities, it would not be able to use information from the outside world at all. Piaget thought about these capabilities and noted that an important facility would be a way of taking in knowledge and adding to previous knowledge to build a picture of the world. That picture would have to change all the time, to take into account all the many new experiences each day brings. Piaget looked at this facility and came up with an idea of how it might work. This idea is outlined below.

Building schemas

The idea is that a baby forms a plan or representation (a **schema**) in its brain about something it experiences. A schema is a mental structure that gives a model of what happens when we do something. A baby does not have language, of course, so the schema does not involve any word or label. That comes later. For example, a baby could have a schema for sucking based on what limited experience it has at first. Then it develops its sucking schema as it experiences more. The baby sucks differently shaped objects and the schema takes all this into account.

The baby is building a schema (a plan of a piece of its world) from its various experiences using a process called **assimilation**. This is the process by which individuals take material into their mind from the environment, which may mean changing the evidence of their senses to make it fit existing schemas. To continue with the example of sucking, the sucking experiences develop and fit into the sucking schema that the baby has. Another example is when a baby moves their hand. They won't know what moving means, or what a hand 'is' but they can develop a schema (mental image) of the muscular experience of moving the hand. Assimilation means altering the input to match the schema and the baby keeps assimilating to build its schema.

At some stage there is such a mismatch between the information being assimilated and existing schemas that a new experience cannot be fitted in (assimilated). At this stage the schema has to change, and **accommodation** is the term used to identify this process of changing the schema to take the new information into account. For example, the sucking schema may not be right for the muscular experience of sucking a blanket, so the schema itself has to be amended. Accommodation occurs and the schema is changed, and then new information is assimilated again into this changed schema.

The accommodation stage occurs in response to an uncomfortable feeling of not understanding (when the existing schema is not enough). This feeling is called **disequilibrium** (unbalance). There is a term for the process of assimilation and accommodation, and this term is **adaptation**. So existing schemas (sometimes the plural is given as 'schemata') are reinforced through assimilation, amended schemas arise through accommodation and the whole cycle of assimilation and accommodation is called adaptation. Adaptation is a change in the way an individual interacts with the world. Once the feeling of disequilibrium has been solved by the schema being developed and changed (adaptation), a state of **equilibration** is achieved (balance). Diagram 5.1 illustrates this process.

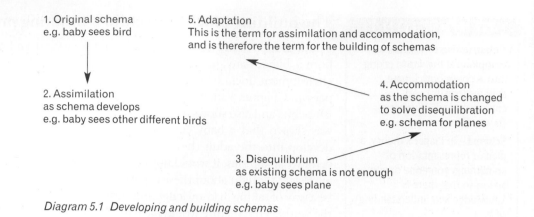

1. Original schema
e.g. baby sees bird

2. Assimilation
as schema develops
e.g. baby sees other different birds

5. Adaptation
This is the term for assimilation and accommodation,
and is therefore the term for the building of schemas

4. Accommodation
as the schema is changed
to solve disequilibration
e.g. schema for planes

3. Disequilibrium
as existing schema is not enough
e.g. baby sees plane

Diagram 5.1 Developing and building schemas

✔ PROGRESS CHECK

Using the terms 'schema', 'assimilation', 'accommodation', and 'disequilibrium',
fill in the gaps in the following passage.

A six-month old baby has already developed a _____ for putting one
large block on top of another. When given smaller blocks the baby uses
_____ and puts one block on top of another as it did with the bigger
blocks. The baby tries to place all sorts of objects one on top of the other.
However, when trying with two balls they do not stand one on top of the other but
one rolls off. The baby experiences _____ . Then the baby learns that
not all objects go one on top of the other, as sometimes one falls off. The baby
needs a new schema about round objects and _____ takes place.
A schema about balls develops, for example, that they roll.

PIAGET'S FOUR STAGES OF DEVELOPMENT

Piaget suggested that children progress through four stages of development from
birth to the adulthood stage. These stages are outlined below and help to show how
we develop cognitive abilities. Remember how we learn according to Piaget. We
learn by developing existing schemas and building new ones by the processes of
assimilation and accommodation.

The four stages are:

- the sensorimotor stage;
- the preoperational stage;
- the stage of concrete operations;
- the stage of formal operations.

It is quite logical to think of cognitive development as being in stages. At that time
(and now) it was thought that children develop physically in stages (for example,
crawling then walking) and language was thought of as stage-like (for example,
babbling, the one-word stage, the two-word stage) so it would have seemed logical
to say that children develop cognitively in stages too. When Piaget was developing
his ideas, it would have been sensible to think of a child as developing cognitively in
stages.

Note, though, that other theories suggest that development is more continuous.
The thing about stages is that each stage is not only thought of as happening at a
particular age and as having differences from the stages before and after it, but that
there is a qualitative change as well as a quantitative one. It is not just that a baby
develops more schemas but that there is difference in the quality of their thinking
as they move from one stage to another. Those who claim we develop continuously
would simply suggest that we change and develop all the time. Learning theorists,

Primary circular reactions – in Piaget's theory, from around 6 weeks to 4 months the baby gains control over its actions and starts repeating them for pleasure (hence the actions are circular). These actions at this age involve only the baby's own body, as it has no control over things around it. So these actions are primary (involving the baby's own body).

Secondary circular reactions – in Piaget's theory, from around 4 months to 8 months the baby has some control over objects around it. The baby enjoys repeating actions for pleasure. So these actions are circular. They are secondary as they involve not only the baby's own body but objects around them too.

Object permanence – knowing that objects have a permanence in the world (exist), so 'out of sight' is not 'out of mind'. Children await the return of an object because they know that it exists even when they cannot see it. According to Piaget a child of around 8 months old, in the sensorimotor stage, develops object permanence.

with their claims that we learn through rewards, punishments and observing others, would suggest that we learn continuously, so in this way they differ from cognitive-developmental theorists who note stages in our development. Piaget suggested stages in our cognitive development. Note that the ages given below are approximate ones. The stages occur at around those ages, but individuals will differ. The idea of discontinuity (stage development) and continuity (continuous development), together with the different theories that take different views of this issue, is discussed again at the end of this chapter.

Stage one – the sensorimotor stage (0–2 years)

According to Piaget, in the early years babies' development focuses on senses and movements. Their cognitive development comes from information they receive from their senses, which comes via sights, sounds, tastes, smells and, importantly, touch. A baby has these sensory abilities and movement is very important – hence the 'sensorimotor' stage, 'motor' referring to movement.

Therefore, early cognitive development relies on input from the senses and babies learn from everything around them. As part of this early development there are specific aspects that Piaget discovered and emphasised. One of these aspects is the development of **primary** and **secondary circular reactions** and another is **object permanence**. These two aspects are outlined here to give examples of how babies develop in the sensorimotor stage.

In the first substage of the sensorimotor stage (up to six weeks old) the baby's learning is mainly about reflexes. By the second substage (from 6 weeks to around 4 months old) the baby begins to be able to repeat actions just for the pleasure of it. For example, the baby might blow bubbles. These repeated actions are called primary (because they are primary to the baby, involving their own body) circular (because they are repeated) reactions. The third substage (from around 4 months to 8 months) brings secondary circular reactions, where the baby again repeats actions for pleasure, but these are secondary because they involve outside influences too. For example, a baby can keep kicking at a bar they can reach with their feet. From 8 to 12 months, the fourth substage within the sensorimotor stage, the baby develops object permanence, as outlined below. A fifth substage (from 12 to 18 months) is when babies develop tertiary circular reactions as they now have enough control over external objects to experiment and see what happens. A sixth substage (from 18 months to 2 years) is where a baby is developing symbols to represent objects (language) and can start problem solving using those symbols as well as actual interactions with objects.

If you have access to a baby up to 8 months old, do some observations (with permission and taking ethical considerations into account – see Chapter 1, p. 14). Note down examples of the above substages. Find an example of primary circular reactions, and one of secondary circular reactions (depending on the age of the babies you have access to).

A baby blowing bubbles – a primary circular reaction!

Developing the idea that objects have permanence

Newly born babies experiment with reflexes and learn to control their own bodies' movements. Then they start to interact with the environment and to move objects

THINK ABOUT IT

Chapter 1 discussed the idea of object permanence so reflect back to that if you need to. Think about how a baby might develop the idea of object permanence, using your knowledge of how schemas are developed.

TRY THIS!

Do some observations yourself to find out how you can interpret from a baby's facial expressions and body language what the baby is feeling or thinking. If you were able to carry out the activity suggested in the second 'Try This!' section in this chapter then you will already have done some research in this area.

1 Try to watch at least one baby of around 4 to 8 months old. Watch its facial expressions and body language and note down in each case what you think the baby is feeling and thinking. How confident are you that you have interpreted the baby's thoughts? Check with another adult whether he agrees with your interpretations. If you both agree, and if all the baby's reactions (facial expressions and other forms of body language) agree with one another (for example, that all the reactions suggest happiness) then you are probably right. This is not really proof, but when most of us agree on these sorts of observations, this is taken as reliable data.

2 If you have permission a good way of doing this task is to video the baby. Then if you are working as part of a class, you could form a group and all watch the video at the same time, making your comments independently. Then discuss your findings and if you find you have made the same interpretations, this would be **inter-observer reliability**. Are you convinced? Most people agree that this is a reasonable way to interpret what a baby is feeling and thinking.

in the environment. Once they have learnt that objects have a permanence in the world they can start to manipulate them more. This also means they need to have gained enough control over their movements to manipulate objects. Gradually, through the sensorimotor stage, babies will learn enough to experiment with objects. Finally, they start to think of objects symbolically and attach words to them, so they can think about them in a different way altogether. Learning that objects have permanence in the world is an important part of this early development.

It has been shown above that at about 8 months babies demonstrate that they know that an object exists even if it goes out of their line of vision. (Remember the ages are approximate, and there are individual differences in the age at which a certain cognitive ability might actually appear.) An adult can play a game with a baby, hiding a toy and then making it reappear, and the excitement and pleasure on the infant's face shows that the baby is expecting the object to reappear. A younger baby, however, loses interest in the toy once it has disappeared. It seems that for a younger baby 'out of sight is out of mind'. So it is concluded that the younger baby does not expect the object to reappear, and has no concept that the object has a permanence when out of sight, whereas the older baby expects it to reappear, and somehow understands that the object has permanence (exists).

CASE STUDY

Reread the case study outlined in Chapter 1 (p. 2), which helps to explain the concept of object permanence.

How can we study the cognitive ability of babies?

It is worth considering here how we study babies. This is because, although Piaget claimed that babies under the age of around 8 months do not have the concept of object permanence, whereas after that age they do know that objects exist, other theorists criticise Piaget's views. There are indeed many criticisms of Piaget's views, and many of these criticisms are because other people have used different methods and by doing so they have come up with different results. In this section Piaget's work is being outlined, but we also need to look at what others have said that contradicts or builds on his work. His basic ideas still tend to stand, but some issues such as the ages at which certain cognitive abilities develop, have been amended in the light of newer research. Piaget's ideas of when a baby develops object permanence have been criticised and it is claimed that infants know that objects 'exist' in the world at a much younger age. What has happened is that other researchers have amended the methods that Piaget used and by developing new methods they have found different things. So looking at methods used is very important.

Generally researchers do accept that observing a baby will yield quite **reliable** data. When we say data are reliable, we mean that if were to do the study again we would get the same results. To test this out researchers do studies more than once (and other researchers also carry out the same study) and data are only really accepted once they are seen to be reliable. There is also **validity** in observing in this way because it is the baby's real behaviour that is being studied, not artificial behaviour in a laboratory. When data are valid it means they do represent real life behaviour in some way. So observing a baby's facial expressions and body language is considered a reliable and valid method.

However, this can only be done when a baby is old enough to react using body language and suitable facial expressions. Perhaps Piaget found object permanence more because by 8 months old the baby was more able to express its expectations (that the object will reappear) then at an earlier age, rather than because the baby did not understand that the object would reappear. If we could study a baby earlier perhaps they would show such understanding – if we used a different method?

Piaget's views on object permanence modified by using different methodology

Some studies have suggested that babies know that objects exist separately (have permanence) by as young as three-and-a-half months. One such study was carried out by Baillargeon, 1993.

In this study babies were seated in a chair that raised them to eye-level facing a table on which is a special piece of equipment – a rotating screen. Picture quite a large rectangular board placed upright on the table with its longest side flat to the table, and hinged on to the table. The board could be rotated so that it could either lie flat away from the baby, be rotated up to an upright position, or lie flat facing the baby. The board could be rotated automatically in a complete semicircle and this is what happened for a little while. The baby could watch the screen flip forwards (to lie down completely at the front), rise to its upright position, and then flip backwards (to lie down completely at the back). Then at some stage, with the baby watching and the screen picked up out of the way, a box was placed behind the screen's upright position, but within the curve of its arc. So if the screen was there and rotating, it would be prevented from going back any further from its upright position because the box would be in the way. The screen was then replaced and the rotation started from the front. As the screen reached the upright position, the box was removed (although the baby couldn't see this), so the screen could rotate back as well. The baby should think (if it can think about it, which is the point) that the screen wouldn't be able to rotate back fully as it has been doing, so it should show surprise when it can do so. If babies do not understand the concept of the box 'having permanence' or the concept of the screen's arc being real, then they should not be put off by 'thinking' that the box will be in the way. The results are that even babies just over 3 months old do show surprise when the screen rotates fully as before. The only reason they would do this is that they understand that the box should stop the arc. Otherwise they would not show surprise as they have happily watched the screen rotate fully before. It is concluded that babies have the concept of object permanence at a younger age than Piaget thought.

Shows the rotation screen and baby watching – then the screen with the box that would stop the rotation.

Other studies have used slightly different methods and found similar results. It is, therefore, now thought that babies develop object permanence at a younger age. However, if you have used Piaget's method to test for object permanence, you probably found the same results that he found. This shows the importance of the method used when drawing conclusions about babies. Although we could now say that Piaget was wrong, it is more usual to say that thinking abilities (cognition) do develop over time, and probably in the same sorts of ways that Piaget outlined – it is just that the ages that he suggested may differ.

✔ PROGRESS CHECK

1   When babies repeatedly wave their arm about without touching anything, apparently for pleasure, what is this called?

2   When babies repeatedly shake a rattle apparently for pleasure, but not seeming to understand fully that moving the arm results in shaking the rattle, what is this called?

3   When a baby can reach for a hidden object or shows understanding that objects exist, what is this called?

Stage two – the preoperational stage (2–6 years)

A child that has moved through the sensorimotor stage now has many capabilities including knowing the permanence of objects and having a great many schemas (for many processes), which are being adapted through experiences. The child now uses language too, although Piaget did not emphasise this part of development as much as other cognitive-developmental theorists did, such as Bruner and Vygotsky.

However, the child at this stage is far from having the thinking (cognitive) abilities of an adult. In the preoperational child there tends to be focus on what the child cannot do, although the many cognitive abilities of a child in the preoperational stage should not be overlooked. A child in the preoperational stage is 'pre' (before) 'operations' (mental operations or processes). Such operations include being able to use logic to combine or separate ideas. The focus is, therefore, on how the child cannot do such mental operations. The child needs continued stimulation so that through the processes of assimilation and adaptation schemas are adapted to form new schemas and knowledge is encouraged.

The child cannot yet conserve volume

Probably the best known of Piaget's experiments involves his so-called **conservation** tasks. Outlining these tasks will also show a very important point about how a child in the preoperational stage is far from being an adult thinker. So the conservation studies are outlined here first. Conservation is a term used to describe our ability to understand that a concept (like volume, mass or number) will stay the same even if something about a situation has changed. So if you have a piece of cake it will stay the same size in total even if you cut it in half (as long as you don't eat any of course). The question is, do young children understand such a concept? If they don't (and it seems that they don't) then they are not yet at an adult reasoning stage, and this is evidence that cognition develops over time and that maturity is needed before certain stages (or abilities) are reached. When children cannot conserve, they are said not to be able to **decentre**. This means they focus on one side of things. The idea is that a child needs to perform mental operations to work out that if one piece of cake is cut into two pieces of cake there is still the same amount of cake. Piaget did not use this example, though, and we need to look at the studies he did.

Experiments to test ability to conserve volume – method 1

Piaget used a method like the one outlined here. Take three beakers or glasses capable of holding the same amount of liquid but with two being short and 'fat' and one being tall and 'slim'. Fill a measuring jug with liquid. (Leave plenty of time to assemble your 'props'. You may not find it easy to obtain glasses of the correct shape.) Use water and avoid a situation where a child participant wants to drink from the beakers (for ethical reasons). Settle the child participant and make sure that you are following all ethical procedures. When you are ready to start, first check that the participant can see the liquid in the jug. Pour two equal amounts of liquid into each of the short 'fat' beakers. Take all the time you need to show to the child that the beakers are holding the same amount and ask them if the amount is the same. Be very clear about the wording of this question. Once this has been established, pick up one of the beakers and pour its contents into the tall 'slim' beaker. Make sure the child sees clearly what you have done but make no comment. Then line up the tall 'slim' beaker alongside the short 'fat' one that still has the liquid in it. Ask the child whether the two beakers have the same amount of water in them. Be very clear about your wording of this question. If the child says 'yes they are the same', then that child can conserve and is beyond the preoperational stage, at least in terms of conservation. If the child says 'no they are not the same' then that child cannot conserve and is in the preoperational stage. This is what Piaget did and he concluded by means of testing quite a few children that children up to around the age of 6 or 7 years tend to be preoperational whereas once they had passed the age of 7 years they were in the concrete operations stage.

As has been shown, Piaget's views on object permanence were criticised once different methods were used to test babies for their understanding of object permanence. Piaget's views on conservation have been similarly criticised and, again, when different methods are used different results are found. However, it is thought that his basic views were correct and, if his studies are repeated, the same results are still found. It is just that the newer studies have built on his theories and modified some of his conclusions.

THINK ABOUT IT

Read the outline of the experiment to test ability to conserve volume showing Piaget's method. Identify any criticisms of the study. You might come up with the main criticism given by other researchers, but don't worry if not. The experiments were quite well controlled and it is not easy to see what is wrong with them.

Experiments to test ability to conserve volume – method 2

Light *et al.* (1979) carried out a study to show that children younger than 7 years can conserve volume if the method is changed. One way of varying the method Piaget used to see if a child could conserve volume is to make the task more realistic. One of the main criticisms of Piaget's work in this area is that a child is likely to go along with what an adult is saying, especially in such a 'test' situation. The child knows that the researcher has already asked if the amount of water in the two short 'fat' beakers is the same. So when the same researcher makes a change by pouring water from one of the short beakers into the tall one, and then asks if the amount of water is the same, a child could think that there was supposed to be a difference and could answer 'no'. It could be that the child is not sure why the researcher made the change so assumes there is a reason, and assumes that something is supposed to have changed.

Researchers repeated the experiment outlined above but this time there was one important difference. One of the two short 'fat' beakers had a crack in it. As the glass was cracked, this would not be a very safe experiment for you to reproduce so just read through what was done but do not do it yourself. The experimenters made sure the crack did not prevent the glass from holding water and was not dangerous. They did not point the crack out at first, and reached the stage where the two short 'fat' glasses had the water in them and the child had answered that the amount in the two short 'fat' glasses was the same. Then they pointed out the crack. Then they poured the water from the cracked short 'fat' glass into the tall 'thin' one. They could even say that they were doing that because the other glass was cracked. Then they continued again with method 1 above, asking the child if the amounts of water in the tall 'thin' glass and in the short 'fat' glass were the same. Children of preoperational age this time were more likely to say that the quantities in the two glasses were the same. So in this case the younger child could conserve. Given a reason such as a crack, the children could conserve. This strongly suggested that a child, given no reason for a change done by an adult, will think that there must be a reason. This type of reasoning could itself be said to show that young children can perform mental operations. However, it must not be overlooked that if Piaget's task is repeated his results are still found. Therefore, it does seem that younger children and older children have different reasoning abilities, even if Piaget's ages and reasons for this were not quite right, and even it is has more to do with their view of adults (that they don't lie) than with ability to conserve.

Another method used is to ask only one question instead of asking 'is the amount of liquid in the glasses the same?' twice. This might avoid the problem of the child thinking that as they have said 'yes' the first time they ought to say 'no' the second time. Here the study would be carried out in exactly the same way as in method 1 but without asking the first question (see Rose and Blank, 1974, who did a conservation study, not quite the same as the one outlined above, and only asked the question after the transformation had taken place). It is assumed that the child realises that the same amount of liquid has been poured into the two short 'fat' glasses and the question to check it is not asked. So when the researcher asks, after pouring the liquid from one of the short glasses into the tall glass, whether the amount is the same, having been asked that before should not sway the child. There is a tendency for younger children (in the preoperational stage) to 'get it right' this time, which is what would be expected given the criticism outlined above. So it is thought that Piaget's method did confuse the younger children. However, note that, again, it did not confuse the older children, so there is still a difference in their type of thinking, which is what Piaget said in the first place. It is generally accepted that we do go through cognitive stages as Piaget predicted, even if all the details he gave are not correct.

The child cannot yet conserve number

There are a number of different conservation experiments but only those to do with volume and number are given here because the principles are the same. The main experiment showing that a preoperational child cannot conserve number is outlined below. The same conclusions are drawn that were drawn concerning conservation of volume. The younger child cannot conserve number but the older child can. However, with a variation to make the task more meaningful the younger child is able to conserve number.

Experiments to test ability to conserve number – method 1

Piaget tested children on their ability to conserve number and found that up to the age of around 6 years they cannot whereas by the age of around 7 (and older) they can. The basic task is to put some large colourful counters in a row. Use around six counters and spread them out clearly (counters from the game Connect Four work well). Make another row to match exactly, using the same number of counters spaced out in exactly the same way. Settle the child before proceeding and make sure all ethical issues are followed. When you are ready ask the child if there is the same number of counters in each row and wait for the child to agree that there are. Then push the counters of one of the rows together so that the row is shorter and the spaces between the counters are smaller. Then ask the child if there is the same number of counters in each row. A preoperational child is likely to say that the number of counters is now different whereas an older child should know that there is still the same number of counters even though one row looks shorter.

The same criticism was made of Piaget's experiment to test conservation of number that was made about his study of conservation of volume. The researcher asks the same question twice – 'is there the same number of counters in each row?' So a child might think that, as the adult has clearly made a change, the 'right' answer is to say that 'no, the number of counters has changed'. So a variation was tried, and this is outlined below.

Experiments to test ability to conserve number – method 2

McGarrigle and Donaldson (1974) carried out an experiment very similar to Piaget's but with a change in the method. The experiment was set up in exactly the same way and the child was asked whether the number of counters in each row was the same. At this stage, when the child has agreed that the number was the same, in Piaget's method the researcher then pushes the counters in one row together a bit so that that one row is shorter. In this variation the same thing happens but the researcher uses a glove puppet to push the counters together. This puppet is called 'Naughty Teddy' and the researcher can comment to the child on what Naughty Teddy has done. This gave the child a reason for the change. The child was then asked whether there is the same number of counters in each row. This time a younger child was more likely to say that there is the same number of counters as before – the child could conserve number. Remember that 'conserving number' means that the child understands that, as no counter has been removed, even if things look different, there will still be the same number of counters there. This understanding shows that the child can perform mental operations and is not pre-operational.

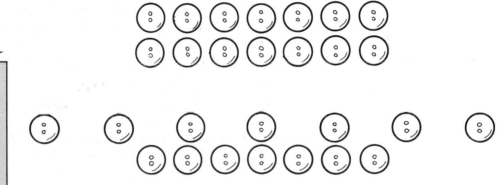

An older child in the concrete operations stage knows that there is the same number of counters even if the length varies

The 'Naughty Teddy' variation of the conserving number experiment shows that children previously thought of as in the preoperational stage (that is aged 6 years or under) could use mental operations, and could conserve, and so would be said to be in the next stage – the concrete operations stage. However, this should not necessarily be taken to mean that Piaget was totally wrong. If Piaget's study is repeated the same results are still found, so, again, it does seem that younger children do show different cognitive abilities from older children. This difference seems to be less about knowing about conserving number and liquid and more about understanding concepts so that when an adult makes a change the child can reason about what has happened rather than just go with what the adult seems to want them to say. So Piaget seems to have been mistaken to an extent. The fact remains though that he did find a difference in thinking abilities, and his ideas about cognitive development happening through stages are still used today.

Experiments to test ability to decentre – method 1

A preoperational child tends to think only of one classification at a time. Another study shows how a child under the age of seven years cannot decentre.

For this study you need to have different categories and examples of the same object. Here pencils are used. You would need long and short pencils, in two different colours. For example, there would be short red pencils, short blue pencils, long red pencils and long blue pencils. To sort the pencils into length and colour involves being able to think about two different categories at once, and preoperational children cannot do this.

Experiments to test ability to decentre – method 2

In the second study different objects are used. You would need a set of identical toy cars, with two different colours (or use blocks). Let's assume that the colours are green and yellow. Then ask the child whether there are more yellow cars or more cars? The right answer would be more cars, as there are green cars too. Children in the preoperational stage find this question difficult. (To be fair, it is rather complicated!)

A preoperational child is egocentric

Egocentrism means having oneself as the centre and not being able to take anyone else's point of view. Perhaps this also shows an inability to decentre because focusing on one side of things would perhaps be the same as not being able to take another's point of view. Piaget claimed that a child in the preoperational stage is egocentric, whereas a child in the concrete operations stage is not. Outlining one of Piaget's studies is probably the best way to explain what 'egocentric' means.

An experiment to test for egocentrism – method 1

Piaget and Inhelder (1956) is probably the most well known study carried out by these researchers. This study is often known as the 'three mountain task'. If you want to copy this study you will need to do some work to build the equipment. On a tray build three mountains, of differing heights and with each mountain separate (papier maché can be used). This would mean that, from certain viewpoints, the largest mountain would block the view of some of the middle-sized mountain and so on. This will be an important part of the study. On top of each mountain you need a different symbol and the usual ones are a house, a cross and a church. Take some photographs of the equipment, making sure that each gives a different viewpoint. It should be clear that in one photograph, for example, the largest mountain with its distinguishing feature on top (such as the house) is blocking some of the other mountains, and in another photograph the smallest mountain is all clearly visible, but blocks some of the largest (and so on). The idea is for the child to sit in front of the equipment and identify their own view of the three mountains from the photographs. The question is whether they can do that. There is also another question that concerns whether then can identify what view someone else has – someone looking at the tray from a different side and from a different viewpoint. One way of doing this is to position a small doll on the other side of the tray and to ask the child to point to the photograph that shows what the doll (not the child) can see. If the child can identify the viewpoint of the doll, then the child is not egocentric. If the child can only identify their own viewpoint, then that child is egocentric. Piaget found (with another researcher who worked with him) that younger children were egocentric, and he concluded that they were in the preoperational stage. He noted the age of children who were egocentric and from that evidence drew up his theory that the preoperational stage lasted up to around the age of six years old. By the age of 7 years children were not usually egocentric and were able to perform that mental operation, so were said to be in the concrete operations stage.

Piaget found that younger children were egocentric and could not take the view of another person so he concluded that one mental operation that children had to develop was the ability to decentre and if the child could not decentre, Piaget thought that they were still preoperational.

Piaget's work has been widely tested and the three-mountain task has been criticised. It is claimed that the task has no meaning for a child. A child in our culture is not usually used to thinking about mountain views and identifying what another can see. There might be a problem with the validity of the method, as it might not measure egocentrism so much as a lack of understanding of the task. Another well-known study was done to test whether children given a more realistic task could decentre at an age lower than Piaget predicted.

An experiment to test for egocentrism – method 2

This was found to be the case. The procedure for this experiment is very similar to the procedure in the three-mountain task. This time, however, the equipment is different. For this task imagine building walls out of bricks such as Lego bricks. Build them in a cross shape. They need to be tall enough to hide toy figures behind the walls, but short enough that in some positions the figures can 'see' each other. The idea is to position the figures in different places and then the child has to say if one figure can see the other or not. One of the figures is a policeman and the idea is that the other figure (or doll) is hiding from the policeman. If the child knows when the policeman cannot see the doll, then that child is taking the viewpoint of another and is, therefore, not egocentric. If a younger child can do this, then this goes against Piaget's findings that younger children are egocentric. In fact young children were able to place the doll figure where the policeman could not see it, and were able to take the viewpoint of the policeman. This is evidence that children can decentre at an age younger than that predicted by Piaget. The idea is that the child understands that the doll wants to hide from the policeman, and so can do the task, whereas the three-mountain task has little meaning for the child, so they cannot do that task.

The argument here is that Piaget was wrong and that children who would be said to be in the preoperational stage are not egocentric. However, it could just be claimed that children leave the preoperational stage younger than Piaget thought. There might still be children who are egocentric and then who decentre – it is just that the ages that Piaget predicted to go with the stages are not right. These ideas are very similar indeed to the claims that children conserve at a younger age than Piaget thought. It seems as though children can do mental operations at an age younger than 6 years, and this can be as young as 3 years. Or it could be that when a task makes sense the children can do it, so what is being measured might be the child's ability to do more abstract tasks that make little sense. An older child might be more capable of doing that sort of task or of obeying instructions.

✔ PROGRESS CHECK

Complete the following sentences by filling in appropriate terms, selected from: conserve, Piaget, volume, egocentric, number.

1 Young children up to the age of around 6 years cannot _____ liquid, which means they don't realise that when liquid from one container is poured into another container without spilling any, then the amount of liquid is the same.

2 Children over the age of about 7 years can conserve both _____ and _____.

3 _____ thought that children aged 6 years and under are _____, which means they cannot take the viewpoint of another person.

TRY THIS!

Observe children in your setting and you will almost certainly see an occasion when a toy is treated as if it were alive. This can be pretend play but it can also demonstrate animism. You could talk to parents and carers of young children and find out if they have an absent friend, or if they treat a particular cuddly toy as a friend. How far do you think this shows that the child thinks objects are alive?

Young children show animism

You probably know enough about Piaget's second stage now to see the general idea that children aged from 2 years to 6 years are developing but not to the extent of being able to perform mental operations in the sense of manipulating ideas. They develop their use of language, of course, and they can also use words to represent things that are not present, so they can 'pretend play'. (Note that both language development and play are looked at elsewhere in this textbook.) However, there is one more idea that you are likely to be able to see often when working with young children. Young children show **animism**. Animism refers to thinking that objects are alive. A child in the concrete operations stage is unlikely to think this, but quite a few younger children do. Piaget's example of animism involved the sun and how it follows us around as we move. Piaget (1960) apparently asked a child whether the sun was alive and the child answered that of course the sun is alive 'otherwise it wouldn't follow us, it couldn't shine.' This child is showing animism.

CASE STUDY

Tom and his friends, whilst at nursery, are having a conversation about the sky and clouds. They are talking about the clouds moving across the sky. Tom comments that one cloud is in a hurry and he talks about the cloud as if it is alive. This is an example of animism.

THINK ABOUT IT

Before reading on, make a list of what cognitive abilities you think a child of 7 years and older has developed. To help you, think about what a preoperational child cannot do, as this will show you what a concrete operational child can do.

Stage three – the concrete operations stage (6–12 years)

You already know quite a lot about the third of Piaget's stages, the concrete operations stage. This is because children aged around 7 years and older do seem to be able to perform more complex mental operations than a preoperational child does.

A child that can use mental operations is no longer preoperational and can decentre and conserve volume and number. Such children are no longer egocentric, which means they can take the view of another person. They can think of more than one classification of things at a time – for example, they can sort long red pencils from short green ones, identifying both colour and length. Piaget thought that being able to classify in this way, and being able to hold ideas in the head so that number stays the same in different situations, are mental abilities, and a child develops them. It is not that when they reach 7 years old they can suddenly do mental operations when they could not before. Rather, it is that children of up to around 6 years old do not show such abilities whereas by 7 and 8 years old they usually can. This strongly suggests that cognitive development is taking place and that is Piaget's main point. Even if some of the abilities do occur at an age earlier than Piaget thought (as shown by alternative experiments), there is still the main point that younger children cannot perform the same mental operations that older children can.

✔ PROGRESS CHECK

Read the following statements and decide whether they are more likely to be true of a child in the preoperational or concrete operational stage.

1 The child can sort bricks according to colour and shape.
2 The child cannot say what a friend can see when the friend is standing in a different place in the room.
3 The child acts as though a tree is alive and talks about it moving its branches to protect the grass below.
4 The child knows that there is the same amount of drink in two glasses, even if the glasses are of different shapes, as long as the same amount was poured into the two glasses in the first place.

In the concrete operational stage of thinking actual objects are thought about. In this stage mental operations require 'concrete' or real objects to be thought about. Children in this stage can deal with objects mentally, for example, imagining three green pens and four white ones, so working out that there are seven pens. However, they need objects (such as pens) to think about. By the next stage (formal operational reasoning) they can think in abstract terms, as explained below.

Some features of concrete operational thought

Children at this stage can decentre. For example, they can pick out short green pencils. They can conserve and they realise that quantity can stay the same even when other properties (such as shape of glass) change. They understand that when something is done, and then changed back again, the original situation is created – the child understands reversibility. They are also no longer egocentric and can see something from someone else's viewpoint.

Stage four – the formal operations stage (12–19 years)

The last of Piaget's stages is when formal operational thinking is achieved. In the concrete operational stage children need concrete objects to develop thinking and to perform operations. In the formal operational stage, actual (concrete) objects are no longer required and mental operations can be undertaken 'in the head' using abstract terms. For example, children at this stage can answer questions such as: 'if you imagine something made up of two quantities, and the whole thing remains the same when one quantity is increased, what happens to the second quantity?' This type of reasoning can be done without thinking about actual objects. However, you may have imagined actual objects in order to achieve the answer. For example, you may have imagined a cake mix made up of margarine and sugar. When the same quantity of cake mix remains, and the sugar is decreased, the margarine must have been increased. In that case you would have been doing concrete operational thinking perhaps – or did you need formal operational thought in order to substitute the abstract ideas ('something' and 'two quantities') with the concrete ideas ('cake mix' and 'margarine and sugar')? These are the sorts of questions to ask and it is not easy to come up with answers. However, you can see that being able to work out totals and quantities without thinking about actual objects is perhaps a different type of cognition (thinking) than the concrete operational thinking outlined above. That is Piaget's main point.

There is some discussion about whether all people reach formal operational thinking.

One way of thinking about this stage is to consider the game 'twenty questions' and another example is 'guess the number'. Both are outlined below.

Twenty questions

This game involves one person thinking of some object and then others in the group trying to guess the object. They can ask 20 questions, but they can only ask questions that need a 'yes' or 'no' answer, such as 'can you eat it?' There is one exception in that the first question is generally 'is it animal, vegetable or mineral?' to give people a start. Children in the concrete operational stage tend to think using objects, so are likely to start by guessing the object, such as by asking 'is it an orange?' When formal operational thinking is reached, however, questions tend to be more abstract, such as 'is it large or small?' Those thinkers ask broader categories to try to narrow down the search.

Guess the number

This game is to try to guess a particular number from between 0 and 2000 in a very short time. The rules are that they can say any number and the person who knows the answer says whether the answer is higher or lower. Some radio programmes play this game and the person who says the number wins money. Formal operational thought is needed. For example, formal operational thinkers tend to say 1000 first, and then they find out if the number is 1000 (in which case they win straight away) or between 0 and 999, or between 1001 and 2000. Assuming the number is lower

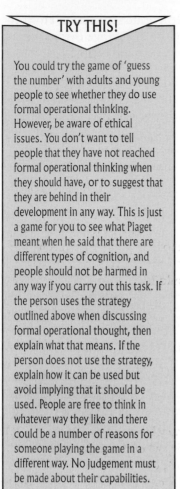

than 1000, they say 500 and find out if the number is 500 (and they win), or between 0 and 499, or between 501 and 999. In this way they can narrow down successfully and quite quickly. Someone in the concrete operational stage might start calling out numbers instead of narrowing down the search, which would be less successful. In practice most adults would try narrowing down the search and would use formal operational thought.

As your course is concerned with young children, no more is said here about formal operational thinking and indeed Piaget too was more concerned about the cognitive development of children than that of adults.

Other theorists emphasised different areas from Piaget and two of those are outlined below. They are the two main names in this area apart from Piaget. Both of these theorists, Vygotsky and Bruner, have useful ideas to add to Piaget's views and they too have influenced early years practice.

VYGOTSKY'S THEORY OF COGNITIVE DEVELOPMENT

Both Bruner and Vygotsky emphasise a child's environment, especially the social environment, more than Piaget did. As you have seen, Piaget looked particularly at how thinking abilities (mental operations) developed. The other two theorists mentioned here do the same, but focus much more on how our interactions with others affect our cognitive development. What we do socially affects how we develop, and both Bruner and Vygotsky recognised this, though they too had different theories. Vygotsky in particular focused very clearly on the role of others in our development, and his theory is outlined before Bruner's.

Vygotsky had a 'social' theory of cognitive development. He saw that people are social beings and do not develop as individuals without influence from those around them. He also saw that language, whilst being a cognitive facility (as it involves thinking), is also very social, as it involves communicating with others. He gave language a larger role in development than Piaget did. Bruner also gave language a larger role. Language development is discussed elsewhere in this textbook (Chapter 6).

Vygotsky thought that language for a young baby is developing but only becomes useful when it enables the baby to communicate with others. At first language is inner speech and it is only later that it becomes a useful tool in our development. For Vygotsky, problem solving is the main focus of a child's development, as children have to solve problems presented to them from birth. This problem solving takes place inside a person's head, and, therefore, involves cognition – indeed problem solving is what thinking is, according to Vygotsky. Where Piaget thought a child developed cognitive abilities in order to deal with the outside world, Vygotsky realised that the outside world actually presents the problems that the child must solve, so the outside world has a great importance in the child's development. In this way children interact with their world, rather than acting inside their own world. They do not, as Piaget thought, just learn to work with their world, but their world (in the sense of the people within it) affects them too. This is why we are saying that Vygotsky's theory is a social one where Piaget's is not.

Cultural influences on cognitive development

Vygotsky (1896–1934) examined cultural influences on cognitive development. When Piaget's work was discussed earlier in this chapter it was suggested that children were more likely to be able to do the tasks if the tasks were changed, and usually the changes meant making the tasks make more sense to the child. Piaget's rather general tasks did show that cognitive abilities between 4 year olds and 7 year olds are likely to differ, but the tasks where children could use their previous experience to make more sense of them allowed them to do certain tasks earlier than Piaget suggested. This is evidence that cultural and learning can affect a child's cognitive development and lead to earlier accomplishment of certain cognitive operations (such as object permanence, which was explained earlier).

Through the influence of culture, such as media, school, and family, it seems that children can achieve more than they would if left to their own devices. Vygotsky talked about the **zone of proximal development (ZPD)**, which refers to the area where a child can accomplish certain tasks and can achieve certain cognitive abilities, but only with the help of others around.

An experiment to test Vygotsky's idea of the need for social support within a ZPD

Wertsch *et al.* (1980) carried out a study in which young children had to build a model truck and there were shapes ready for the task to be completed. To complete the task the children had to look at the model and then copy it. It was arranged that their mothers would be present and the mother would look at the model. Young children were much more likely to refer to their mothers, see their mother looking at the model and then look at the model themselves to complete the task. Older children, who were better at the task, did look at the model but did not need the mother's example. So the younger children's ZPD included being able to do the task with help. However, the older children could do the task and did not need to move into the ZPD for that task (their ZPD would include the inability to do more complex tasks than the one outlined here without support and so on).

Although not specifically recognised by Vygotsky, it has since been found that the role of culture is domain specific which means some abilities don't seem to need cultural influence to develop and others do. One ability where the affect of others is not found is the ability to make sense of photographs, charts and so on. So some cognitive abilities probably do respond to the influence of others, whereas others do not. However, in general it does seem to be the case that cognitive development is affected by others around and by cultural effects.

BRUNER'S THEORY OF COGNITIVE DEVELOPMENT

Bruner's theory of cognitive development is not the same as Piaget's. However, like Piaget, he did think that development could be broken down into stages. He did not talk about stages as such, but talked about different ways of representing the world. He thought that a young baby would use an active way of representing the world. He called a way of representing the world a **mode of representation** and he called this first mode the **enactive mode**. A young baby would develop by actively engaging in the world, for example by putting objects in their mouth. The second mode of representation according to Bruner is the **iconic mode**, and 'iconic' really refers to pictures. So as the child grows it can use mental pictures to represent the world and does not need actual objects quite so much. The final and third mode of representation is the **symbolic mode**. Language is what we use for symbols, so basically Bruner meant that language helps us to develop cognitively. Piaget suggested that children passed through stages, leaving one stage to enter another. Bruner's ideas are slightly different because he recognised that instead of relinquishing one mode of representation for another as they grow older, children retain earlier modes of representation. As adults we are, therefore, able to represent the world through all three modes. Those of you who have a physical skill such as playing the piano or driving a car will recognise that, when proficient, you no longer consciously think about what you are doing – you are using the enactive mode.

Experiment testing a symbolic mode of representation

Bruner and Kenney (1966) devised a task. There was a board with nine squares and shapes that became gradually taller and fatter at the same time. Children had to copy the design on to another board and they could do that. This was taken as evidence that they had an iconic mode of representing the world as they would have a picture of the board to model on. This was a reproduction task and they reproduced the display. The second task was harder. It involved copying the display but this time reversing it. This was called a transposition task. If the thinnest and narrowest piece was on the left hand bottom square then the child had to start with that on the right hand bottom square, for example. To do this it was thought that the child had to think symbolically, using language such as 'most thin', 'tallest', and so on. They had to reason verbally and only the older children could do this task which reinforces Bruner's claim that using verbal reasoning is a cognitive ability that develops with age.

The transposition task could be done by 79% of seven year olds but none of the five-year olds could do it. The reproduction task was done correctly by 60% of the five-year olds and 80% of the seven year olds.

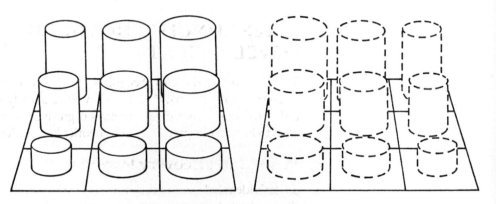

An idea of the apparatus used in Bruner and Kenney's experiment

INFORMATION PROCESSING APPROACHES TO COGNITIVE DEVELOPMENT

Piaget's theory looked at stages of cognitive development, assuming that over time a child would mature and develop more and more complex ways of thinking. Bruner also thought that there were stages, even though he thought of them as ways of representing the world that develop as a child matures. However, another view is that cognitive development is a development of the way the brain handles the flow of information that comes into it via the senses. The brain makes sense of in some way, and then produces an output of some sort. This is about information processing and such theories are known as information processing theories.

It might help to think of a computer because it is said that there is quite a lot in common between a computer and the human brain. Both are taking in information as input (though in different ways of course). Both are working on the information and processing it. Then both produce an output.

The information processing theories of cognitive development focus on three stages in just this way. First, the information is received and encoded. Then internal processes take place such as memory storage or problem-solving strategies. At this stage new information is linked to existing information. Finally cognitive structures are altered as a result of this processing and the individual learns new ways of interacting with the world. The hardware of this process is the size and capacity of the units in the brain doing the processing and the software is the strategies and capabilities of the brain.

As information processing is a flowing process, which would in theory never stop as input is continually being received (maybe not while we sleep, but that is another story), then this theory is quite different from Piaget's stage view. The information processing theories would see cognitive development as being a continuous process. Piaget's theory would fit into the idea of **discontinuity**. This means that he proposes that cognitive abilities in one stage are both quantitatively different in that the child cannot do certain things in one stage they can do in another and qualitatively different in that the child is different in the quality of what they can do. Bruner similarly suggests that children that use a symbolic mode of representation have different experiences in a quality sense as well as just more experiences in a quantity sense. Information processing theories (and other approaches in psychology such as the behaviourist approach and social learning theory, which were outlined in Chapter 4) represent **continuity** in that they think that development is continuous rather than in stages.

> ## DEFINITIONS
>
> **Discontinuity** – refers to theories that suggest we develop in stages, and we are both different in quantity and quality when we move 'up' to the next stage.
>
> **Continuity** – refers to theories that hold that development is not stagelike and happens all the time. We all develop with all our experiences.

BRIEF CONCLUSIONS ABOUT COGNITIVE DEVELOPMENT

Theories, such as theories of cognitive development outlined in this chapter, might be interesting in their own right but they should really also be useful. It might be interesting to know how a child develops cognitively, but we would expect such theories then to inform our practice. Such theories have indeed been applied in education.

Piaget and discovery learning

Piaget's ideas led to discovery learning principles. For example, Piaget's ideas suggest that a child develops by interacting with the environment, such as co-ordinating their muscles when very young and developing conservation skills when they are older. From this theoretical viewpoint, 'teaching' is not really going to be the best way forward for a child if teaching is defined in a narrow way and means telling children something or showing them how to do something. Children can only work within their cognitive abilities and, for example, a young child in the preoperational stage, according to Piaget, cannot take the view of another so should not be expected to. Facilitating their learning becomes more useful than teaching. This is called allowing for discovery learning. Many materials must be made available so that children can explore their world in as much depth and breadth as possible and so have as many experiences to assimilate, accommodate and build as many schemas as possible. Computers can help to provide materials and stimulation.

Those of you working with children under 3 years may have come across treasure baskets and heuristic play. These were ideas for exploratory play developed by Elinor Goldschmeid. The treasure basket is specifically designed for babies of about 8 months old who can sit on their own. They are given a basket full of small objects made of natural materials that are chosen to appeal to all of the baby's senses. For instance there may be an orange for taste and smell, rattles and rustly paper to hear, fir cones and cotton reels to explore (there are a lot of possibilities). The role of the adult is to make sure that the objects are safe and to monitor babies as they explore all the objects in front of them.

For toddlers the idea was refined into heuristic play (from the Greek word *heuriskein*, which means 'to discover'). Heuristic play is designed for a group of toddlers. Sacks, or large tins are obtained and each is filled with a collection of 10 to 20 of the same item. Items used need to be safe, and again challenge all the senses. They can include lengths of chain, cotton reels, shells, fir cones, corks, wooden spoons, etc. The role of the adult is to set the area up attractively and monitor the children as they play whilst trying not to enter into any interaction with them. At the end of the session the toddlers help sorting the objects as they go back into the containers.

Vygotsky and reciprocal teaching

Vygotsky emphasised the role of others in setting problems for a child just outside where they are comfortable with tasks. This means going into children's ZPD and challenging them to try something slightly harder than they can achieve – but not so difficult that they cannot achieve it without help. It is not only the teacher that can lead a child through 'zones' to stretch them so that they can develop. Peers and other classmates can also take this role and can learn from one another, on the principle that they are unlikely to all be at the same level in every area. Teaching works better if the teacher helps a child to move forward rather than instructing the child, and there is the idea of reciprocal teaching. For example, children could help one another in a group to develop reading. A text is read through. Then someone in the group summarises what it is about and the others discuss this summary. Together they work out what the text is about, and the teacher supports the discussion rather than leading it. In this way children can help themselves to develop.

Bruner, scaffolding and the spiral curriculum

Bruner's ideas led to 'scaffolding' and the idea of a spiral curriculum. With the idea of developing and building a child's symbolic thinking, Bruner emphasised thinking itself rather than actual knowledge. The aim would be for a child to develop problem-solving skills, for example, and then be able to transfer those skills to other situations. Education becomes not so much giving knowledge as developing thinking skills. In order to achieve this subjects would be taught at levels of gradually increasing difficulty, in a sort of spiral, so the child is building understanding skills as well as learning knowledge. Training in this way will lead to children being able to solve problems by themselves, which is the aim. Like Vygotsky, Bruner, therefore, emphasises the need for others to help a child to develop these skills, and in this way Vygotsky and Bruner differ from Piaget.

TRY THIS!

If you are working with children aged 3–6 look at the Foundation Stage Curriculum Guidance document.

1   Look at the section that describes the underlying principles of early years education. Can you see the influence of Piaget, Vygotsky and Bruner in this?

2   Look at the different areas of the curriculum. How do these areas relate to the academic subjects you learned when you were at school? How does this relate to Bruner's ideas?

ANSWERS TO 'TRY THIS!' PROBLEMS

Here is a list of possible assumptions about babies and their psychological (and physical) development, from the 'Try This!' section on p. 76.

✓ 'Babies need stimulation.' Without it they do not seem to develop normally. See Chapter 3 on the effects of privation and deprivation.

✓ 'Babies cannot fend for themselves.' Unlike some animals they need 24-hour care at the start. See Chapters 1, 2 and 3, on evolution theory, attachment and bonding.

✗ 'Mothers make better early carers than fathers.' This is not the case although the roles of mothers and fathers usually tend to be different. Babies can attach either to mother or father – the main caregiver, whoever that is, is the main attachment figure. Chapter 3 looks at this.

✓ 'Babies cannot stand up at first.' However, they do have a walking reflex when very newly born.

✗ 'Mothers naturally love their babies.' Ask around to find out if this is the case. It is generally thought now that there is not a natural response but this is not proved. Culturally we are conditioned to love babies and most mothers do, however, this may not be an instinct.

✗ 'Some children are born naughty.' This could be the case, but is very hard to test. In any case, it is very unlikely that any characteristic is wholly nature or nurture, and this would include 'naughtiness' (whatever that is).

✗ 'Children should be talking by the age of 2 years.' Usually they would be talking and it might be worth checking out why they are not. However, there are plenty of cases where a child is a 'late talker' and yet develops without any problems.

FURTHER READING

Bruce, Tina (1987) *Early Childhood Education,* Hodder & Stoughton, London.
This is an easy read, recommended for all students.

Cohen, D. (2002) *How the Child's Mind Develops,* Routledge, Hove, Chapters 2 and 3.
This is an easy read and recommended for students studying at Level 3 and higher.

David, T., Goouch, K., Powell, S. and Abbott, L. (2003) *Birth to Three Matters: A Review of the Literature Compiled to Inform the Framework to Support Children in their Earliest Years, DfES,* Nottingham, Chapters 2 and 5.
This book is particularly recommended for students on higher level courses.

Donaldson, Margaret (1978) *Children's Minds,* Fontana/Collins, Glasgow.
Although this is an old text, it can be considered a classic and is recommended for all students at Level 3 and above.

Goldschmied, E. and Jackson, S. (2004) *People Under Three. Young Children in Day Care,* 2nd edn. Routledge, London.
This book is suitable for students studying at Level 3 and above and contains valuable information on the treasure basket and heuristic play.

Lindon, J. (2000) *Helping Babies and Toddlers Learn a Guide to Good Practice with Under Threes,* The National Early Years Network, London.
This is a very easy read and is useful for students studying at all levels. Chapter 5 contains a good section on exploratory play.

KEY TERMS

You need to know the meaning of the following words and phrases. Go back through the chapter to make sure you understand them:

Accommodation
Adaptation
Assimilation
Constructivist
Continuity
Decentre
Disequilibrium
Discontinuity
Egocentrism
Enactive mode of representation
Equilibration
Iconic mode of representation
Inter-observer reliability
Object permanence
Primary circular reactions
Reliability
Schema
Secondary circular reactions
Symbolic mode of representation
Validity
Zone of proximal development

KEY NAMES

Bruner
Piaget
Vygotsky

Language development and IQ

INTRODUCTION

This chapter examines both language development and IQ. These different aspects of development are included together in this chapter partly because they both illustrate how questions about the influences of nature and nurture are important when studying such characteristics. Language development is examined in some depth because it seems to have such an important role to play in a child's development. Stages of language are outlined, as well as what is expected of children as they grow. Theories of how we acquire language are reviewed, including the idea that we have a biological device that sets us up to acquire language, and that learning from environmental influences is also very important. Non-verbal communication is also examined as it is useful to understand some ideas about things like body language when working with children. Then the concept of intelligence is examined, including the idea that there are probably many kinds of intelligences and the issue of what intelligence really is – does it exist? The main concept examined here is IQ because what we measure is IQ rather than something called 'intelligence'. IQ measures different capabilities and seems to develop with age, which is interesting. Another question how much of our IQ (capabilities) is determined from conception and how much is affected by our nurture. The fairness of IQ tests is considered, paying particular attention to the role of cultural knowledge in IQ tests and whether they can be culture fair.

LANGUAGE DEVELOPMENT

This chapter will be looking at two different but interrelated topics: language development and the measurement of intelligence. There are different theories involved and different factors affecting the development of these two characteristics. Both, however, involve aspects of genetic influence linked with aspects of environmental effects, so both involve the nature / nurture debate that has been discussed in many of the other chapters in this textbook. Language development is looked at first.

Children start to develop language from before birth and it seems that they are biologically prepared to use language. Chapter 2 considered some biological aspects of the foetus and newly born infant that suggest that there is a biological aspect to language development, and these are briefly outlined below. However, infants in different parts of the world clearly learn different languages and so there must be an environmental influence to language development. Chapter 4 discussed learning theories and these are used in this chapter to give one explanation about how we might learn our particular language.

'Language' has been taken by some, to mean the whole communication system of language that includes speech, or at least words, as in sign language. There is another type of communication, non-verbal communication, which is studied briefly later in this chapter.

Characteristics of human language

Many different species communicate, including dolphins, bees and lions, but no other species has all the same characteristics that humans have in their language. Human language uses symbols and has rules that mean that speakers can use and understand lots of different sentences and phrases. For example, we can say 'the cat sat on the mat' and know what that means, but we can also say 'the pig ran on the treadmill' and know what that means, even if it is unlikely and even if that sentence has not been heard before. This is what makes human language different – we can understand utterances that we have not heard before.

A symbolic system

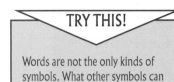

TRY THIS!

Words are not the only kinds of symbols. What other symbols can you think of?

If you have studied Chapter 5, which looks at cognitive (thinking) development, you will have come across the term 'symbolic' when looking at the way Bruner thought we develop ways of representing the world for ourselves. The symbolic stage is the final stage according to Bruner, and the advantage for humans here is that being able to use symbols as language means that we can represent ideas and things in our minds and so develop ways of thinking about them. It is because we have symbols for things that we develop our thinking abilities as we do. Piaget and Vygotsky had different ways of looking at how language fits in with cognitive (thinking) development but also had a role for language, as is explained later in this chapter. So the ability to use symbols is important for the way humans develop. Language is symbolic because it uses symbols for meanings. Symbols generally have a meaning that is understood by others. We all have to mean the same thing when we talk about a bird, for example. However, symbols can be anything really – we can use any word to represent any object as long as we share that meaning with others. This does happen when groups of individuals develop their own language, which can be called slang, and this form of almost private language can help to fix a group together. For example, children can develop this sort of code and parents are excluded, which is part of the point of doing it. Symbols do not necessarily have to have a shared meaning. For example you may have a piece of music which has a special meaning for you and no one else.

A rule-governed system

Language also has rules. Symbols must usually have shared meaning and be combined in a way that everyone understands. There have to be rules. In English rules include the order in which the words are put together in a sentence, for example, the word 'the' goes before the noun to which it is referring. We must say 'I went to the shop' not 'I went to shop the'. This last sentence is starting to have a different meaning, and could become 'I went to shop the thief', which would have a completely different meaning. This example shows the importance of rules.

A productive system

Human language is a productive system in that there can be many ways of combining the symbols and the rules to make completely new utterances that can still be understood. We can produce all sorts of new sentences and phrases. It is a very flexible form of communication.

Modes of language

There are different language modes – or ways of communicating using language. When we learn a new language we tend to study reading, writing, speaking and listening as we need all these aspects of a language. A lot of research focuses on speaking a language but these other modes are also important. Signing is often studied too and is a form of speaking. Writing is taught but speaking is acquired, and this aspect of language is investigated in what follows.

An infant preparing for language development – turn taking

From before they are born children are developing in ways that will help them develop language. For instance a child's hearing is well developed at birth. The interactions that infants have with their caregivers are working towards the development of language. Chapter 2 mentioned turn taking, for example. New babies have been shown to have the ability to stick out their tongues in response to adults doing the same. Babies also pattern other movements, including babbling and blowing bubbles. If their caregiver speaks, babies move their mouths in speech-like movements and makes noises, as if preparing for speaking.

Modelled gestures and how an infant copies them

Turn taking is important as, in order to use language successfully at any age, the speaker and the listener must obey the rules and take turns in one or the other role. Two people having a conversation need to know when to listen and when a response is appropriate. Babies seem to use this patterning from a very young age and seem to be biologically ready to do this, although learning can also take place during the interactions that babies have with their caregivers. The infant is even learning turn taking when feeding. A feeding baby may pause and then the mother will jiggle the breast or bottle to start the infant feeding again. There are also what are called **protoconversations** (Bateson, 1975), which refer to interaction patterns between the mother and baby where the mother speaks when their baby stops babbling or when the mother finishes the baby's 'conversations'. These protoconversations seem to be preparing babies for later speech.

Stern (1985) emphasised the importance of sensitive mothering – which was discussed in Chapter 3. Mothers who are sensitive to their infant's needs tend to have babies who have formed a more secure attachment. These infant-mother pairs are more likely to enjoy turn taking and engage in reciprocal (turn-taking) behaviours. This would involve starting and finishing conversations together.

Developing language – the need to start conversations

Young infants tend to mimic others and practise turn taking but they do not actually start conversations. They are restricted to babbling, which is really practising sounds and they develop language according to reactions to their babbling. However, it is not until they are slightly older that they actually start conversations or use language for themselves. First attempts at using language are not likely to be verbal in any case. Children are likely to point to what they want rather than ask

DEFINITION

Protoconversations – interaction patterns between mothers and babies where the mothers speak when their babies stop babbling or when the mothers finish the babies' 'conversations'.

DEFINITIONS

Speech stream – a continuous set of sounds that would be speech to an adult but to a young baby is just a stream of sounds with no gaps.

Motherese – the term for the special way that adults speak to babies, for example, using a higher pitch and emphasising words more clearly, with rhythm. This seems to help an infant to learn to separate sounds into words and so to learn to distinguish speech.

DEFINITION

Phonemes – sounds that are treated the same even if not the same, for example 'key' and the same sound in 'ski' have the same phoneme ('key'/'ki').

for it. This can be at the age of around 8 months. Pointing is found in all cultures (for example, Butterworth, 1995) so is thought to be instinctive. When babies point, others respond and from these responses the baby learns better what works. So from about 12 months old infants become better at obtaining what they want as they can point, look at and vocalise to communicate to others. As they develop language, children stop pointing quite so much and their communication becomes more verbal than physical.

Keeping conversations going

Once children have learnt to initiate conversations and they know about turn taking, they have to learn to maintain conversations. Older children are more likely than younger children to wait until another speaker has finished before starting their own part of the conversation (McLaughlin, 1998). Younger children might be able to take turns well enough but their own part of the conversation can be rather irrelevant so it is hard to keep a conversation going. For example, if children under 2 years old are asked questions they usually only answer about one-third of the questions asked (Pan and Snow, 1999). They do not focus well on actual conversations, even though they wait their turn before speaking. However, by the age of 3 years they are answering about half the questions asked. Children are also more likely to answer questions than to ask them. This means that their conversations with adults are the most successful and young children do not converse well with their peers. By the age of about 4 years, though, children are good at conversations and it is from this age onwards that many adults enjoy their conversations with children very much.

Developing speech

Although babies' hearing is quite well developed even at birth, it takes longer for them to be able to distinguish sounds enough to separate them, which is needed for them to understand speech. For a young baby a sentence would be a continuous stream of sound, called a **speech stream** (Jusczyk, 1997). Infants do learn to separate sounds into speech and this might be partly because of the way adults speak to them. Adults speak to infants in a more rhythmic way and using a higher pitch. They emphasise words differently too. This is called **motherese** or infant-directed speech. By around 7 months babies manage to separate words and to start to make sense of uninterrupted speech.

Hearing speech sounds

Sound categories used in speech are called **phonemes**. Phonemes are sounds that are treated the same even if not the same, for example 'key' and the same sound in 'ski' have the same phoneme ('key'/'ki'). In English we treat that sound the same even though it is slightly differently pronounced whereas in Chinese the example of the 'key' and 'ki' sound are treated differently and Chinese speakers differentiate between those two sounds. This is what makes it difficult to learn new languages – phonemes differ. Infants have to learn to discriminate between phonemes in their own language. This is similar to them having to distinguish words.

Distinguishing between phonemes – innate or learnt?

The study of how infants can distinguish phonemes is not easy given that very young babies are tested. One way is to use habituation. Habituation occurs when a baby gets used to something. It is assumed that a baby sucks on a dummy or something similar more when it attends to or is interested in something and then it stops sucking when it becomes bored (or used to) something. A baby is presented with a sound and sucks and shows interest. Gradually the baby loses interest and becomes habituated to that sound. If another sound is introduced the researchers can tell if the baby can recognise the new sound as different by whether the baby starts to suck again. For example, if the sound is 'ba' and is repeated, when the baby stops sucking it is assumed that it is bored with that sound. If the sound is changed to 'pa' and the sucking starts again it is assumed that the baby can recognise that this is now a different sound. Using this technique it has been found that an infant of around 1 month can distinguish between a 'ba' and a 'pa' sound. As these infants are only 1 month old this tends to suggest that being able to discriminate between sounds is an innate ability, although it is possible that it is learnt because babies can hear whilst still in the womb.

By 6 months infants can distinguish between many different phonemes including those that adult speakers of the same language cannot distinguish. However, after that age infants start to focus on the language they hear so by the age of 12 months they can discriminate between phonemes in 'their' language but not the phonemes of other languages. It seems that they have an innate predisposition to distinguish between phonemes in general but that gradually learning takes over and they begin to discriminate only between phonemes used in their own language.

Learning to speak – from crying to babbling

Babies can make out speech sounds before they can produce them. Babies need to be able to control the mouth, lips and tongue as well as the vocal cords before they can speak. They all go through the same stages of being able to produce sounds, which tends to suggest that this is an innate or in built maturation or biological process. Remember that if all babies in all cultures follow a similar pattern for any developmental task then it is likely that that behaviour or ability is instinctive.

- Birth to 2 months. From birth to around 2 months babies use cries and coughs and these appear to be simply reflex reactions. Some say that babies use different crying for different needs but parents cannot distinguish cries if they are played them back on a tape recorder so it is not shown that this is the case. It is more likely that a parent works out what the baby wants by environmental factors such as how long ago the baby was fed or whether the nappy is wet or not.

- Two months to 4 months. From between 2 months and 4 months the baby begins to laugh and to combine sounds. There is reciprocal 'cooing' for example, as the parents returns the sounds, and there is turn taking, as discussed in Chapter 2.

- Four months to 6 months. From between 4 months and 6 months, babbling is found. Infants produce a range of sounds. Babies start to combine sounds from between 6 to 10 months old. They seem to be experimenting with sounds. Infants do not produce all known sounds when babbling, however, all babies do babble so it does seem to be a genetic tendency and they produce the same range of sounds whatever the language they are exposed to. As many deaf children babble this is more evidence that this is an innate ability.

- From 7 months. By seven months old deaf babies tend to stop babbling, so it seems that from about 6 months babies need to hear sounds in order to develop their babbling into speech. Infants in institutions also do not vocalise much, which tends to suggest that hearing others speak, and interacting with others is important.

- From 10 months. Babies from 10 months onwards not only vocalise quite a lot but start using a large range of tones too, ready for actual speech, which needs many different rising and falling patterns such as when a question is posed. Table 6.1 summarises the move from reflexive sounds to complex babbling.

Learning to use language, and learning grammar

As mentioned earlier language is not just words but also grammar and rules are involved. **Syntax** is the word for the way words are related to one another to form sentences. Chomsky, whose theory is discussed later in this chapter, thought there were two levels of syntax – the surface and the deep structure. Some sentences are ambiguous such as 'the eating of the dogs was terrible', which could mean either that the dogs were eaten, which was a terrible thing, or that they ate in a very bad way or a very unhealthy way. This shows that the surface structure can have more than one meaning. Sophisticated language use means that the deep structure is easily understood, but clearly syntax and grammar rules are quite complex and a child has to learn to grasp all the rules.

Table 6.1   Developing control over sounds in preparation for speech – universal stages

Age of baby	Stage of vocalisation
Birth to 2 months	Cries, coughs, sneezes – reflex actions as the required physical control is not present.
Two months to 4 months	Cooing and laughing occur and adults repeat these sounds back to the baby. They reciprocate and turn taking occurs.
Four months to 6 months	Babbling is found in all cultures and the same sorts of sounds are made. Deaf babies babble.
Six months to 10 months	Sounds are combined though not into words. Deaf babies cease babbling so it seems that sounds from others need to be heard.
Ten months onwards	Babbling, and also ability to modulate (rise and fall) sounds that are produced so that the babbling begins to sound more like the language babies hear around them.

The one-word stage

When children learn to use language, they go through similar stages. The first stage is the one-word stage. This occurs between 10 and 18 months and it is thought that the single words used actually represent more in the way of thinking than a single object.

For example if a toddler says the word 'car' the same surface structure can have different deep structures such as 'look at that car', 'I want that toy car', or 'I'm frightened of that car'. We understand what the toddler means by looking for contextual clues.

Golinkhoff and Hirsh-Pasek have researched in this area (1995). They used 17-month-old babies and showed them two videos, each presenting a different scene. An example is that one video shows a dog licking a cat and the other shows a cat licking a dog. As the videos played the infants hear one of two sentences, for example, 'the dog is licking the cat' or 'the cat is licking the dog'. It was found that infants looked longer at the video that matched the words, which suggests that there is good understanding of sentences even if the children are in the one word stage.

Signing the word 'eat' shows how language does not have to be vocal

The two-word stage

The two-word stage occurs when the child is between 18 months and 2 years old. Children use two words together and they seem to fit together as if being sentences without joining words. They are not just two random words. For example, the child can say 'kick ball'. Children are likely to use words they hear often.

Moving towards complete sentence use

From around 2 years old children start to use complete sentences and the difference between what they can produce at the age of 2 years and what they can say at 3 years is very marked. There are common grammatical errors made as a child develops their speech. One error is **over-regularisation**. This means that children learn a rule and then use it even when not appropriate. For example, they learn to add '-ed' to make a verb past tense, and then add '-ed' even when a verb is not regular – so, for example, 'thought' becomes 'thinked'. Children also make mistakes with plurals and add an 's' when inappropriate. For example, they can say 'foot' – but the plural would be 'foots'. Table 6.2 outlines the different stages of language production.

Table 6.2   The different stages of language production

Approximate age of child	Language stage	Description of stage
Between 10 and 18 months	One-word stage	One word can be used for a number of meanings, for example 'milk' can mean 'I want some milk' or 'there is some milk'.
Between 18 months and 2 years	Two-word stage	Two words are used together to communicate. It seems as if the two words are a sentence but with lots of words missing, for example 'kick ball' rather than any two words just put together.
Between 2 and 3 years	Moving to use of complete sentences	There is very rapid progress made at this time and the difference between what 2 year olds can produce and what they can say at 3 years old is very marked.

Is language an innate ability or a learnt one?

There is evidence to suggest that language has an innate element in that we are biologically prepared to develop language in some way, and evidence that we learn particular languages through social influences. Therefore, it seems that there is both a 'nature' and a 'nurture' aspect to language. When it is said that language is acquired this means that it develops from abilities that we have and when it is said that language is learnt then this means that it comes from environmental input. Evidence is outlined in this section.

Biological underpinning for language development

In Chapter 2 it was explained that the foetus can hear sound before birth and it seems that very soon after birth babies can recognise their mothers' voices. Clearly the sound system is ready to receive input and language will be one of the first inputs that the child will decode. Indeed in Chapter 2 it was suggested that babies can even distinguish 'their own' language from a 'foreign' language, which is added evidence that we are ready to develop language from an early age.

Chomsky (1982) studied language development and suggested that there is evidence that humans have what is called a **language acquisition device** (LAD). One piece of evidence he used to claim that we have the inbuilt capacity to develop language was that if all language was learnt then why do young children incorrectly impose grammatical rules such as adding '-ed' to a verb incorrectly (for example, 'wented')? They would not have heard such words so must be using some innate (inbuilt) tendency or device to impose these rules.

DEFINITION

Over-regularisation – means using grammatical rules even when they don't apply – for example, adding '-ed' to a verb to make it past tense but doing this for 'thinked' when it should be 'thought'.

DEFINITION

Language acquisition device (LAD) – the term used for an in-built biological readiness to decode and use language. Evidence comes from our tendency, for example, to use grammatical rules but incorrectly when young – and we could not have learnt this incorrect grammar.

Another piece of evidence that suggests that the tendency to develop language is innate is that all babies babble the same sounds. It is only later (around 6 months old) that babies will start to use only the sounds of 'their' language. If all babies babble the same sounds then this suggests that that is an innate tendency as it is found in all cultures regardless of environmental aspects.

A third piece of evidence that we have an instinctive need to use language is that even deaf babies babble and tend to develop language too. Babbling does not rest on hearing sounds so it seems to be innate. If deaf children use incorrect grammar when signing (and they do) then this again suggests that there is a biological tendency to develop language.

These three pieces of evidence are used to suggest that language development has, at least in part, a biological aspect to it even if the particular language used is developed through learning and interacting with the environment.

Chomsky's evidence that language is an innate tendency in humans can be summarised as follows:

- Language requires the ability to understand deep structure from surface structure and the same surface structure can represent more than one 'deep' meaning. We could not really learn this ability to decipher deep meaning from surface structure.

- The environment only provides information about surface structure.

- Sentences that children hear are often complex and ungrammatical but they still understand them.

- Children don't receive very much feedback about the grammar of their sentences but they still develop correct grammar.

- Children acquire their own language quite quickly and relatively easily.

Children use words they have not heard (such as 'thinked') and they use correct structure eventually even though it is often not corrected when originally it is wrong. This strongly suggests that humans have an innate ability to develop language, even though the particular language they develop must itself be learnt.

Others have claimed that parents do provide their children with good grammatical sentences much of the time. However, adults do use shorter sentences when they speak to children. There is a simplified use of language. Even so, Chomsky would still point out that there is this deep meaning that must be interpreted from the surface structure and this is something that is done over and above learning each sentence and each word, so there is evidence of at least this type of innate ability. Similarly, the tendency to overregularise, as outlined above, does support the idea of some innate tendency, because words like 'foots' are not heard but are created by the child. It is usually concluded that we have an innate predisposition or tendency to learn language but that we do not have any innate knowledge of language (Maratsos, 1999).

THINK ABOUT IT

If you have already read Chapter 1 or Chapter 4, recall what was said about the different theories of learning, as those theories are used here to explain language development.

Learning a particular language

Although the ability to apply rules to language, and going through different stages of language acquisition, can be innate tendencies, children must learn their own languages and it is thought that this is done by reinforcement and imitation.

Operant conditioning principles can help to explain language acquisition

Operant conditioning can help to explain how we learn our particular language. The mechanisms of operant conditioning are outlined in Chapter 4. Children learn that particular sounds represent particular things or actions and this is not innate. One study was done to show this. Tincoff and Jusczyk (1999) showed 6-month-old infants two videos of their parents, with both showing at once side-by-side. The infants looked longer at the video of the mother if they heard the word 'mummy' and longer at the video of their father if they heard the word 'daddy'. This suggests understanding of the words. If videos showed a man and a woman whom the infant did not know, this effect was not found.

One way in which a child might learn a word is if using the word achieves some purpose. If children say 'milk' and receive a drink of milk, they are more likely to use the word again. The response reinforces the action of using the word. This is a form of operant conditioning where the law of effect is at work. The law of effect states that if a response is pleasurable then the effect will be to do it again, and if using the word 'milk' is successful, then it is likely to be used again. One type of reward is to get the required object or action (such as receiving the milk to drink) and another type of reward is parental attention. So sometimes a word might be repeated because it gets a good reaction from the parent, and babies like attention.

Children do make mistakes though. They may learn through reinforcement what a bird is, both by looking at pictures of birds and seeing them in the garden or flying around. Then they might use **overextension** and might refer to every flying object or every object with wings as a 'bird' even if it is a plane. This again reinforces the idea that there is some innate tendency at work when language development takes place, and over extending might be part of that innate predisposition. Similarly, **underextension** can occur when a word is used only for one specific object rather than for all such objects. Perhaps the word 'bird' is only used to apply to one particular object in the house, such as a special ornament, rather than all birds. Operant conditioning cannot account for these sorts of occurrences and this is evidence that language development relies on both learning and an innate predisposition.

Social learning theory and language acquisition

Imitation and the principles of social learning theory can help to explain how we learn our particular language too. The mechanisms of social learning are outlined in Chapter 4. Social learning theory also includes the idea that reinforcement is important for learning, so it would agree that rewards can lead to learning. However, social learning theory states, too, that we learn through imitation of role models and through modelling on others, particularly **significant others**. Significant others are those who are particularly important to us. Language can be learnt through modelling and young children copy their parents' speech just as they copy other behaviours. This can explain why some expressions run in families, and how accents are acquired.

An input model to explain how we learn language

Krashen (1985) has suggested an input model to explain how we learn language. This model helps to show how we need both innate structures, such as a language acquisition device, and learnt knowledge. The input model suggests that we hear 'input', which becomes understandable – for example, the baby starts to decipher sounds and we have to hear speech to start learning a language. Some sort of device in our brain, like a language acquisition device, has to be present to help with understanding. We use acquired knowledge about rules in this way. There is also learnt knowledge from the environment, which is used to decipher any input. We learn a language with the acquired knowledge about rules and the learnt knowledge from experience.

The relationship between language and thought

Having suggested that language development is a complex process that involves biological processes, innate mechanisms and interaction with the environment so that a particular language can be learnt, it is also important to link the idea of language development to cognitive development. If you have read Chapter 5, you will have learnt about cognitive (thinking) development. It was suggested that cognitive development relies on biological processes and the development of certain abilities such as understanding that the mass of an object remains the same even if the shape of it is altered.

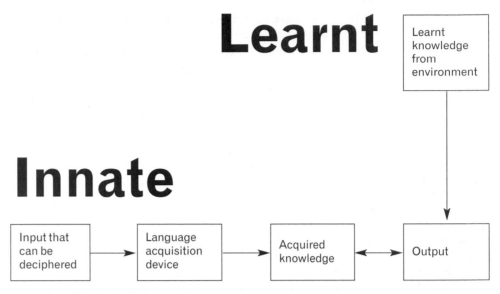

An outline of Krashen's input model

Cognitive abilities tend to develop as we grow and mature from babies to adolescents. Some theories suggest that these abilities can be speeded up by help from adults and by giving opportunities to learn, as was explained in Chapter 5.

Chapter 5 also suggested that, whereas some theorists think that cognitive development relies on language development and needs language as a tool for thinking, others think that language development simply occurs as cognitive development occurs – that cognitive development must come first. This has led to some discussion about whether cognitive (thinking) development guides our language development, or whether there needs to be a certain level of language ability that then guides our cognitive (thinking) development. Does the use of a particular language guide our thinking? In some ways the answers to this issue are not really important when considering childcare, however, they do pose some interesting questions about child development and so the different approaches are outlined here.

There are three main arguments. One school of thought suggests that we need to develop cognitively before we can develop language and the way we develop cognitively guides our language itself. Another school of thought suggests that we need language of some sort before we can develop certain levels of thinking, and that the language we learn affects our thinking. There is a final view that a child develops language and develops cognitively, but separately. Then the two abilities combine as the child develops further. These three views are briefly outlined below.

Language has to be developed before we develop cognitively

There is a view that we develop our language and it guides or limits our thinking. For example, if our language has lots of words for rain (for example, 'sleet', 'showers', 'downpour', and 'mist') then our thinking about rain will be more complex than if our language only had one word for rain. This view is called **linguistic relativity** because it claims that language dictates our thoughts and our thoughts are relative to the language we use. Two researchers, Sapir and Whorf, came to this conclusion separately. They said that, as we develop language, our language will help us to cut up nature into objects. If you were an artist you would know a lot of different words for 'red' colours (for example, 'magenta', 'crimson', 'red', 'pink', 'ruby' and 'vermillion') and would actually see the different colours in nature and in the world. If you are not an artist and only know the colours 'pink' and 'red', then you will only see pink and red. At least this is the claim.

There are those that criticise this idea. For a start if there is no word for something it would be hard to describe that thing and hard to talk about it, but that does not mean we cannot think about it differently. We might perceive many shades of red but we cannot talk about them without the words. So the limits of our language would not be the limits of our thinking – it would just be harder to talk about different perceptions (such as different colours of red) without the words to describe them. It might be the case that in some cultures there are different words to describe something. For example, they could talk about aeroplanes, which can be described in various ways such as glider, biplane, fighter, seaplane or passenger, but there might be no similar words in a language where planes are not commonplace. This does not mean that those who use the other language cannot see the difference between a seaplane and a biplane.

If we are limited by our language, and can only think about things we have words for – or at least if our thinking is limited by the words we have – then this can have quite a strong effect on our development. In one culture if everyone is limited to the same extent then this limitation might make no difference. For example, everyone in the culture might have the same difficulty in distinguishing between colours, so they would at least be equal. But consider what happens when, within one culture, there are language differences and they are said to limit thinking? This issue was considered by Bernstein and has great importance for the development of the child. Bernstein's findings are outlined below.

Limited by language code

Bernstein (1961) claimed that there are two main language codes used by children and that teachers and others treat the child differently according to the code used. This idea links to labelling and self-fulfilling prophecy, both of which are considered in more depth in Chapter 9. Bernstein argued that the two linguistic codes were used in different social circumstances. Bernstein was a sociologist, not a psychologist, and he considered the social situation and class differences rather than individual development. Bernstein talked about a restricted and an elaborated code. By **restricted code** he meant the use of short and often unfinished sentences that are often ungrammatical. Using a restricted code relies on shared understanding between the speaker and the listener, and there is shorthand involved. For example, a family might understand a reference to 'fonenge' but nobody else might. (It is shorthand for 'fire engine' and comes from a shortened form pronounced by a very young child.) By **elaborated code** Bernstein meant more formal language with correct grammar and no shorthand. Bernstein claimed that if elaborated code cannot be used then thinking is limited. It has been suggested that some working-class people cannot use elaborated code and that this means they (and their children) would not think in a complex way. It could also mean that teachers, for example, might judge those who use an elaborated code as more intelligent. This might be, for example, because those using elaborated code use correct grammar, or because a restricted code is less easily understood so they don't understand the child as well, as they don't share their meanings. Using this theory it would be claimed that teachers tend to be middle class and use an elaborated code and children who use the same code 'speak their language'. This has implications for a child's development, as considered in Chapter 9.

Others have looked at language codes too and considered issue such as race and how a different use of English such as a different race might use, might similarly affect a child's development. This issue is considered later in this chapter, when IQ is considered.

Language comes as we develop cognitively – thinking comes first

There is a view that says that we develop cognitively and then our language fits in with that thinking. So if our cultural view is about sharing and co-operation, and our thought processes are shaped by this cultural view then our language will emphasise sharing and co-operation. The view that thinking comes before language has some evidence to support it. For a start, babies begin thinking at a very early

DEFINITIONS

Restricted language code – refers to a shortened version of language that relies on shared meanings and where incorrect grammar is often used.

Elaborated language code – refers to 'proper' language use, with correct grammar and no shorthand.

age, as has been shown in Chapters 2 and 3, which look at the development of sociability of the baby, and Chapter 5, which looks at cognitive development. Mental events that do not need language occur very early on, such as problem solving (if you have studied Chapter 5, link this to the idea of developing operations) and expressing thoughts such as pain and pleasure. It is likely that our ancestors could think before they developed language use and thinking allowed them to plan and organise. It is hard not to think of them doing this before they developed language. No other animal has a language like human language and yet other animals must surely think. Experiments that try to teach animals to use language have had some success although not complete success because no other animal has the necessary jaw and tongue shape for human speech. However, some chimps have learnt to use language very successfully using a computer keyboard to indicate words and phrases. This tends to suggest that the chimps have good thinking ability and can learn how to apply language to things. Piaget would agree that language stems from cognitive development, not that it is necessary for thoughts to develop.

Piaget's view of language

Piaget focused on cognitive development. His view of language development follows his main theory that a child develops cognitively through maturation (biological processes). Young children are egocentric and can focus only on themselves, so their language is dominated by their own view and by themselves. Language helps children to identify objects and to understand how to discuss objects that do not exist. Preoperational children tend to use language literally, so when they talk about clouds moving they tend to think of them as being alive. So, for Piaget, thought comes before language and language is used alongside the development of cognitive processes. Refer back to Chapter 5 to see how this view fits with Piaget's main theory.

Bruner's view of language

For Bruner, language has a more central role in cognitive development and the child does not reach the third mode of representation (way of thinking) until language can be used to create symbols for things. This third way of thinking is called the symbolic mode, which underlines the importance placed on being able to use language for this stage to be reached. Refer back to Chapter 5 to see how Bruner's theory has this special role for language.

Language and thought develop separately then come together as a child develops

Vygotsky proposed that language and thought develop separately until about the age of 2 years. Vygotsky realised that animals were very capable of thought but not capable of producing language. He also thought that language was more than just a tool for thinking. So he thought that babies developed thought and language separately at first. He claimed that babbling was speech without thought (**pre-intellectual language**) and that recognising people and things (which babies do) was thought without language (**pre-linguistic thought**). From around the age of two years the child uses language with thought to develop further. Language can then start to direct a child's thinking.

Non-verbal communication

Spoken language is usually accompanied by non-verbal cues and, even over the phone, the person speaking uses gestures, even though they cannot be seen. Non-verbal cues can also be used on their own to communicate, although 'use' is probably not the right word as we usually don't really control our non-verbal communication. In fact non-verbal cues can often contradict a verbal message. For example, we can welcome someone into our home whilst still giving negative cues such as folded arms and a non-smiling look.

DEFINITIONS

Pre-intellectual language – Vygotsky's idea that babbling and crying are the beginnings of speech but without thought. So language and thought are said to develop separately up to the age of about two years.

Pre-linguistic thought – Vygotsky's idea that recognising objects is the beginning of thinking but without language. So language and thought are said to develop separately up to the age of about two years.

Reasons for non-verbal cues

Non-verbal behaviours can occur for a variety of reasons. Patterson (1983) listed some of them:

- they provide information about feelings and intentions;
- they are used to regulate interactions, for example by signalling the end of a conversation;
- they can be used to express intimacy;
- they can be used to establish control or dominance;
- they can be used to achieve a goal, such as when pointing to get something

Types of non-verbal communication

Much research into non-verbal behaviours has been done in the field of social psychology, and not specifically looking at children, however, children do use non-verbal cues in the same way that adults do. This may mean that such cues are innate or that the children model on those around them. What is important is that a child can communicate (and receive information) using non-verbal cues. Non-verbal communication can be through gaze, facial expression, body language, touch or interpersonal distance. Interpersonal distance is examined further in Chapter 9. Social norms can affect our use of non-verbal cues and this shows that they can be controlled to an extent – for example, we might be happy that someone has lost his job but we are likely to hide our smiles, although there should be other cues that can be picked up. This suggests that there is an element of learning involved in non-verbal communication as if it were entirely instinctive we could not control it. However, as it seems that we cannot completely control our non-verbal communication, then there could be innate factors involved, perhaps through evolution and the idea of survival of the fittest.

Individual differences in the use of non-verbal communication

There are some individual differences in ability to use and decode non-verbal signals. For example, it has been found that, in general, women are better than men at using non-verbal communication. This could be because of the way girls are brought up to be more expressive or that females are innately better at non-verbal language. There is no real evidence to suggest that some people are simply better at picking up non-verbal signals than others but you might agree that this is the case. It is not really known why.

Gaze and eye contact

One important type of non-verbal communication is using gaze and eye contact. When two people are communicating they tend to spend about 61% of the time gazing. A gaze lasts about three seconds. Eye contact is really a mutual gaze and two people together spend about 31% of the time holding eye contact. A mutual gaze (eye contact) lasts less than 1 second. We seem to seek a lot of information by looking into people's eyes and indeed this can be uncomfortable if the person is a stranger. Too little eye contact can also be disconcerting. People wear dark glasses on purpose, sometimes, to avoid having to make eye contact. This can protect privacy for one person – or can seem like a threat to the other person. We seem to get information about people's honesty, their competence and attentiveness from gaze. Children will do the same thing. One study asked mixed couples to talk to one another for ten minutes and then gave the individuals false information about how much gazing had taken place, (Kleinke and others, 1973). Males liked their partners more if there was said to be more gazing than the average, though this was not the case for females. Both sexes liked the other less if it was said that there was less than average gazing, even if this was not true, so we seem to think that if we gaze more it means we like someone, though there are some gender differences here.

Women engage in more eye contact than men do and people with lower status use more eye contact than those of higher status. Perhaps these findings correspond and women see themselves as having lower status. There are cultural differences in gaze too, with white adults spending about 75% of the time gazing when listening and 41% of the time gazing when speaking. However, North American blacks gaze more when speaking than listening. Such differences might be important if we interpret character of a person by non-verbal cues and these could be misinterpreted if different cultures were involved and indeed different genders too. A white speaker could interpret a black listener's low rate of gaze as rudeness and a black speaker may interpret a white listener's high rate of gaze in the same way. Gaze can indicate dominance and if an adult gazes more at a child than the child does at the adult this might be interpreted as control, which can have implications for the relationship between the adult and the child.

Facial expression

It has been said that there are a small number of facial expressions and that they are universal. If this is the case it suggests that they are innate. Distinctive patterns of facial muscle position indicate these emotions, which are fear, disgust, happiness, surprise, sadness and anger. Surprise is indicated by a dropped jaw and raised eyebrows, for example. When shown photographs depicting these emotions people from many different cultures can very accurately distinguish them, which does give evidence to them being universal (for example, Ekman and others, 1987). There are, though, cultural differences in what facial expressions it is appropriate to display and on what occasions. In Japan people are taught to hide negative emotions and to smile instead, and in quite a few cultures men are discouraged from showing emotions.

Posture and gesture

Kinesics is the study of body posture and gesture. **Illustrators** are body movements that accompany speech. **Emblems** are body movements that stand in for speech. **Postures** are positionings of the body to give meaning and **gestures** are meaningful body movements and postures. Postures include the use of hands to give directions (illustrators). A wave of the hand in greeting would be an emblem and a gesture. Some emblems are specific to a culture and some are fairly universal. We point to our selves to indicate 'self' whereas in Japan they put a finger to the nose. In Britain drawing a line across the throat would mean someone has 'had it' whereas in Swaziland it means 'I love you', which is quite a difference! As with gaze, cultural differences in posture and gesture are important and there can be important consequences when getting it wrong. It is not possible to know all the different non-verbal cues for all cultures of course, but it is worth bearing the differences in mind when interpreting non-verbal communication with others, including with children. High status tends to give a relaxed open posture, with the body leaning backwards and legs comfortably apart. Low status tends to give a more rigid and upright posture, with arms close to the body and legs and feet together. People who like one another lean towards one another and tend to face one another. These sorts of cues tend to be automatically translated (within the same culture anyway).

Touch

The importance of touch was outlined in Chapter 2 when looking at how more contact between mothers and their babies in the first hours and days of birth seemed to mean that the mothers formed a stronger link with their children even years later. We use touch a lot to give and receive information as adults too. Touch is used to communicate affection, to be playful, to control or draw attention, and to accomplish tasks. Children use touch in these ways just as adults do. Studies have shown the importance of touch. For example, Crusco and Wetzel (1984) found that

DEFINITIONS

Kinesics – in non-verbal communication, the study of body posture and gesture, apart from the face.

Illustrators – in non-verbal communication, body movements that accompany speech.

Emblems – in non-verbal communication, body movements that stand in for speech.

Postures – in non-verbal communication, positionings of the body to give meaning.

Gestures – in non-verbal communication, meaningful body movements and postures.

both male and female customers left larger tips when they had accidentally been touch on the hand by the waitress than when they had not. You can see how useful knowledge of body language is, although it is not very ethical to use knowledge in this way!

Encouraging language development in young children

As the sections on language acquisition have shown, it looks as if there are many influences on children's language development. As early years practitioners, one of your important tasks is to promote language development in the children you care for. Table 6.3 summarises the various theoretical approaches and the implications for practice.

Table 6.3 Practical suggestions for encouraging children's language development

What psychologists tell us about language acquisition	Implications for practice
Children start to hear in the womb and have good hearing at birth	If we want children to concentrate on language then the environment should make this easy for them. The radio and TV should not be on all the time. Background noise should be kept at a minimum.
Children are born with an innate predisposition to be sociable. Language development is encouraged by the close responsive relationship with a sensitive adult	The key person system should be encouraged in childcare settings. The younger the child the more important this is. Early years practitioners should be talking to babies in ways that are similar to the ways their mothers/main carers talk to them – infant directed speech. Surround babies with a language-rich environment, using care giving routines as opportunities for promoting language development. Use songs and rhymes. If the child's 'home' language is not English try to learn some songs in the other language. As children grow older, listen attentively to what they say and answer their questions fully. As a key person you may understand what they are trying to say better than anyone else, so be prepared to translate and support their attempts to communicate with other children and adults. Use open questions to encourage a response.
Children learn through positive reinforcement	Show you are pleased when babies/children respond to your conversations or initiate conversations. Praise older children for using words correctly and by following instructions correctly. Encourage non-verbal communication by playing games such as pat a cake, playing finger games and waving bye bye.
Children model their behaviour on significant adults	Start sharing books with babies. Take every opportunity to increase their vocabulary by pointing things out to them, etc. Do not use inappropriate language or children will copy.
Learning another language helps children in all areas of learning	Children who are learning English as an additional language should be encouraged to use their 'home' language in nursery. If possible employ early years practitioners who speak the languages of the children. Liaise with parents so that you have tapes, books and other resources in the child's 'home' language.

THE DEVELOPMENT OF IQ – INTRODUCTION

The rest of this chapter focuses on the development of intelligence – and looks at issues such as what intelligence is and whether it can be measured. It is this difficulty of definition that makes us talk about IQ rather than intelligence. IQ is the abbreviation for 'intelligence quotient', the term given to a way of measuring an individual's ability. If you know people's IQ it tells you how able they are in relation to others. An IQ of 100 is average. A higher score than this suggests that the individual is more able in certain ways than average; lower than this suggests that the individual is less able than average. This is an area of psychology that has caused much controversy. It is therefore a good idea to read this part of the chapter critically, asking questions such as what intelligence is, whether there is any such thing, whether it is innate or learnt and whether it limits our thinking.

Very young children cannot really have their IQ measured. Instead, DQ (developmental quotient) is measured – and so DQ is also discussed, with the same reservations. Recently there has been interest in emotional intelligence, though this is discussed in Chapter 9 when social and emotional development are considered.

Defining intelligence(s)

A concept such as intelligence needs to be defined before it can be discussed. **Intelligence** is a general term for an individual's abilities in ranges of tasks such as vocabulary, verbal reasoning, number and problem solving. It might also refer to the ability to learn new material, and **emotional intelligence** covers abilities such as dealing with people and adjusting to new situations. It has been claimed that there are multiple intelligences, which means that the above abilities (for example, verbal reasoning and problem solving) are not the only types of intelligence that are relevant. For instance a musician may be highly musically 'intelligent' or able; a gymnast may have a highly developed form of bodily kinaesthetic 'intelligence' or ability.

Measuring intelligence(s)

One main aim of measuring intelligence was to improve children's chances, because it was thought that if children of lower intelligence were given additional help and teaching then they would improve. This was the aim of those like Binet (1857–1911) in France. They realised that such measurement would allow them to decide who would receive additional help. Galton (1822–1911), however, a pioneer of intelligence testing, believed in positive eugenics. Eugenics refers to using the idea of evolution and genetic transmission to mate the best genes with the best genes and produce the best possible race. Galton wanted to use a measure of intelligence to decide who would pair off with whom to get the best race, which is not the same aim as Binet's at all. At the start of the nineteenth century, most people believed that intelligence was a genetic characteristic and not to do with learning. It is probably true that many people still believe that now, and in Chapter 2 it was explained that evidence seems to suggest that about 50% of our intelligence is genetic and the rest given by environmental factors. It was Binet's approach that led to the continued interest in intelligence, not Galton's.

Intelligence tests were devised because there was a need to measure intelligence. They have been much revised; however, such tests still exist today. What Binet, with a colleague, Simon (1873–1961), did was quite simple. They devised tests and found out what children in certain age groups could achieve. What most of them could achieve became the norm for the age group. Having set the norm they could then use the tests to see which children were 'normal' and which were below or above normal for their age.

Finding an IQ score

Binet developed the idea of mental age. **Mental age** is the person's test score compared with the age of children who can usually achieve the same test score. If people's test score was that of a six-year old, they have a mental age of six, even if they are really only five-years old. Their 'real' age was called their **chronological age**.

Stern developed a way of turning this idea into a score by finding an **intelligence quotient (IQ)**. IQ is calculated by dividing the mental age by the chronological age and multiplying by 100. So if a child has a mental age of six and a chronological age of five, their IQ is $(6 \div 5) \times 100$, which is 120. When researchers from Stanford University in America revised the original test and used the idea of

IQ the test became known as the Stanford-Binet IQ test and this is still used. This test measures children's IQ and there is an adult version too. The idea is that a normal IQ would be 100. This is because when a mental age is the same as a chronological age (and this would be the norm) then the result is always 100. For example, a mental age of 6 and a chronological age of 6 times 100 gives 100. It is accepted that a normal IQ score would fall between 85 and 115 and either side of those scores would be either a low IQ (below 85) or a high IQ (above 115).

What do IQ tests actually measure?

Intelligence seems to cover a lot of areas including creativity, verbal reasoning, mathematical ability, vocabulary and problem solving. Tests don't really measure all these things. There would need to be different tests for different parts of what we call intelligence – and tests would also measure willingness to solve problems and the wish to succeed, because test performance would depend on these sorts of factors too. Thurstone (1938) researched this area and concluded that there must be different types of intelligence as he saw from his research that people who seemed to be intelligent in one field (such as maths) were not intelligent in other fields (such as creativity). Thurstone separated social intelligence from non-social intelligence, and academic intelligence from non-academic intelligence. He also separated mechanical from abstract intelligence. So Thurstone thought that there were different types of intelligence.

Then another researcher, Guilford (1982) followed Thurstone's ideas and looked for different factors that were measured in IQ tests. He suggested that there were up to 150 factors or kinds of intelligence. Gardner agreed that there are different kinds of intelligence. Gardner (1983) is one of the best known researchers to discuss the idea of multiple intelligences and he settled at first on seven different kinds. He is still researching in the area. Gardner's seven categories are broad and include athletic skill and social grace, so they are not always about what we might call intelligence.

On the other hand, others think that there is indeed one thing called intelligence. Spearman (1927) held the view that there was one general intelligence (g), which is the amount of mental energy someone brings to a task.

Yet another view is Sternberg's (1984) who thought that there are three sides to intelligence. The first side is the traditional idea that intelligence links with cognitive abilities, as traditionally believed from the start of IQ testing. It could be called being 'school smart'. The second side is concerned with how well people adapts to their culture, and is to do with being 'street smart'. The third part is to do with experience and adapting to new things.

Currently there are those who agree with Spearman and think that there is this general intelligence, and those that follow Gardner's ideas and think that there are multiple intelligences. The issue is not resolved.

You can see that it is by no means easy to say what intelligence is and that there are differences of opinion about this. Also, even if it were clear what it was, it would be hard to measure. The only measure we have is to see what most children of a certain age can do and say that that is a normal level of intelligence. Intelligence, then, is 'what an intelligence test measures', and an IQ score is simply a measure of how someone fits in with what others of a certain age can do. This is quite a long way from saying that something called 'intelligence' actually exists, and it is also a long way from saying that it is an innate characteristic. Perhaps it is this difficulty of pinning down what there is to measure that leads studies to find that about half of 'it' is genetic and half is affected by environment. It has been said that IQ is a measure of how children fit in with others of their age. Also, as tests are set up in certain cultures and IQ is a measure of how a child compares with other scores on that test, then intelligence is measured within a particular culture, and so can be affected by cultural knowledge and customs. If IQ is affected by culture then it is not measuring something innate, so there is good reason to think that IQ can be improved by environment (including teaching and stimulation).

How far can IQ be improved by environmental factors?

It has been shown above that intelligence is not easy to measure. Chapter 2 showed how characteristics like intelligence do have a genetic underpinning but that many different genes are likely to be involved and also that only about 50% of intelligence that seems to be attributable to genes. Chapter 3 looked at how children are treated in the early years, including the type of attachment they form, and it was said there that privation (when no attachment is formed) can lead to very poor development. Deprivation (when an attachment is broken) can also have very serious consequences for the child, and some studies claim that it can lead to juvenile delinquency, poor achievement at school and difficulty in forming relationships both in school and in later adulthood. Studies outlined in Chapter 3 often referred to IQ as a measure of how privation and deprivation had affected a child. It was shown (for example, by Skeels, 1966) that privation was related to low IQ but that, even with poor quality care, IQ could rise if the child received some attention and affection. Another study showed that privation led to low IQ but that, with special attention, such a poor start could be overcome (Koluchova, 1972, 1976). Such studies do strongly suggest that IQ can change over time and that stimulation and good quality care can lead to improvements in IQ, even if there are others that suggest it is harder to overcome a poor start. This is all evidence that IQ is affected by environment (even if there is also a genetic basis).

It is really because we believe that IQ can be affected by environment that this topic is included in this book. If IQ was completely genetically given then there would be no opportunity to improve it and to improve a child's life chances in this way, so we would presumably take a different view about education.

Using IQ tests and drawing false conclusions

One important problem with IQ tests is that we tend to see them as scientific and true. If people are given an IQ test and obtain a good score they are quick to claim that they are intelligent. If they obtain a low score they see themselves as unintelligent. We accept the validity and reliability of the test(s). There are, however, doubts about both these issues. A valid test is one that measures what it claims to measure and it is suggested above that intelligence is not a single thing that can be measured in any case. One problem with validity is that there are cultural factors built into the tests, and people without particular cultural knowledge might do badly because of that, rather than because they are unintelligent. When drawing conclusions from the results of an IQ test we need to take such factors into account. Of course, these problems are well known and tests have been devised that are called **culture fair**. Even so, it is difficult to find a test that does not rely at all on previous knowledge, so there are still doubts about conclusions drawn. A reliable test is one where if you do it again you get the same results. However, it might be that performance depends on other factors such as how people feel on the day they take the test, or how motivated they are.

Cultural differences can lead to IQ differences – can tests be culture fair?

Earlier in this chapter there was discussion of how use of a different language code might affect development at school, and it was said that teachers use an elaborated code, so children limited to a restricted code might not do as well because they would be seen as less able. Issues such as language code can also affect how well a child does on an IQ test and cultural differences can affect success on a test. This issue has been quite widely researched now. If we judge people by how well they do on a test, and there is bias because there are items they would have difficulty with, not because of lack of intelligence, but because of lack of experience, then this is not a fair test. There is the underpinning idea that intelligence is innate, and if a test is measuring innate ability but requires certain experiences then that is not fair.

The debate about whether tests were culture fair began when Jensen (1969), discussed the finding that whites did better than blacks on IQ tests (scores of whites were around 15 points higher). He suggested that this was because of a genetic superiority. There were studies done to look at this issue – which was seen as a very serious one, given the racist aspects to the claims. Scarr famously carried out a study looking at black children adopted into white families and found that the younger they had been adopted the nearer to 'white' scores their own scores were (Scarr and Weinberg, 1976). There were other studies too – for example, the scores of poor children increased if families that were well off adopted them. These studies suggested that there were environmental aspects to IQ scores – if they could improve when environment changed, then it seemed that environment affected performance. Environmental effects were thought to be things like schooling, level of poverty, and types of experiences. For example, Japanese children tend to do better than American children (in general) and it is not thought that there is a genetic reason – rather, their schooling is somehow better. Following these studies, IQ tests were looked at again to try to eliminate cultural bias in them.

One problem with drawing up **culture fair tests** is that language tends to be culturally biased as outlined above. So pictures and non-verbal instructions were included and tests that were self-explanatory were included. However, there is no completely fair test because experience will help people to work out what is wanted. For example, you might need to find a matching shape and that might be obvious, but you would need to know the rules about this. Although they might seem obvious in one culture they might not be obvious in another.

Intelligence has genetic (nature) and environmental (nurture) aspects

As has already been claimed, intelligence seems to have both genetic and environmental aspects. Chapter 2 briefly looked at genes and their effects on our behaviour and twin studies were explained as they are often used to show whether some characteristic is innate or learnt. Identical twins (MZ) share 100% of their genes whereas non-identical (DZ) twins share 50% of their genes, as do all brothers and sisters. If identical twins are more similar in IQ than non-identical twins this can be taken as suggesting that there is a genetic aspect to IQ. However, it could be claimed that identical twins are brought up in the same environment and treated more similarly even than non-identical twins in a family, so there is still an element of environmental effect involved. Moreover, no study shows that identical twins have exactly the same IQ, which they would if it were totally genetic (or at least their IQ would be very similar each time). So studies have been done using identical twins but choosing twins that are reared apart – which means they are brought up in different households, so they don't share their environment. If identical twins still have a very similar IQ, then this does seem to be evidence for a genetic influence. Studies have indeed found that the IQ of identical twins reared apart is very similar. Bouchard *et al.* (1990) carried out the Minnesota Study of Twins Reared Apart and found correlations of from +0.69 to +0.78 for identical twins reared apart (+1 is a perfect correlation and means that 100% of the time there is agreement, so you can see that +0.7 is very high – 70%).

Another way of studying whether intelligence is genetic is to look at children who have been adopted. If the IQ of the children is compared with the IQ of the adopted mother and the IQ of the biological mother, and if intelligence is genetic, then you would expect the children's IQ to match the biological mother's more than the adopted mother's. The Texas Adoption Project involved just such a study. Horn

(1983) compared 469 children. It was found that the children's IQs did indeed match the biological mother's more than the adopted mother's. However, the scores were +0.28 for the biological mother and +0.15 for the adopted mother. If +1 is a perfect (100%) correlation, then these figures are rather low. The difference is not very great either. Even though there is some evidence here for the involvement of genetic factors in intelligence, there is also a lot of room left for environmental factors.

Of course there have been other studies and in general, taking all the evidence into account, as outlined in Chapter 2 it is thought that intelligence might be 50% down to genes and 50% down to environment.

Developmental quotient – measuring very young children

There are tests for looking at the IQ of very young infants – as young as 9 months – but they are clearly going to be different in style from tests that look at older children. The Bayley Mental and Motor Scale is a test used on infants and devised in the 1930s. A problem is that when infants were tested at 9 months and then again (using a different test) at 5 years, there was very little link between the same child's two scores. This either casts doubts upon the usefulness of the tests or shows that IQ changes over time. The most likely explanation is that the tests measure different abilities – and this suggests that intelligence is not one thing. Tests for very young children tend to measure motor abilities and skills (such as being able to point or grasp) whereas tests for older children measure verbal and cognitive skills. Since the 1930s other IQ tests for infants have been developed but in no case did their earlier scores match their later scores. Indeed it seems that IQ is not stable until the age of around 10 years – or at least that is what was found by using the various testing and comparing results of a child as it grows.

More recently, though, it has been thought that there are some aspects of intelligence that are stable over time. For example, when a score is found by seeing how easily a 4 month old can recognise a new stimulus (like a new sound) and then that child is tested again at the age of five years using the Stanford-Binet IQ Test, then there was a correlation of +0.60 which is quite high. Perhaps being able to recognise new stimuli at four-months is a basic memory skill. However, of course, as has been shown, there are many factors to intelligence and there could be many other reasons for this finding. Basically there is still a lot that needs to be learnt about intelligence – once it has been decided what that is!

How useful is the concept of IQ in early years care and education?

As we have seen, any measure of intelligence appears to be particularly unstable until children reach about the age of 10 years and, as such, the concept of intelligence has little relevance to early years care and education. There is one area where one can see the influence of this approach and that is the use of schedules of development or norms of development in the assessment of babies and young children. Although these have a place in child health surveillance they are less useful as a tool in childcare and education.

Good early years practice is less interested in a child's abilities compared with the abilities of others, than in treating children as individuals and providing appropriate care and learning experiences for the individual child.

One aspect of personality that is related to how well a child does in a school situation is the disposition the child has towards learning. In previous chapters we have seen that children are active learners. They have a natural curiosity to investigate and make sense of the world. In childcare and education settings it is important that we foster and encourage curiosity, exploration and a thirst for knowledge. In this way we will be providing the conditions for children's abilities to flourish.

KEY TERMS

You need to know the meaning of the following words and phrases. Go back through the chapter to make sure you understand them:

Chronological age
Culture fair tests
Elaborated language code
Emblems
Emotional intelligence
Gestures
Illustrators
Intelligence
Intelligence quotient (IQ)
Kinesics
Language acquisition device (LAD)
Linguistic relativity
Mental age
Motherese
Overextension
Over-regularisation
Phonemes
Postures
Pre-intellectual language
Pre-linguistic thought
Protoconversations
Restricted language code
Significant others
Speech stream
Syntax
Underextension

KEY NAMES

Bernstein
Binet
Bruner
Chomsky
Galton
Gardner
Guilford
Jensen
Piaget
Sapir
Simon
Stern
Sternberg
Thurstone
Vygotsky
Whorf

FURTHER READING

Cohen, D. (2002) *How the Child's Mind Develops,* Routledge, New York, Chapter 7 (on measuring intelligence).
This is an easy read and recommended for students studying at Level 3 and higher.

David, T., Goouch, K., Powell, S. and Abbott, L. (2003) *Birth to Three Matters: A Review of the Literature Compiled to Inform the Framework to Support Children in their Earliest Years,* DfES, Nottingham, Chapter 4.
This book is particularly recommended for students on higher level courses.

Gardner, H. (1992) *Multiple Intelligences,* Basic Books, New York.
This is a classic that describes the theory of emotional intelligences. It is recommended for students studying on higher level courses.

Gopnik, A., Meltzoff, A. and Kuhl, P. (1999) *How Babies Think,* Weidenfeld & Nicolson, London.
This book is essential reading for students studying at Level 3 and above. Chapter 4 is particularly recommended for this topic.

Mukherji, P. and O'Dea, T. (2000) *Understanding Children's Language and Literacy,* Nelson Thornes Ltd, Cheltenham.
Chapters 2 and 3 are particularly relevant. This book is recommended for students studying at all levels.

Whitehead, M. (1999) *Supporting Language and Literacy Development in the Early Years,* Open University Press, Buckingham.
This book is recommended for students studying at Level 3 and above. It gives excellent suggestions as to how to apply theory in the practical situation.

7

Gender and moral development

INTRODUCTION

This chapter looks at how we develop gender-appropriate behaviour and moral behaviour. Similar important theories are used to explain both, so we will look at them in the same chapter. The discussion of gender examines the biological underpinnings of gender-specific behaviour and what 'biologically' each sex is likely to be 'programmed' to be like and do. It examines learning theory to see how our gender roles could be learnt through the mechanisms of operant conditioning and social learning theory. It goes on to look at Freud's theory, because the psychodynamic approach has a special way of explaining both gender and moral development. Finally, gender schema theory is discussed. Gender schema theory suggests that we develop ideas of how our own gender should become and we act accordingly.

Moral development can also be explained using psychodynamic principles, and these are outlined. Both Kohlberg and Piaget had cognitive developmental theories of how we develop moral behaviour to suit our society. So does learning theory. These explanations are outlined.

GENDER DEVELOPMENT

We will discuss how far gender is innate or genetic, and how far it is affected by environment. It would be useful if you recall what you have already studied about the nature/nurture issue – for example, the idea of how genes work (outlined in Chapter 2). It would also be useful if you recall some basic ideas about the main approaches to psychology (outlined in Chapter 1). As you might expect, learning theories (discussed in Chapter 4) are important, as are theories of cognitive development, (discussed in Chapter 5). Freud's ideas will also be looked at in greater depth. If you are not very familiar with the main assumptions of the above approaches then look upon this chapter as a good opportunity to become familiar with them.

There is sometimes confusion between the words 'gender' and 'sex'. When a baby is born one of the first questions asked is 'is it a boy or a girl?' This is a question about the sex of the child. Is the child anatomically a boy or a girl. 'Gender' is slightly different. It refers to sexual identity, especially in relation to society or culture, and includes an understanding of the behavioural expectations of being male or female.

It might be natural to think that boys and girls are born with certain tendencies according to their gender and this is almost certainly true. There could be some basic tendencies that are sex specific and these are discussed below. However, considering that there are different gender-specific behaviours in different cultures, it is not the case that all our gender specific behaviour comes from our biology. It seems very likely that much of it is learnt. This section considers what is likely to be

TRY THIS!

Talk to a variety of different people, some your own age, some older and someone from a different culture from your own and ask them if they can describe the typical behaviour of a boy and a girl.

biologically given in the way of sex differences in behaviour and what is likely to come from environmental influences.

There are various explanations for why we develop particular gender-specific behaviours.

Biological explanations for gender development

Most people expect there to be at least an element of our gender specific behaviour that is attributable to genes. Males are biologically different from females. Only one pair of the 23 pairs of chromosomes in humans is different in males and in females, females having an XX pair and males having an XY pair. This gives our sex, which is the biological fact of our make up. In fact some people do have some variation on this theme, for example, rarely there is an XXY combination, but basically most people fit the above definition of male and female. The natural tendency is to produce a girl (XX) and only if testosterone is present, which it is when the Y chromosome is present, will male genitalia develop in place of female genitalia. The chromosomal difference is linked to the release of hormones and it is the hormones that make the visible (and invisible) differences between the sexes. So if there is release of androgens, for example, then these control the biological fertility of males and so on, whereas release of oestrogens control female patterns of menstruation and maturity. Both males and females have androgens and oestrogens but usually males have more androgens and females more oestrogens.

One piece of evidence for biological differences can be seen in instances where a foetus receives excess androgens because androgens are given to the mother during pregnancy to reduce the likelihood of miscarriage. If that foetus is female then the girl, with more androgens than usual, does tend to show more aggressive and 'tomboy' behaviour as she grows up and tends to be less 'feminine' – for example, preferring male activities. This is called **androgenital syndrome**. So it seems that biological differences can lead to behavioural differences.

In some cases of androgenital syndrome the girl babies were designated as boy babies at birth and treated as boys for a little while as it took time to realise that a mistake had been made. It was found that if the mistake was put right (including surgery) at around 18 months old then the girl seemed to develop normally. However, if the mistake was not realised until nearer three years old serious problems were more likely. This suggests that biological factors have quite a strong influence and also that upbringing has a strong effect too. As with other areas where the nature/nurture issue has been discussed the focus is on the interaction between innate factors and learnt ones, and the two are not easily separated.

Studies with animals have investigated what happens if an animal is injected with the 'wrong' hormone. When monkeys carrying a female foetus were injected with the male hormone testosterone, after birth female progeny subsequently acted more like males. The monkeys were more assertive and more independent than normal female monkeys, for example. Increasing oestrogen levels for male animals gives more female behaviour and this has been done sufficiently (with animals) to be a fairly firm conclusion. Of course generalising results from animal studies to humans might not be totally reliable. However, the evidence that hormones affect behaviour is quite convincing.

It is hard to draw conclusions about the role of hormones at the moment, partly because testing on humans is difficult as well as expensive. In humans, levels of hormones also vary during the day, which makes study difficult. Blood tests have to be taken many times a day, which is, again difficult. It is generally thought that hormones do not affect human behaviour as much as they affect animal behaviour, perhaps because of the role of the brain.

Male babies in general are heavier, more active and more irritable than female babies are. They are less hardy, sleep less well and are less easy to comfort. Female babies, in general, walk and talk before boys. Of course there are many individual differences and these tend to be more important in explaining differences between babies than do sex differences. As regards innate skills, it is thought that males are better at spatial skills and mathematics skills whereas females are better at things to do with language and judging emotions. Studies have found some differences between males and females – but the situation is not all that clear. For example, Newcombe and Dubas (1992) found that the girls at 16 years old who were better at spatial skills (such as doing a jigsaw or parking a car) were those who had, at the age of 11 years, rated themselves to be quite masculine. So it might be characteristics of masculinity that lead to better spatial skills, not sex at birth. One must always take into account the effect of environment and learning. For example, with regard to mathematics skills Byrnes and Takahira (1993) found that boys are better at such skills because they are more often taught them.

Evidence that gender roles come from nurture not nature

The previous section presented some arguments that sex-related behaviour comes from our nature – in other words it is genetic. However, there are other gender-related behaviours that seem to come from our upbringing. When other cultures are studied it is clear that there is some gender-specific behaviour that is different in different cultures. Then again, there is much that is the same. It is tempting to think that where there are differences then this suggests that that behaviour is learnt and where there are similarities between cultures that suggests that such behaviour is innate. Of course, females tend to be physically weaker. If it is found that females have roles that are less physically demanding in each culture, then the biological factor is probably driving the cultural behaviour, rather than the role itself being biologically given so it must be remembered that biology and environment continually interact.

There was one set of cross-cultural studies that was thought to show that gender roles are not biologically given – but the problem is that those studies have been questioned so their findings are in doubt. Margaret Mead was an anthropologist who studied three different groups of peoples in the Pacific region (1920s and 1930s) and found quite marked differences in the different gender roles. One group was the Arapesh. Both males and females were gentle and co-operative, and they shared their roles including childcare. Another group was the Tchambuli, where male children were encouraged to be artistic and creative, spending their time making themselves look pretty. Women took the lead and did the organising. The Mundugumor were the third group. Both males and females were aggressive and argumentative. Children received little attention and had to fight for what they wanted. These three groups show how different the roles of the different genders can be. There was some doubt as to whether the researchers tended to see what they expected – which is understandable really as it must be difficult to observe neutrally. However, even if the results are not as solid as all that, there is still the suggestion here that gender roles can be different in different societies, so learning might be taking place.

As you can see there can be problems in drawing conclusions from studies – it is difficult to be absolutely sure that the findings are valid and reliable. It is worth mentioning another study that is supposed to show the strong influence of nurture on our gender specific behaviour, but in fact now has a different ending. This is a famous case and is worth outlining even if just out of interest as it shows difficulties in studying real people. John Money carried out a strange case study. It involved identical twin boys one of whom, in the 1970s, had a planned castration as a response to an accident during a routine operation. Although it may seem a strange decision, it was thought that the boy could be brought up as a girl, with some surgery and treatment (giving of hormones and so on) and that this would be a successful way of overcoming the 'accident'. The other twin remained a boy. Remember that they were identical twins so shared 100% of their genes. It was thought that if the 'girl' became a girl without difficulty then this would show that gender behaviours are all learnt and that biology has nothing to do with it – except for the physical and hormonal differences, which can be adjusted by medication. Up until quite recently it was reported that this 'experiment' had been a success and that 'Brenda' had been successfully reared as a girl. That would probably have been the current situation, too, if 'Brenda' had not revealed her identity and written her story. 'She' had reassumed a male identity and was called 'David' by then and he said that, contrary to the claims made, he had always felt odd, even though he did not know the full circumstances until his early teens. He said he had preferred boys' games and knew there was something wrong without knowing what. David married and seemed to be reasonably settled in his existence as a boy, although very recently he committed suicide. His twin brother had committed suicide years before. There is a lot to be learnt from this case study. Psychologists have to take great care when 'using' humans in this way. However, as the story is from David and not from the psychologists involved, we can't really make judgements without the full facts. What is true is that we can no longer claim that in this unique case environment had overcome biology – indeed this case now seems to be evidence for there being a strong biological basis to gender roles and gender behaviour.

Learning theories and their explanations for how gender development occurs

There are studies that have shown that one way in which gender behaviour does seem to be learnt is by the types of actions and reactions parents demonstrate with the offspring. Studies in this area (for example Fagot, 1978) have shown that parents treat boys differently from girls. Even when mothers are asked to look after another mother's baby without knowing the gender of the baby, they act according to how the baby is dressed and choose what they consider gender-appropriate toys and gender-appropriate behaviour. Examples of gender appropriate-behaviour would be cuddling a girl closer and bouncing a boy on the lap. Examples of gender-appropriate toys would be a hammer rattle for a boy and a soft toy for a girl. Fagot (1978) studied 24 American families, each with a child of around 20 months old. She visited the families five times and watched parent and child interaction for about 1 hour each time. She noted that girls were encouraged to ask for help when it was needed, to dance, to take an interest in girls' clothes, to play with dolls and to stay near to a parent. They were discouraged from running around, climbing and being too active. Boys were encouraged to play with trucks and blocks in an active way and to manipulate objects. This would help to build strong muscles. They were discouraged from playing with dolls and from asking for assistance. They were discouraged from doing anything parents thought of as feminine. Girls were discouraged less for being 'masculine' than boys were for being 'feminine'.

These studies suggest that children are reinforced to act in a gender specific way. They are rewarded for appropriate behaviour by their parents' reactions, such as smiles and approval. They are not rewarded for inappropriate behaviour. These factors can be explained by principles of operant conditioning. The law of effect says that if something is pleasurable, that action is repeated, and this is positive reinforcement in action. There might even be punishment for some inappropriate behaviours – such as a smack.

Social learning theory suggests that learning takes place by imitation and modelling. This theory would suggest that girls engage in feminine behaviour (what is thought of as 'feminine' in their culture) because they model on their mothers and female role models. Boys model on their fathers and male role models. Both operant conditioning and social learning theory can help to explain gender specific behaviour within a culture. Chapter 4 outlines mechanisms of operant conditioning and social learning.

There is some evidence that mothers and fathers react differently to gender appropriate and gender inappropriate behaviour. Levy *et al.* (1995) found that females are more likely to be tolerant when behaviour is not seen as appropriate than males. Fathers may see part of their role as being to guide their children regarding gender-appropriate behaviour.

CASE STUDY

In the private nursery where Farida works there is a large selection of dressing-up clothes. These clothes include outfits for role play, which have been carefully chosen to be gender neutral. The selection of clothes also includes examples of children's clothes from a variety of different cultures as well as a couple of pretty party dresses. Farida has noticed that Ben, one of her key children who is 3 years old, loves dressing up. He particularly enjoys wearing a frilly, pink party dress and has got into the routine of putting it on as soon as he arrives in the morning.

One day Ben's father comes to pick him up and asks to speak to Farida. He says that one of the other parents has telephoned his wife and told him about Ben wearing the dress. He explains that he does not want Ben to grow up a 'sissy' and he wants Farida to stop Ben wearing the dress. As he speaks to Farida he looks stressed and angry.

Farida knows that little boys often like to wear dresses and gently explains to Ben's father that she understands that he might be worried but that, in her experience, children, left to their own devices, move on to other interests. She suggests to Ben's father that they make no comment to the child about his attachment to the dress as paying attention to this may strengthen the behaviour.

Freud's theory of gender development

Freud developed the psychoanalytic approach, which was briefly introduced in Chapter 1. His ideas are used in child psychology but not as often as the other approaches. They are discussed here and will be returned to in Chapter 8, as the psychodynamic approach is used as one way of explaining play. Freud's ideas on gender development can be explained using the general assumptions of Freud's theory, so the theory is detailed here and then briefly repeated when looking at moral development as a reminder that the same principles apply.

One way of outlining Freud's ideas is to split them into three sections:

- the two instincts that guide us;
- personality;
- psychosexual development.

These three aspects are closely linked, but it is useful to separate them for the sake of clarity. When the three aspects are understood, then the way we develop both our moral self and our idea of our own gender are quite easily outlined using the concepts.

Two main instincts that drive us

Freud thought that we have an amount of energy to use and that we cannot add to that energy. Hopefully we have enough energy to do all that we want to do in life but sometimes we use up energy hiding past experiences, for example, and this does not leave us with enough to move forward. This energy is in the form of two basic instincts. One instinct is **libido**, which is life instinct, and includes sexual desires. The other instinct is **thanatos**, which is the death instinct and includes hostility to

DEFINITIONS

Id – Freud's term for the demanding part of our personality that can be seen in the baby, who is all 'I want . . .'

Superego – Freud's term for the conscience part of our personality as well as for the ideal we have of what we should be like. It is the 'you can't have . . .' part of the personality.

Ego – Freud's term for the part of the personality that balances the demands of the id and the control of the superego and makes decisions in reality.

DEFINITIONS

Oral stage – Freud's first stage of psychosexual development where pleasure centres on the mouth. Aged around 0 to 2 years.

Fixated Freud's term for when we are 'stuck' in one of the psychosexual stages and have not achieved satisfaction at that stage, so we use energy in keeping any dissatisfaction unconscious.

Anal stage – Freud's second stage of psychosexual development where pleasure focuses on the anus. Aged around 2 to 3 years.

Phallic stage – Freud's third stage of psychosexual development where the child becomes a sexual being and, for example, sexually desires the mother and hates the father because he sees him as a rival. Aged around 3 to 5 years.

Latency stage – Freud's fourth stage of psychosexual development where, in psychosexual terms, there is little development. Aged from around 5 years to puberty.

Genital stage – Freud's fifth stage of psychosexual development where, from puberty, the young person starts to form what Freud thought of as 'normal' (opposite sex) relationships.

others. Really the death instinct is focused on ourselves (we live and then we die) but Freud thought that we use defence mechanisms. Defence mechanisms work to hide our thoughts in our unconscious mind, so that they do not consciously bother us. So we hide threatening thoughts such as those about death or about our inappropriate sexual desires. Defence mechanisms include repression (forgetting), projection (focusing the feelings onto someone else) and denial (ignoring the feelings all together) – and there are others. So defence mechanisms avoid us knowing harmful thoughts, and a death instinct would be focused on others instead of ourselves. So we have an instinct to live and this includes sexual desires and we have an instinct to die and this brings anger and hostility, which can be projected onto others.

Freud's view of personality

Freud thought that the personality is made up of three parts. One part is the **id**, which is the demanding part of our personality. The id comprises our instincts and if you imagine a baby with no thoughts other than what they want and need, then that is the id. The id is present at birth and remains the same throughout our lives – it demands what will satisfy it. Needs and desires are instinctive and include warmth, food, drink and sexual satisfaction. Another part of the personality is the **superego**. This does not develop until the age of around 3 years. The superego is our conscience and our image of what our ideal self should be. This comes from our parents and interactions with society, as we learn what is right and what we should be like. The third part is the **ego**. This is the reality part of the personality and develops after about the age of one year. The ego works to balance the demands of the id with the control of the superego. Think of the id as 'I want', the superego as 'you can't have' and the ego as trying to keep both satisfied.

Freud's view of child development (psychosexual development)

Freud mapped out five stages of child development. He linked these to various times in a child's development when certain areas have importance to the child. He thought that, at first, the baby focuses all attention on the mouth and called the first stage the **oral stage**. The baby sucks everything. This stage occurs during the first year. Anyone stuck (fixated) in the oral stage will show oral characteristics such as smoking, thumb sucking or comfort eating. **Fixated** is Freud's term for when we are 'stuck' in one of the psychosexual stages, have not achieved satisfaction at that stage, so use energy in keeping any dissatisfaction unconscious.

The second stage has a focus on the anus and is called the **anal stage**. This happens between 1 year to 3 years old. Children focus on their faeces and potty training can have an impact at this stage. Anyone fixated at the anal stage will show either retentive characteristics such as meanness or being excessively tidy, or expulsive characteristics such as being very messy or enjoying messy pursuits such as pottery. The third stage is the **phallic stage**, where children focus on their genitals. Freud did think that children are sexual beings and have sexual feelings, though instinctively rather than consciously. The third stage can start at around the age of 3 years old.

The fourth stage is the **latency stage**, when little changes in terms of psychosexual development.

The fifth stage is the **genital stage**, at puberty, where, if the rest of the child's development has gone well, the young person will form opposite-sex relationships. This is the final stage according to Freud.

Drawing aspects of Freud's ideas together to explain gender development

Freud thought that gender development occurred in the third stage of psychosexual development, the phallic stage. He had a rather complex theory about this. He thought that in the phallic stage the boy has sexual feelings. Of course these are unconscious. Freud suggested that a boy has sexual feelings for his mother. A girl has sexual feelings for her father. Freud spelt out more about the boy's development, so this is dealt with here first. The boy has sexual feelings for his mother but also fears his father. The father is seen as a threat because he is a rival for the mother's affections. The id is guiding these sexual feelings and the thanatos instinct generates hostility towards the father. The boy also loves his father, because he is his father. So there are contradictory feelings of love and hatred towards the father and the boy feels great guilt because of these feelings. The guilt comes from the superego, which is the con-science given by society and parents. Guilt and fear of the father leads to castration anxiety as the boy focuses on the penis and his anxiety focuses on this area.

One way of overcoming this guilt and fear is to 'become' the father and to identify with the father in this way. The boy takes on the father's attitudes, sex roles and moral values and in this way possesses the mother too. The ego chooses to satisfy the id's demands by this identification process and it resolves the guilt. This demonstrates how the ego acts as a mediator between the demands of the id and the control of the superego.

This idea of a boy wanting his mother, hating his father and resolving guilt by identifying or 'becoming' the father is called the Oedipus complex after a Greek legend where Oedipus killed his father and married (unknowingly) his mother. When the boy identifies with his father and takes on all his father's mannerisms, views and attitudes, then he becomes male too in that he takes over all the male behaviour of his father and this is how he develops his gender-specific behaviour.

The girl sexually desires her father and has feelings of hatred towards her mother. The girl, however, does not suffer from castration anxiety so her fear of her mother is not as strong as a boy's fear of his father using the same mechanisms. One other mechanism is involved here and that is that the girl desires her father, partly because he has a penis and she does not, so this is a way of possessing one. Freud did not have such a clear outline of the process for girls as he did for boys. However, he did think that girls had penis envy. One way or another girls identify with their mothers just as boys do with their fathers, but in a less intense way because penis envy is not as strong as castration fear. This would tend to mean that girls are less 'female' than boys are 'male' although there is little evidence for this. Freud referred to the process of a girl identifying with her mother to avoid feelings of hatred and jealousy as the Electra complex, to match the boys' Oedipus complex.

A young girl scolds a doll, as if copying how her mother might scold her. This is internalisation and illustrates how the girl has learnt moral values and gender behaviour from her mother.

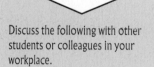

TRY THIS!

Discuss the following with other students or colleagues in your workplace.

How have cultural expectations of the behaviour and the role of women and girls led to unequal opportunities? What can early years practitioners do to promote equality of opportunity for girls?

Achieving an understanding of gender

Children first become aware of their gender at around the age of 3 years, according to Thompson (1975) – this is when they achieve a **gender understanding**. Younger children are able to say what sex they are but seem to have little understanding of the differences. Young children do not understand that their gender will remain constant. This is perhaps because of their limited cognitive ability.

Gender constancy refers to the understanding that gender remains constant, and that a girl is always a girl, for example. Gender constancy is achieved usually by the age of 7 years, if not before.

Gender schema theory

The idea that there is an element of learning when developing gender-appropriate behaviour is widely accepted. It is also accepted that a child has to be cognitively ready to accept such ideas. Bem (1981) has combined these two ideas and has developed the **gender schema theory**. Children reach a point where they can combine all that they have learnt about what is appropriate for which gender through operant conditioning and social learning theory with their cognitive understanding of **gender identity** and **gender constancy**.

How gender role affects us

We have seen how gender behaviour can be linked both to biological differences and learned behaviour. In the past, and still today, opportunities for girls and women have been limited by cultural views on appropriate behaviour and roles for women in society.

It is not just girls that have been disadvantaged. Recently there is concern that boys are doing less well academically than girls are in the educational system. One of the reasons may be that the behaviour we see in many boys in nursery is viewed as negative. Most early years practitioners would agree that boys have a tendency to be more boisterous and to prefer rough and tumble play outside than quieter play in the home corner or the graphics table. Early years practitioners frown upon many of the boys' enthusiasms. For instance boys love 'super hero play' and pretending to fight with sticks and guns. Until recently this type of play was actively discouraged as it was thought to encourage violence and aggression. More recently it is becoming recognised that early years practitioners need to take a more reflective approach. We should be building on boys' enthusiasms and use their play as an opportunity to deliver the early years curriculum. For example one nursery recognised that Spiderman fascinated many of the boys. They incorporated a Spiderman theme into all their planning and found that boys were motivated to engage in activities that usually held little interest for them.

MORAL DEVELOPMENT

Any society needs children to grow up to follow its rules. This chapter looks at how children learn these rules, drawing on the theories discussed in Chapter 4. It also looks to see if moral development is related to cognitive development and whether children pass through stages in their understanding of moral issues. Moral issues include issues such as conforming to social rules and giving help to others. Moral development includes how we learn what is right and wrong.

What is moral behaviour?

In any society there is a view as to what is right and what is wrong. A moral way of behaving is right; any other way is not moral and is wrong. In general, in most cultures, aggressive behaviour is seen as anti-social and is not a moral way of

Pro-social behaviour – behaviour that helps others and is acceptable by society.

Altruism – when helping behaviour is carried out at some cost to the helper.

Anti-social behaviour – aggressive behaviour that is not accepted by society. There is some intention to harm.

behaving – it is not right. Similarly, in most cultures, helping behaviour is seen as pro-social and is a moral way of behaving – it is right.

Pro-social behaviour includes being kind to others and helping them. At the same time this sort of behaviour can also be rewarding to the 'helper' who receives thanks and appreciation. An example of pro-social behaviour is helping an elderly neighbour with her shopping. Your reward is her grateful thanks and, perhaps, a cup of tea.

Altruism is one type of helping. Truly altruistic behaviour is helping others for no reward at all and at a cost to oneself. An example of this would be a passer by who rushes into a burning house to save an unknown child, with no thought for personal safety.

Aggressive behaviour (**anti-social behaviour**) almost always results in disapproval. However, disapproval can be rewarding if it means attention is given. Even attention that is bad (such as punishment) might be better than no attention at all. In general, though, we encourage pro-social behaviour, we are impressed by altruism and we don't like aggressive behaviour. This is a Western view, perhaps, but is fairly universal.

There might, however, be different definitions of what is pro-social and what is anti-social in different societies. This is because social norms differ between societies. For example, in a society it might be a pro-social act for a man to open a door for a woman, but in another society that might be viewed in a different way, and might even be seen as anti-social. Indeed within one society that act could be viewed differently by different people. Some women might be grateful for such an act; others might see it as male dominance. So acts cannot always be deemed pro-social or anti-social; sometimes it also depends on the individuals concerned. This is what makes defining moral behaviour difficult. It is really the intention that is pro- or anti-social, not the act itself. Anti-social or aggressive behaviour occurs when someone intends harm or at least sees that harm will be done and does nothing to stop it. Someone can push into someone else accidentally and it is not seen as an aggressive act, whereas if the push is deliberate it is seen as aggressive.

Approaches to moral development

Infants are not old enough to know right from wrong and cannot engage in moral behaviour. Their thought processes are not developed enough to understand such issues and their language is not developed enough to have an understanding of behaving appropriately. Of course, there might be some genetic factors involved and, for example, some children might be more naturally aggressive than other children, but this is very hard to prove. Most of the study of moral development is concerned with how social norms are learnt and how children are encouraged to be pro-social and discouraged from being anti-social.

The influence of learning theory is looked at before discussing cognitive developmental theories and, finally Freud's explanation for how we develop moral behaviour is examined. Learning theory looks at moral behaviour, cognitive developmental theories look more at thinking, and psychodynamic explanations look at feelings as well as behaviour and thinking.

Learning theories and their explanations for how moral development occurs

Learning theories focus on how we learn behaviour and so focus on learning to behave in a moral (or non-moral) way. Learning theory includes the mechanisms of operant conditioning. The basic idea is that we repeat behaviour that has a pleasant consequence because we like rewards. We do not repeat behaviour that has an unpleasant consequence. We avoid being punished because it is not pleasant and we avoid bad experiences. Consequently, one way of teaching children to behave in a moral way is to reward their pro-social behaviour. This can be done simply by praising them and by giving smiles as positive reinforcement. Another way of teaching moral behaviour is to punish bad behaviour. However, as was explained in Chapter 4, a problem with punishment is that it can be the only form of attention a child gets and so can be a reward in that sense. The punisher is also modelling anti-social and aggressive behaviour, so the child might then copy that, thinking that it is the right way to act. So punishment is not a very effective means of teaching a child moral behaviour.

Classical conditioning can also be used to explain how we learn to be good. It is thought that punishment is linked to pain and fear, and that these are natural responses. If some act is punished, then that act becomes linked with pain and fear and so will not be carried out again. This suggests that punishment can work in these circumstances. In general, however, learning theorists do not favour punishment as a way of teaching moral behaviour, as it seems to be more counterproductive than useful.

Another learning theory is social learning theory. This theory focuses on the principle of imitation and on the importance of role models. As just explained, punishment can be a model and a child can then imitate such behaviour. However, similarly, pro-social behaviour can be modelled and so can be encouraged. A child can learn moral behaviour by having good behaviour to copy.

Social learning theory has often focused on how aggression might occur because of modelling and has been used to explain problems of showing violence on the media. Bandura's studies were discussed in Chapter 4 and it was shown that children do copy violent acts, at least in experiments. Also boys tend to copy male models more than girls do and, although both boys and girls copy aggressive acts, girls are more likely only to be verbally aggressive whereas boys are more likely to copy physical aggression too. Children tend to repeat aggressive acts that they see rewarded more than they repeat aggressive acts that they see punished. So it seems that children should not watch violence – or if there is violence that they are likely to see, it should at least be punished.

In fact, as with most explanations of such behaviours, there is more to it than that. It is suggested that if a child watches aggression on the media, they are less likely to copy it if they have a pro-social model in the family. So if their parents do not model aggression, and if their parents watch a programme with them and explain how the aggressive acts are wrong, then that can make a difference as to whether the child copies the aggression they see or not. A problem with experiments is that they separate variables like violence as portrayed by the media without taking into account all the other variables such as the reactions of other family members when a violent programme is being watched. Nonetheless there does seem to be evidence that children use imitation and modelling, and if society wants to promote pro-social behaviour then that should be modelled, not violence.

Cognitive developmental theories and their explanations for moral development

Piaget produced an important theory of cognitive development that considers the issue of moral development, in particular how we develop moral thinking. This theory is covered in Chapter 5 and focuses mainly on the need for a certain level of thinking ability before certain aspects of development can be reached or understood. A baby is in the first stage of cognitive development, the sensorimotor stage, and this stage does not include reasoning, so a baby would not have a sense of moral behaviour.

In the second stage, the preoperational stage, a child's thinking is limited and there is a strong focus on the self. The child would find it difficult, if not impossible, to take anyone else's view into account. Therefore, a child in that stage of reasoning would find the idea of right and wrong difficult to deal with. Children in that stage, however, can learn absolute rules and so can be told what to do. This is called **heteronymous morality** because children think that the rules cannot be changed.

DEFINITIONS

Heteronymous morality – the first stage of moral reasoning according to Piaget. In the preoperational stage (between 2 and 7 years old) children can learn what is right and wrong but cannot themselves reason about it. They can learn the rules.

Autonomous morality – the second stage of moral reasoning according to Piaget. In the concrete operational stage (from the age of around 7 years) a child can understand that rules can be broken, and can carry out moral reasoning for itself.

This is not really moral reasoning but they can abide by the rules and so do know what is right and wrong.

By the third stage of cognitive development, which is about from the age of 7 years, a child should be capable of moral reasoning to an extent, although complete abstract reasoning would be difficult for them. Children in this third stage (concrete operations) can understand rules and can negotiate changes in them, so are able to deal with moral issues and rules of what is right and what is wrong. This is called having **autonomous morality**.

Another cognitive developmental theory that looks at cognitive development is Kohlberg's theory (1932). Kohlberg set out to build on Piaget's ideas. Kohlberg proposed that there are levels of moral development so his theory, like Piaget's, was a stage theory. Note that Kohlberg's levels of moral development, again like Piaget's, only really focuses on older children and the first level goes from the young child up to around the age of 12 years, with other stages then moving through adolescence to adulthood. So, again, it is seen that a very young child is not considered to have developed in a moral sense. This underlines the point that perhaps young children should not be blamed for doing wrong – even though they are blamed for anti-social acts and are then treated as 'naughty'. Kohlberg outlined three levels of moral development, and each of the three levels itself has two stages. Kohlberg's levels and stages are outlined in Table 7.1.

Table 7.1   Kohlberg's levels of moral development

Level of moral development	Description
Level One. The level of preconventional morality. Lasts up to around 12 years.	Stage 1 – younger children are concerned with the outcome of behaviour not with motives. So an act that has bad consequences is a bad act, even if the intention was good. Stage 2 – older children think that what is good is what gives them and others pleasure, and what is bad gives hurt.
Level Two. The level of conventional morality. From between 13 and 16 years.	Stage 3 – moral behaviour is what makes people popular, in particular the children themselves. They do what gives them a reward. Stage 4 – rules must not be disobeyed because that brings punishment. Children are good to avoid guilt and punishment.
Level Three: The level of post-conventional morality. From the age of 16 years.	Stage 5 – it is believed that the wider community's interests should be put above those of the individual. Ideas about justice and fairness are apparent. Stage 6 – philosophical reasoning is encountered, getting to grips with the deeper meanings of what is right and wrong and why.

There are problems with Kohlberg's work. For one thing, he asked males and so his theory should only really be said to apply to males. The stages he found were in the society he studied and might not be found in all societies. However, you can tell children stories yourself and find that there is some evidence for Kohlberg and Piaget's ideas. Piaget had a story about cups and you can use a similar story to find out for yourself that young children do have a different type of moral reasoning from older children. The story goes a bit like this:

> John was thirsty but his mother told him to wait and she would get him a drink later. He did not wait though. He picked up a cup to fill it with milk and then dropped the cup, breaking it. In the meantime his brother Henry was trying to help his mother to get ready for visitors. Henry picked up a tray with four cups on it and carried it into another room. He dropped the tray on the way and the four cups were broken.

KEY TERMS

You need to know the meaning of the following words and phrases. Go back through the chapter to make sure you understand them:

Altruism
Anal stage
Androgenital syndrome
Anti-social behaviour
Autonomous morality
Ego
Fixated
Gender constancy
Gender identity
Gender schema theory
Genital stage
Heteronymous morality
Id
Latency stage
Libido
Oral stage
Phallic stage
Pro-social behaviour
Superego
Thanatos

KEY NAMES

Bandura
Bem
Fagot
Freud
Kohlberg
Mead
Money
Piaget

Then the child is asked who was the naughtiest, John or Henry? A young child will see the consequences of the actions and, as John only broke one cup and Henry broke four cups, will say that Henry was the naughtiest. An older child, however, will take intentions into account and will say that John is the naughtiest because he was told to wait whereas Henry was trying to help. This sort of story helps to show the difference in thinking between young and older children.

Freud's theory of moral development

Freud's ideas about moral development come from his general theory about psychosexual development, outlined earlier in this chapter. Children develop a conscience when the superego develops, from the age of around 3 years. This comes from interactions with parents, peers, media and all other social interactions. Children identify with their same-sex parents through the Oedipus and Electra complex. This identification is a thorough one. They don't just copy the parent – it is as if they become the parent and take on all the parent's attitudes and behaviours. So the child adopts the moral stance of the same-sex parent, and that is how moral behaviour is learnt.

Some conclusions

It is thought that a child has to be cognitively ready to understand moral issues as these involve discussing what is right and wrong, which are abstract concepts. At the same time children learn the rules by mechanisms such as operant conditioning and social learning theory. They probably learn the rules before they understand the principles, which is worth bearing in mind. However, a child can know right from wrong without being able to argue about the principles involved. Freud, as you might expect, had his own view on how we develop moral behaviour, but his views still include an element of learning from parents and are similar to the ideas of social learning theory, which also focus on identification with significant others.

FURTHER READING

Cohen, D. (2002) *How the Child's Mind Develops,* Routledge, New York, Chapter 4.
This is an easy read and recommended for students studying at Level 3 and higher.

Dowling, M. (2001) *Young Children's Personal, Social and Emotional Development,* Paul Chapman Ltd, London.
This book is useful for students studying at Level 3 and is essential reading for students on higher level courses.

Holland, P. (2001) *We Don't Play with Guns Here,* Open University Press, Buckingham.
An excellent book about boys' play in nurseries and the reactions of early years practitioners. Essential reading for all students at Level 3 and above.

Siraj-Blatchford, I. and Clarke, P. (2000) *Supporting Identity, Diversity and Language in the Early Years,* McGraw-Hill, Maidenhead.
This book has a good section on gender identity and is suitable for students on Level 3 courses and above.

Play and friendships

INTRODUCTION

This chapter examines play and friendships. There are many different types of play. Piaget described three types to go with his first three stages of cognitive (thinking) development. Others have categorised play, too, emphasising how it tends to move from solitary play at first, through to social play and then play with rules. There is general agreement that a child needs to have a certain level of cognitive development to play with rules or for pretend play, as well as for other types of play.

We will consider what play is for. The chapter will then discuss friendship patterns and look at how friends develop, who is popular, and what advantages there are to having friends.

The topics of play and friendship are related because children develop peer relationships through play and gradually form friendships. As with the other topics that have been investigated in this book, various theoretical approaches are used. These approaches have been discussed in other chapters and Table 8.1 summarises them.

Table 8.1 Some basic theories and assumptions used in child psychology, which help to explain play and friendships

Theory/Approach	Brief outline of assumptions
Learning theory	• Involves operant conditioning (we do again what we get rewarded for) • Involves social learning theory (children imitate role models) • Focuses on our 'nurture' and behaviour
Piaget's theory of cognitive (thinking) development	• There are four stages of cognitive (thinking) development • The first stage is the sensorimotor stage (the child learns through senses and muscle movement) • The second stage is the preoperational stage (the child has limited reasoning and thinking abilities) • The third stage is the concrete operational stage (the child can do mental thinking without actual objects but needs to think of object, so limited) • The fourth stage is the stage of formal operations (where there is the ability to do abstract thinking) • Focuses on how we develop thinking capacity
Biological approach	• Gives a great deal of very important information about our genetic make up and inherited characteristics, as well as how we develop physiologically • Gives our 'nature'
Psychodynamic (Freud's) approach	• Claims we develop through five psychosexual stages – oral, anal, phallic, latency, and genital • We develop the three parts of the personality (id, ego and superego) through these stages • Focuses on our emotional development

Table 8.1 continued

Theory/Approach	Brief outline of assumptions
Social approach	• Emphasis is on how our interactions with others affect both our everyday behaviour and our early development • We do not live in a world alone, and we are not passive in our own development – we actively develop in a social world that affects us
Social constructivist approach	• This uses the social approach and firmly claims that children (and adults) actively construct their own world within a specific culture and particular norms and customs • It is not that our nature and nurture form us – we actively engage in the process, and so do others and our interactions with others

Note that the social approach is mentioned in Table 8.1. Theories discussed in earlier chapters tended to see the child as passive whereas in this chapter there is more focus on children as active human beings who develop by enquiring about things and by seeking out others. Chapter 9 continues with this theme and looks at social and emotional development, as well as examining issues such as the effect of stereotyping and labelling on a child's development – issues that are clearly 'social' in nature, as they examine how others affect us.

PLAY

Play is an enjoyable activity that is done for its own sake and without obvious immediate purpose. An example of play in babies is when an infant drops an object repeatedly, or bangs objects together to make a noise. In **free play** children choose what they do and what they play with. It is valuable in helping children to develop their skills and their imagination. There is also **directed play**, which is likely to be found in places such as nurseries, because there children are likely to be directed towards certain activities even if only because of what is laid out for them to play with. Directed play focuses on activities that will allow a child to explore and strengthen their natural abilities.

Types of play and definitions

Different types of play tend to go with different theories because theorists have produced different explanations and terms. It is useful to have a list of terms and definitions, so these are given here first. Table 8.2 lists some types of play, and gives brief definitions. Then theories are outlined to explain each type in more detail.

Table 8.2　Types of play

Type of play	Brief explanation
Sensorimotor play	Play is with objects to give pleasure – for example, if objects make a noise. Cognitive development thus takes place – for example, learning how to move objects
Unoccupied play	When a child is not engaged in a specific activity
Onlooker play	When the child just watches others
Solitary play	When a child plays alone, away from others
Parallel play	Playing near others but alongside, not interacting
Pretend play	When objects are used as something else or to mean what they don't usually mean
Symbolic play	Piaget's term for pretend play – when objects are used as something else or to mean what they don't usually mean
Associative play	When more than one child is doing the same thing with others
Cooperative play	When more than one child is interacting sharing tasks to get something done

Table 8.2 continued

Type of play	Brief explanation
Sociodramatic play	Pretend play with social role playing as well
Functional play	Involves simple body movements or actions with objects
Constructive play	Making things with objects
Dramatic play	Acting out roles in a pretend game
Games with rules	Playing with publicly accepted rules
Social play	Incorporates all the kinds of play that include social roles, such as dramatic play, games with rules and sociodramatic play
Physical activity play	Involves physical activity often without objects
Rough and tumble play	Involves wrestling, kicking, chasing, tumbling and rolling on the ground – and similar activities

DEFINITIONS

Sensorimotor play – playing with objects to give pleasure, for example, if objects make a noise.

Symbolic play – when objects are used as something else. Piaget's term for pretend play.

Games with rules – playing with publicly accepted rules.

DEFINITIONS

Pretend play – when objects are used as something else or to mean what they do not usually mean.

Solitary play – when a child plays alone, away from others.

Social play – incorporates all the kinds of play that include social roles, such as dramatic play, games with rules and sociodramatic play.

Scaffolding – is where an adult helps a child to play, for example, modelling a pretend game, and then the child gradually learns such games for itself so that at first the adult supports the child's play, and then later this support is not needed. In other words at first there is scaffolding and then the scaffolding can be removed.

Play and cognitive development – Piaget's stages of play

Piaget's theory of cognitive development outlines four stages of development, and there is a link between these stages and types of play. The type of play depends on the level of cognitive development.

Piaget's first stage is the sensorimotor stage, where children develop through moving within their environment, such as waving their arms and, when they have sufficient muscle control, shaking a rattle to enjoy the movement and the sound. This is **sensorimotor play**. Early play therefore, according to this theory, involves muscle movement and sense data such as sounds.

Piaget's second stage is the preoperational stage, when a child finds it hard to do complicated mental operations. Play is, therefore, very basic and doesn't involve devising rules. As children move from the sensorimotor stage to the preoperational stage, they are able to carry out pretend play, which in this theory is called **symbolic play**. Their cognitive development is such that they are able to pretend about objects. Indeed this is a stage where animism occurs, where children can think that an object is actually alive. More detail about Piaget's stages can be found in Chapter 5.

Games with rules occur when the child is in the third stage – the stage of concrete operations. At this stage rules can be understood and a child is capable of altering rules to suit a situation. For example, an older child can 'bend' the rules to let a younger child win. It can be seen here that cognitive development is important, and play, relying as it can on thinking processes, develops alongside the development of cognition. Thus children can only be expected to play according to their level of understanding.

Pretend play

Studies have been done to look specifically at **pretend play**. For example, one study (Haight and Miller, 1993) made videos of nine children playing at home. The children were 12 months old when the study began and it ended when they were 4 years old. It found that, in the beginning, there were children whose pretend play was **solitary play** – in other words they played alone. However, around 75% of the children's pretend play was **social play**. First they played with mothers and then with peers. This suggests that play linked not only with cognitive development (it helps in learning motor movements and in understanding the properties of objects, for example) but also with social development. There is also the implication that play and social interaction themselves encourage cognitive development. Adults in an infant's life seem to have a **scaffolding** role in the development of pretend play. At first they are heavily involved, for example by demonstrating pretend play, but then gradually that support is withdrawn and children engage in pretend play on their own. This is usually by the time they are around 3 years old. This idea of scaffolding was outlined in Chapter 5 when cognitive-development was considered.

An example of pretend play – this child is putting the doll to bed

Interacting with peers

Young infants do not interact with those of their own age in any real sense of playing with them, however young babies will show an interest in other babies, especially if the babies are familiar to them. They are around 2 years old when they begin to develop peer relationships. Lewis *et al.* (1975) looked at mother and infant pairs where the infants were aged around 12 to 18 months old. If two mothers with their infants shared a playroom (they had not met before) then the infants stayed close to their mothers as you would expect because they are at the age when they would show separation anxiety (Chapter 3 outlines this area of study, looking at attachments). However, the infants did look at each other quite a lot and showed interest, suggesting that they were moving towards the time when they would interact. Perhaps it is the loosening of the attachment bond by around 2 years old that enables children to start to build peer relationships. Before the age of 2 children are more likely to interact with adults, although they will often show interest in another child.

The effect of siblings

Having brothers and/or sisters (**siblings**) can affect how a young child interacts with others. Older siblings can play with a younger child but, unlike adults, they can be hostile or uninterested. A well-known study (Dunn and Kendrick, 1982) looked at 40 first-born children who were around 2 years old when a new baby was born in the family. The findings of the study showed that the older child took a lot of interest in the infant and cared for it. However, there was also hostility. Hostility was often directed towards the parents although some jealousy was actually directed at the baby. This study is important as it shows that even quite a young child can have strong feelings towards a younger sibling, and this demonstrates their state of mind. A particular point about their state of mind is that they are able to understand what their younger brother or sister is thinking – this ability to understand what another person is thinking is called '**theory of mind**' and is an important theory when it comes to looking at child development.

Research has also shown that younger children tend to have more highly developed social skills than their older siblings. This may be because if they want to join in the play of their older brothers and sisters they have to work very hard at it and be charming. Older brothers and sisters often make it hard for younger siblings to join in.

Theory of mind

As young children develop they have older children to set an example of how to interact and to help them to learn about social behaviour. The siblings can learn how to support one another, and how to annoy one another. This suggests that a young child has an awareness of the likes and dislikes of the older child. Piaget's theory of cognitive development, which is outlined in Chapter 5, suggests that young children are **egocentric** and cannot take the view of another person. However, studies like that of Dunn and Kendrick (1982) and outlined above suggest that a young child has a theory of mind. A theory of mind means an ability to put oneself in the mind of another.

There is a procedure often used to test theory of mind. There are several variations but the procedure is similar across studies. Imagine two dolls – Anne and Sally – a researcher, a child, and a pretend situation. The child watches the researcher who plays out the pretend situation with the two dolls. Anne and Sally are 'in the same room' when Anne 'puts' a marble under one of two plastic beakers turned upside down on a table. Both of the dolls have 'seen' this action so 'know' that the marble is under the red cup not the blue cup. The child has watched this, so knows that too. Then the researcher 'walks' Sally out of the room. Sally cannot see what happens next. Anne then 'moves' the marble to the blue upturned cup. The child knows that the marble is now under the blue cup. The question is will the child understand that Sally will think that the marble is still under the red cup? If the child does understand that Sally would not know that the marble has been moved, then the child has a theory of mind and can see the world through another's point of view. If, however, the child thinks that Sally would look for the marble under the blue cup – which is where the child knows the marble is – then the child has no theory of mind and cannot take the view of another. The child will not understand that Sally does not know what the child knows.

This procedure tends to show that 4 year olds have a theory of mind but younger children do not. However, studies of younger children with their siblings, such as Haight and Miller (1993), suggest that young children can understand the thoughts and feelings of another (such as that they are upset and feel pain). Studies of theory of mind strongly suggest that this is just what autistic children find difficult and this issue is looked at again in Chapter 10, when 'abnormal' behaviour is discussed.

All the above suggests that play is an important element in developing cognitive abilities, and that social skills are also developed through play. Being able to interact with others such as adults (for scaffolding and modelling) and siblings also seems to help children to learn cognitive and social skills. This is not to say that the 'only child' has difficulty in developing, because this does not seem to be the case. There must be many ways of developing cognitively and socially. If there are siblings this seems to affect development but there seem to be few problems if there are not.

Categories of social participation – as play becomes social

Although Piaget's stages of cognitive development help in understanding how play develops according to the child's level of thinking, one common way of describing play is to outline the actual sequence of peer interaction that seems to take place from babyhood through to the older child. Observations have shown that there are clear stages. One well-known study was carried out by Parten in 1932. She watched children of different ages from 2 to 4 years old and noted their type of play according to how much they interacted with other children. How far children play interactively and co-operatively with others is called **social participation**. Parten's stages are outlined in Table 8.3.

> **DEFINITION**
>
> **Egocentric** – the term for young children's inability to take the viewpoint of other people. They see things through their own eyes.

> **DEFINITION**
>
> **Social participation** – is how far a child plays interactively and co-operatively with others.

Table 8.3   Categories of social participation (from Parten, 1932)

Type of social participation	Description	How develops with age
Unoccupied	Child not engaged in activity	Decreases
Onlooker	Child watches, not joining in	Decreases
Solitary	Plays alone away from others	Decreases
Parallel	Plays alongside but without interacting much, using same materials	Decreases
Associative	Child interacts and does same thing	Increases
Co-operative	Child interacts and actively shares task with others to achieve goal	Increases

As would be expected from what has been said above, social participation increases as the child grows older and others become more important in play. The child spends less time alone or playing alongside other children, and spends more time playing with others. Not only are children more involved with each other as they get older but the size of the groups grows too. A study of over 400 children in Israel (1981) aged 5 to 6 years, when playing outdoors, found that there was a lot of group activity and the size of the group grew with age too. Parten observed some children not involved in any activity and this was called **unoccupied play**. Then there were children who simply watched – this was **onlooker play**. Some children played alone, and this was called **solitary play**. Others played alone but alongside others and shared the same materials – for example playing separately in the same sandpit. This was called **parallel play**. Other children associated with one another in that they were interacting whilst doing the same thing, and this was called **associative play**. The final category was **co-operative play**, where children worked together to achieve the same goal. It should be noted that children do not 'pass through' stages of play in the same way that we describe children 'passing through' Piaget's stages of cognitive development. Rather these types of play persist as more advanced forms of play are added to the child's repertoire

Smilansky's four stages of play

Already two theories of how play can be categorised have been outlined. Piaget suggested three stages of play to go with his first three stages of cognitive development. Parten found six categories of play when considering how social it is, ranging from no activity to full co-operative play. Smilansky (1968) suggested four stages of play development and developed Piaget's ideas. Smilansky's stages are outlined in Table 8.4. As outlined above, Piaget developed the idea of symbolic play, where objects can

Table 8.4   Smilansky's four play stages

Stage of play	Description
Functional	Simple body movements (corresponds with the sensorimotor stage)
Constructive	Making things with objects. More mature than sensorimotor play, but not pretend
Dramatic	Pretend play, specifically acting out roles
Games with rules	Playing a game with public rules such as football

become symbols, and this is pretend play. It was Smilansky who developed the idea of **sociodramatic play**, which is pretend play but with role playing too, such as playing spacemen and aliens. Smilansky thought that play developed through **functional play**, which involved motor movements, through **constructive play**, which is slightly more focused, to **dramatic play**, which is pretend play and often involves social roles. The final stage is the same as Piaget's and involves the child in playing according to accepted rules.

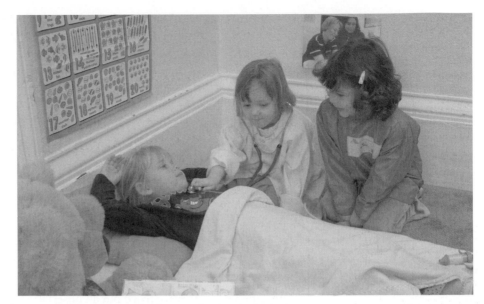

An example of sociodramatic play – pretend and role playing

A play hierarchy

Theorists have categorised play in many ways, as the studies mentioned above and numerous others show. However, there are some basic assumptions about play, its role and how it develops. It was clear that both cognitive and social development are helped through play and that play stages follow the child's stage of cognitive and social development. Smilansky developed a categorisation of stages of play and Parten developed a categorisation of social participation.

Rubin *et al.* (1978) created a play hierarchy so that play could be observed and children's play could be categorised according to their cognitive and social development. For example, a child could be associating with others and acting out roles in dramatic play. This would be pretend play using social roles. It would show that level of social participation, and that the child was not actually co-operating with others but could associate with them. This would be associative dramatic play. You might have a group of children engaged in domestic role-play in the home corner. One child might be a baby pretending to cry, another might be the child's mother and a third the doctor. These three children would be acting out a story and directing themselves as they go along. A fourth child might also be in the home corner dressed as a nurse, but on the sideline and not actively joining in. This child would be participating in associative play rather than co-operative play.

Problems with categorising play

A problem with developing categories and stages, such as stages of play, is that children rarely fit exactly into categories. For example, a mature child who can engage in co-operative play might have some time engaged in solitary play out of choice. Also dramatic play, where social roles are acted out, can include functional play, where things are built. So the idea of a judging a child's level of development by means of a hierarchy is not as clear cut as the above outline seems to suggest. Another important criticism is that physical play is not dealt with in the above three ways of categorising play (Piaget's, Parten's and Smilansky's).

Physical activity play

Quite a lot of play involves physical activity, often without objects. Pellegrini and Smith (1998) suggested three developmental phases in physical activity play. The first type of physical activity play they suggested was where there were bodily

TRY THIS!

Undertake observations of children of various ages in your workplace/placement. A time sample method is useful for this. That is you observe the child for a minute or two every 15 minutes during a session. You need to record what the child is doing, with whom (adult or children) and the type of play you see (if any).

Analyse your results using the theories of play previously outlined. Do your observations lead you to conclude that children of different ages play in different ways?

Rhythmical stereotypes – refers to physical activity play found in babies, such as kicking legs and waving arms.

Exercise play – refers to running, jumping and climbing, found in young pre-school children.

Rough-and-tumble play – refers to play fighting, which involves activities such as chasing, tumbling and rolling on the ground, kicking and wrestling. This tends to occur in school-age children.

Physical activity play – involves exercise play, rhythmical stereotypes and rough-and-tumble play

TRY THIS!

In your placement or workplace undertake an observation of a group of children in the outside play area. Use the information from this chapter to try and categorise the type of play you see. Can you identify rough and tumble play? Does it seem to be the boys who are playing in this way?

movements such as babies use, for example, kicking legs and waving arms. They called this **rhythmical stereotypes**. Second there is **exercise play**, which involves jumping, running and climbing – these are whole body movements that can be done with or without others. The third category is **rough-and-tumble play**, which refers to play fighting, and involves activities such as chasing, tumbling and rolling on the ground, kicking and wrestling. This tends to occur in school-age children. Table 8.5 gives Pelligrini and Smith's categories of **physical activity play**.

Table 8.5   Categories of physical activity play (from Pelligrini and Smith 1998)

Type of physical activity	Description
Rhythmical stereotypes	Like a baby's movements, kicking legs and waving arms
Exercise play	Jumping, running and climbing, with or without others
Rough-and-tumble play	Play fighting including wrestling, chasing, and tumbling and rolling on the ground

Humphreys and Smith carried out an observation in 1987 and found that rough-and-tumble play took up about 10% of playground play activities. Children enjoy rough-and-tumble play, especially boys. Most of the time rough-and-tumble play does not lead to real fighting according to studies such as Schaefer and Smith (1996).

What is play for?

Play seems to have an important function in helping a child to develop in various ways. Play seems to help us to develop socially, as well as in cognitive and language development. Physical play helps to develop muscle strength and may have had a role in preparing humans for later activities such as fighting. Rough-and-tumble play as outlined above may have had that role.

Helping social, cognitive and language development

Play seems to have certain functions. Some researchers think that play is necessary for normal development. For example, Smilansky (1968) thought that sociodramatic play was important for normal social development to take place. She thought that preschool settings should encourage sociodramatic play and plan for it, to encourage social development. She carried out her studies in Israel and noted that immigrant children were not only not showing much sociodramatic play but were also behind in language and cognitive skills. Other studies, such as some carried out in America, also found that disadvantaged children had these deficits in language, cognitive and social development. This could be because parents did not use scaffolding to develop dramatic play. The conclusion that sociodramatic play gives successful language, cognitive and social development was drawn, although, of course, an unstimulating environment can itself cause developmental problems, as outlined in Chapter 3 when looking at attachments and lack of or broken attachments. It is thought that sociodramatic play had a strong role to play in normal development and should be encouraged. Such play involves a lot of language interchange, and social negotiation, as well as symbolism in that objects have to represent other objects. All these things are thought to be important in developing language, cognitive and social skills.

Studies were done to see if encouraging sociodramatic play would improve language, social and cognitive development. Play tutoring was used to encourage children to develop sociodramatic play. Play tutoring involves teachers in taking children on trips to stimulate them (such as to a zoo) and then providing some appropriate materials for the children to reproduce situations. Staff could also model such play to provide scaffolding. Some children received play tutoring and some did not (they were the control group). Then researchers checke children who received play tutoring developed in any different who did not. Studies during the 1970s and 1980s found tha improve with play tutoring and the conclusion was drawn th dramatic play did help with a child's development. However, t improve no matter what the teachers did, which suggests that it might just have been the extra attention and stimulation that led to the improvements rather than any specific 'training'. The teachers also knew whether a child was receiving peer tutoring or was in a control group and this may have affected the situation, because of their interactions with the child based on this knowledge. This idea of how people can subconsciously affect the behaviour of others is looked at in Chapter 9, when the effects of labelling and the self-fulfilling prophecy are examined. Others tried studies using play tutoring, but making sure that teachers did not know which condition children was in (whether they had the tutoring or were part of a control) and they also tried to equal out the stimulation the children received. These studies did not find the same effects as the first studies (see, for example, Smith, 1988). It was concluded that stimulation from adults is what works, rather than actually promoting the use of pretend play. So play helps with language, cognitive and social development and that these are improved if the child receives plenty of stimulation from adults. Activities such as social pretend play do seem to be important too.

Helping build strength

Physical play helps to build up muscles and rough-and-tumble play, in particular, may be useful in building fighting strategies. This may have had a survival value. It may be that children learn their place in a **dominance hierarchy**, and that they can then use this when they are older to make judgements about appropriate behaviour. A dominance hierarchy refers to a child's understanding of an order in dominance, which is the ability to 'win'. Children learn that there is an order in who is likely to win in certain situations and they learn their place within that order. Pelligrini and Smith (1998) researched this area.

Play therapy

Play can be used as a therapy, according to the psychodynamic approach. Problems that children may have due to repressing some traumatic event or maintaining unwanted thoughts in the unconscious can be uncovered through play. Axline (1971) studied a child called 'Dibs' and this case study can help to illustrate how play is used as therapy. Through therapy the child can confront conflicts and find ways to resolve them. The therapist observes the child playing with toys. For example, Dibs seemed to be having hostility to his father when he buried a doll.

Cultural variations in play

There are cultural variations not only in how play is supported and what is encouraged. It is important to note that children in all cultures play, which is evidence that play is an innate tendency, presumably, therefore, useful in terms of our development. It might be that in some cultures children are at work, for example, watching the family cows, but they still play tag at the same time. What they play with may differ but materials are still adapted for play. For example, children can use reeds, leaves, stones, teeth, shells and wood. Scaffolding is found in all cultures too. Scaffolding was explained in Chapter 5, where cognitive-development was outlined. It involves adults helping and supporting children until they can do something for themselves. Adults provide guidance and support and encourage skills so that the child won't fail but without doing everything for the child. Children learn through social interactions with adults, who are more competent, and they learn various culturally related activities.

Bronfenbrenner's ecological model

Bronfenbrenner (1979) suggested an ecological model for play, which emphasises its role in developing appropriate skills for a particular culture (or ecology). Children's environment and adults within their particular culture are very important in providing guidance for their play because they must learn appropriately for their culture.

Parental roles in play in different cultures

Parental roles in supporting play seem to vary between cultures. Whiting and Whiting (1975) suggest that children in more complex cultures play with more complexity, perhaps reflecting cultural needs, and parent support reflects these differences. In more complex cultures children seem to have more free play opportunities where they can explore more. In other cultures there is not this leeway because children are needed to help with economic support of the family – they must do their share of the work.

In some cultures adults think of themselves as play partners with their children more than in other cultures. American and Turkish mothers seem to think it is appropriate for them to play with their children, for example, whereas Guatemalan and Mexican mothers do not (see, for example, Farver, 1993 and Haight, Parke and Black, 1997).

When adults are involved in children's play they have different ideas of what is suitable depending on the culture. For example, European-American mothers tend to emphasise independence and self-expression whereas Chinese mothers emphasise social harmony and respect for rules (see Haight *et al.*, 1999). Japanese mothers tend to focus on social interactions and communication in play whereas American mothers tend to use play to teach world knowledge (see, for example, Tamis-LeMonda *et al.*, 1992).

Parental and teaching roles – spiral learning

The idea of spiral learning fits mainly into the Western approach to play as learning. Chapter 5 discusses Bruner's ideas about cognitive development. The idea of a spiral curriculum comes from Bruner's views – that a child need scaffolding of a sort whilst learning but that the child also needs to learn without support, so support must be there when needed then withdrawn when it is not needed. In this way learning is as if in a spiral, with children gradually developing skills and knowledge, building on what they can do and being supported to learn and to be able to do more.

The child is like a scientist, researching and learning, with the adult supporting as needed. Play is part of this learning as the child explores and tries things out. This is experiential learning and there is a cycle of learning, with children trying something out, thinking about it, perhaps getting some support, then incorporating their thinking and experiences until learning has taken place and they move on to something else, with that new learning ready to support them. This self-organised learning, with adult support and scaffolding where necessary, is more likely to be firm and solid learning because the child is an active learner in the process.

Play and losing

Chapter 4, where learning theories were outlined, emphasised that using punishment when encouraging learning is not a successful means of reinforcement because children may learn that some form of aggression or punishment is appropriate, and they may also find the punishment reinforcing because attention is given. Positive rewards are considered more productive although there may be a place for punishment, if only in the form of removing children from a situation until they behave appropriately. It is using these ideas that leads to the notion that losing is not good for a child because positive reinforcement (which winning would bring) is more productive. There is a tendency now for competition to be avoided so that children do not 'lose'. In Chapter 4 the idea of learned helplessness is also outlined, and this suggests that if we keep trying at something and do not succeed then we will stop trying. Children who keep putting a hand up to answer a question and are never asked will stop putting their hand up, for example, according to this idea. So it might be thought that if a child keeps losing they will stop trying. On the other hand you could argue that people do lose (at least not everyone wins) in social situations, so children must learn that losing is acceptable and they must learn about losing. Engaging in social activity can affect self-esteem too, as discussed in Chapter 9, and losing may affect self-esteem in a negative way. There are many reasons why losing is not a good experience, and for the most part it is best for a child not to lose. However, it is perhaps worth bearing in mind that learning to lose is also a skill a child needs to develop.

FRIENDSHIPS

The development of understanding of social relationships, and the development of certain types of play, show that friendships between children do not occur until a certain level of development is reached. This is probably a certain level of cognitive development, language and social development. Many factors are needed, including appropriate social skills. As was shown earlier, children from around 18 months and maybe earlier do take an interest in other children although, probably because of separation anxiety, they are unlikely to do much more than watch others playing. Only older children engage in co-operative play, which would be the sort of play you would expect between friends. There are other factors involved too, such as whether children have brothers or sisters, and this might affect their level of social skills. So you would not expect actual friendships to develop until around 4 years old. Parten (1932) showed different levels of social participation as a child develops and her observations underline this idea that friendships will not occur until a certain stage of development is reached. By school age, peer groups are important to children. Some children are popular, others are lonely and some have a small group of friends, or even one close friend. Researchers have observed children in nursery schools to see what patterns of friendships are likely to develop.

Studying friendship patterns – sociometry and sociograms

One way in which patterns of friendships are studied is to build **sociograms** (Clark *et al.*, 1969). These consist of large circles showing children's play partners. Diagram 8.1 shows how a sociogram is constructed.

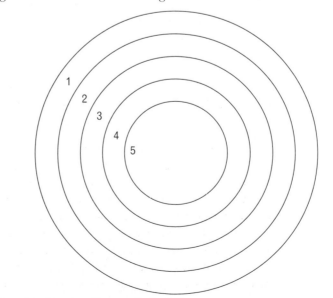

Diagram 8.1 Constructing a sociogram

Five circles are drawn up. Those children who play with only one other are represented by a symbol in the '1' circle, and those who play with four others (for example) are represented in the '4' circle. Boys are represented by a triangle and girls by a circle. Then lines are drawn between the triangles and circles to show which child plays with which other child. More lines mean how often they were seen playing together. Therefore, for example, two circles joined by three lines in the '1' circle means that two girls play together, don't play with anyone else, and were observed playing together three times.

The technique of building sociograms to study relationships within a group or groups is called sociometry. Observations can give friendship patterns but interviews can be used too, such as asking children who their main friends are, or to name three class members that they like best. With interview data the researcher can draw arrows to show which child says they like a certain child, and the arrows can be two headed if that child says they like them too. Children can also be asked who they like least. It was found using these sorts of questions that those children who seemed to be liked most, could also be in the 'liked least' category for some class members. It was not that everyone always liked the same person.

Coie *et al.* (1983) carried out a study that suggested that there are five types of child. There are popular children, neglected children, rejected children, average children and controversial children. Their categories are outlined in Diagram 8.2 below.

TRY THIS!

In your workplace/placement have a go at undertaking a sociogram using the method outlined above. This method is good to use with children who do not have well-developed language skills. For older children you may like to try the interview method.

Diagram 8.2 Sociometric status categories (from Coie et al., 1983)

Different types of sociometric status and the effect on a child, especially for rejected children

There might be problems with being a 'rejected' child. A child could be rejected due to poor social skills. Dodge *et al.* (1983) watched 5-year-old children to see how they joined in with groups. Children who are popular watch and wait and then join in a group as they have seen what is required to join in. Neglected children remain, waiting and watching, and don't actually join in. Rejected children, however, do try to join in but they interrupt the play and are disruptive. It has also been found that rejected children do not spend so much time in co-operative play or in social conversation as do average or popular children (Ladd, 1983). They also spend more time fighting and arguing, play in smaller groups and play with younger children. Rejected children, when older, also seem to do less well at school (Wentzel and Asher, 1995). Neglected children in school were liked by teachers later and quite well motivated.

When more studies are done, however, it can be seen that rejected children can fall into different categories. A Netherlands study found that aggressive rejected children can be impulsive and dishonest too. However, they also found rejected submissive children who were shy but not aggressive and who did not do badly at school. It seems that only rejected aggressive children have problems later in school. It is not easy to sort out all these variables. For example, rejected aggressive children, when older, can be rejected in the sense defined above, but might in adolescence actually be well liked in a group of similar adolescents.

Improving social skills

One way of improving a child's popularity – and this seems particularly important for rejected aggressive children – is to improve their social skills. Dodge *et al.* (1986) looked at social skills and suggested that there are five steps to an interaction with a peer. A child would see what another child is doing. Then the second step is to interpret this information. The third step is to look for an appropriate response. The fourth step is to select the best response and then the fifth and final step is to enact that response. Is there a part of this process that a rejected child gets wrong? It has been found that rejected children seem to misinterpret the behaviour of others (step 2) and to select aggressive responses (step 4). However, some rejected children just seem to react aggressively when they see others playing together well and they might not be rejected in other situations. Sutton *et al.* (1999) looked at English children aged between 7 and 11 years and found that those said to be ringleader bullies by others were not bad at social skills. They were quite good at hurting others without adults finding out, for example. They were not very good at understanding the feelings of others though, but scored highly on theory of mind tasks, so could put themselves in the place of another. From these conclusions it was thought that some social skills training could be useful and training has been provided in sharing, negotiating, joining in and being assertive (but not aggressive).

TRY THIS!

Depending on the age of the children you work with, look at the appropriate curriculum guidelines. What section deals with developing social skills?

If a five-year-old child had difficulties developing appropriate friendships with others in the class, how might you help?

Stages of friendship

From a study of children, both in Scotland and Canada (Bigelow and La Gaipa, 1980), it was suggested that there are three stages in friendships and in how friendships are seen by children. Children aged from 6 to 8 years old see friendship as being about shared activities, living near and having similar expectations. From between 9 and 10 years old children consider shared values and rules to be more important. Then, from aged 11 to 12, children talk about understanding and sharing things about themselves, as well as having shared interests. This suggests that physical activities are what define friendships early on but that there is a shift towards more psychological factors, such as understanding one another, in older children.

Friends do seem to be similar in many respects. Their characteristics are similar, such as how co-operative they are, whether they are shy, helpful or sociable. Researchers have studied how friendships help a child to develop. Newcomb and Bagwell (1995) looked at various studies and summarised their findings into four main features that interactions between friends have that other interactions do not have. These features are:

● friends play together more and have more intense social activity;

● there is more reciprocity and intimacy in interactions;

● there is more frequent conflict resolution between friends;

● friends help one another in tasks more and criticise one another more constructively – so they accomplish tasks better.

Friends seem more able to compromise, can negotiate better to do a task and produce more ideas together than non-friends do (Fonzi *et al.,* 1997).

Advantages of having friends

Hartup (1996) looked at the advantages of having friends, finding that:

● it is important to have friends;

● high-status friends are best;

● it is important to have good quality friendships.

Children with friends are not lonely and do better. However, having a high-status friend can be useful, for example, when dealing with bullies. Two low-status friends may have problems as they cannot help one another much when in trouble. Low-quality friendships can lack trust and so can be less useful than high quality friendships. It is hard to show that having friends can help development, though it does seem likely. Parker and Asher (1987) looked at the findings of many studies to see if they could find a link between friendship patterns and later problems. The problems they looked at were dropping out of school early, being involved in juvenile and adult crime, and having mental health problems. There did seem to be a link between those who had few friends and those who dropped out of school early. There also seemed to be a link between aggressiveness in school and crime later. They probably did not turn to crime just because they did not form friendships. It might be that a certain sort of person has difficulty in forming friendships *and* is likely to turn to crime. However, if they had been able to develop friends at school, this might have helped to alleviate some problems. There seemed to be less of a link between being shy and withdrawn at school and having later mental health problems. Overall school friendships do seem to be important.

Sex differences in play and friendships

In Chapter 7, which looked and moral and gender development, it was shown that boys and girls do play differently. For example, between the ages of around 2 and 4 boys in general engage more in physical activity and rough-and-tumble play, whereas girls engage more in domestic play or dressing up. However, there are many activities where there are few gender differences at this age. Children of this age do, however, usually choose play partners of the same gender. By around the age of 6 years sex segregation in the playground is very common. In general boys prefer outdoor play and team games whereas girls prefer indoor play and often play in pairs. Even by the age of around 10 years boys still prefer team games, tend to be more aggressive, and tend to play in quite large groups whereas girls are more orientated towards adults, play in smaller groups and are in general quieter and more empathic.

These differences may be due to biological differences, as outlined in Chapter 2 and Chapter 7. Collaer and Hines (1995) suggest that male sex hormones lead boys to be more physically active. However, social learning theory (which is outlined in Chapter 4) suggests that adults model appropriate gender-specific behaviour, which children copy and learn. Parents reinforce caring behaviour in girls, for example, as suggested in Chapter 7. However, if children learnt most of their gender-specific behaviour from modelling why would boys engage in play fighting as that is not likely to be modelled by parents or teachers? The cognitive-developmental approach suggests that children gradually adopt a gender identity and this is what leads to gender-specific behaviour. This is a form of self-socialisation as the child not only models on adults or others but comes to realise what is appropriate. A good way of summarising how children develop gender differences in their play behaviour is to say that some of the behaviour comes from biological underpinning and some is learnt from modelling on others and by being reinforced by them. There is also the aspect of realising what is appropriate, and this comes as cognitive abilities develop. Add to that the importance of social interactions and the development of social skills, and you can see that different approaches all contribute to our understanding of this area. These approaches are the biological approach, the learning approach, the cognitive-developmental approach and the social approach. Refer back to Table 8.1 for a review of these approaches.

KEY TERMS

You need to know the meaning of the following words and phrases. Go back through the chapter to make sure you understand them:

Associative play
Constructive play
Co-operative play
Directed play
Dominance hierarchy
Dramatic play
Egocentric
Exercise play
Free play
Functional play
Games with rules
Onlooker play
Parallel play
Physical activity play
Pretend play
Rhythmical stereotypes
Rough-and-tumble play
Scaffolding
Sensorimotor play
Siblings
Social participation
Social play
Sociodramatic play
Sociograms
Sociometry
Solitary play
Symbolic play
Theory of mind
Unoccupied play

KEY NAMES

Dunn and Kendrick
Parten
Piaget
Smilansky

FURTHER READING

Dowling, M. (2001) *Young Children's Personal, Social and Emotional Development*, Paul Chapman, London.
    This book is useful for students studying at Level 3 and is essential reading for students on higher level courses.
Lindon, J. (2001) *Understanding Children's Play,* Nelson Thornes Ltd, Cheltenham.
    This is an easy read and suitable for students on all childcare and education courses.
Tassoni, P. and Hucker, K. (2000) *Planning Play and the Early Years,* Professional Development Series, Heinemann Educational.
    This book is an easy read and is suitable for all students on childcare and education courses.

Social and emotional development and social influences

INTRODUCTION

Social and emotional development are both very important aspects of a child's development. A child is a social being from the start and cannot develop normally without social influences, as the effects of privation show (see Chapter 3). This chapter will begin by considering the humanistic approach, which has a particular view on how we develop, focusing quite clearly on ourselves as individuals but also on how we fit within society. The humanistic approach focuses on esteem, belonging and self-worth. Erikson's theory is considered next. This falls within the psychodynamic approach, although it could be said to be more modern than Freud's precisely because it focuses more on social development than on psychosexual development. Erikson concentrates on how we develop our identity and our personality. Emotional development is considered because it is an aspect of our development that could be said to have been neglected by early theorists and recently it has been seen as being of great importance in how we develop. The final sections of the chapter focus more directly on social influences on our development, partly to show how important they are and partly to show how destructive they can be unless fully understood. In courses such as the one you are undertaking it is very important for you to be aware of such issues, especially when you become a childcare practitioner, and you will see why when you study the material. For example, by stereotyping a child or not dealing with your own prejudices you might affect the child in a very negative way

As is clear from Chapter 5, children are not little adults – they are different not just in size but in many other ways too, including their thinking and problem-solving abilities. Early theories in psychology focused very much on our reasoning and cognitive (thinking) development. A focus on social issues followed later. It is fairly recently that emotional development has become quite an important area of study. Perhaps it is the case that we have needed to look at basic needs before studying 'luxuries' such as whether we are happy. This chapter addresses such issues.

SOCIAL DEVELOPMENT

Children develop socially from birth because from this time there will be interactions between the infant and others. When 'abnormal' functioning is considered in the next chapter, you will see that aspects of abnormality can come from environmental influences including from abnormal social interactions. It is important to note, however, that there are many causes for abnormal behaviour, such as biological and genetic causes, so it is not that poor social interactions cause all types of abnormal behaviour. This chapter will help to show that social interactions do have a strong role to play in how we develop and how our personalities develop.

Biological bases for social development – we are ready for it at birth

Chapter 2 looked at biological bases for infant behaviour including factors such as innate sociability and how an infant seems to have inbuilt preferences, for example, for human faces. The baby engages in reciprocal behaviour – for example, a mother makes a sound then the baby makes a sound – and seems to be born with useful characteristics such as these so that social behaviour can develop. The baby can recognise the main caregiver's voice quite early on, for example. Evolution theory holds that humans have developed in the way they have because the fittest of the species survive. It seems that aspects of a baby's abilities such as voice recognition, face recognition, the ability to smile, and a preference for turn taking have developed because they aid survival. Babies that can attach to their main caregivers would have been more likely to survive, and so those genes would have survived too. So the characteristics that enable a baby to develop as a social being – characteristics that aid interaction with others – seem to suggest that humans are innately social and that social development is an important part of a child's development.

Developing socially through attachment and other survival traits

Chapter 3 developed the idea that babies are social beings and looked at attachment, separation anxiety, stranger fear, the effects of deprivation and what happens if a baby is privated (which means that care is non-existent). Aspects of development such as monotropy (having one main caregiver), and multiple attachments (when the baby attaches to many individuals such as mother, father and relatives) were examined and helped to show how important social development is for the child.

Developing social competence – living in a social world

Robert Selman studied how children develop social competence as a way of promoting their social relationships. Social awareness can be developed through group work and interacting with peers and others. He thought that disagreements must be dealt with in an open way and there should be co-operative learning activities and a focus on social and ethical issues. These ideas follow on from Vygotsky's views that children learn well by interacting with others and through peer tutoring, for example. Vygotsky's views were discussed in Chapter 5. Social competence can be linked to emotional intelligence, which is outlined in more detail below. Selman felt that those with good social competence would do better in a social world – and that social competence had to be practised. It is not something that we learn and then retain for ever, which is an important point. Social competence helps children to interact in a social world, and gives children moral rules and reasoning, which helps to build a successful society.

Approaches to psychology that take social factors into account

Chapter 1 outlined some approaches to psychology, one of which is the social approach. Most of what is presented in this chapter falls within the social approach, though two other approaches are also considered – the humanistic approach and one theorist within the psychodynamic approach. It would be worth turning back to Chapter 1 and briefly reviewing Table 1.1, which outlines the main approaches in psychology. Focus in particular upon the humanistic approach, the psychodynamic approach and the social approach. Briefly review the social constructionist approach, which goes as far as to say that we cannot study ourselves at all without considering social influences upon us, as there is no such thing as a person or personality unaffected by cultural and social influences. These sorts of issues are dealt with in this chapter.

The humanistic approach

The humanistic approach is useful in this section as it emphasises how individuals develop their personalities and their sense of self through interacting within a social and cultural setting. The main focus is on the individual, not on society, but it is clear from this approach that individuals who keep a distance from others will perhaps find it hard to achieve their goals and fulfilment. For example, one aspect of the humanistic approach suggests that to fulfil one's potential it is necessary to have a sense of belonging and to have recognition from others. This approach is outlined here and it was also outlined in Chapter 1, so you may already be familiar with the basic claims of the approach.

The humanistic approach only really started around 40 or 50 years ago. This may seem a long time but in comparison with other approaches it makes the humanistic approach a relatively modern one. The approach turned away from the psychodynamic approach partly because it was felt that psychodynamic theorists viewed people as having something wrong with them because of their experiences – for example, people can become fixated at a certain stage and, therefore, be held back. Those within the humanistic approach also felt that behaviourists treated people as unthinking and programmable – it is suggested that if rewards are offered we do something and if punishment is given we stop. The humanistic approach sees human beings as basically good and free. Healthy humans are free to choose what they do and what they become – it does not rest only on their social interactions or on how well they attach with their main caregivers. This is not to say that social interactions do not affect us but that we have power to do something about them and we can choose what happens. Those within the humanistic approach think that each individual's goal is to **self-actualise**. The term self-actualisation refers to what humans seek more than food, sex and safety – they want to grow and develop their potential and if they achieve this development then they are said to have self-actualised.

> ### DEFINITION
>
> **Self-actualisation** – the term used by humanistic psychologists to indicate when people have achieved their personal goals and have developed their potential.

Maslow's hierarchy of needs

One well-known person within the humanistic approach is Abraham Maslow (1908–70) and his theory is used in many fields from business studies to psychology. Maslow thought that other approaches focused too much on how individuals fulfil basic needs such as hunger, thirst, sex and the need to escape from pain, and that it was more productive to focus on something more positive, as people seek things for their own sake as well as to satisfy needs. Maslow thought that needs included social needs, such as a person hungering for more acceptance at work, and he did not just focus on physiological needs such as hunger. Maslow (1968) thought that humans were different from animals just because they not only had the same needs but also took pleasure in positive and enriching experiences such as enjoying music. These sorts of experiences, and enjoying problem solving such as doing crosswords, are what make us human. From these ideas Maslow developed a hierarchy of needs. By this he meant that he accepted that humans had basic physiological needs (such as hunger and thirst), and social needs (such as the need for esteem and to belong). However, he also wanted focus on self-actualisation needs. He suggested that there is a hierarchy of these needs with basic physiological needs at the bottom, social needs in the middle and self-actualisation needs at the top. He illustrated his theory by means of a triangle, to show that self-actualisation needs were at the peak, and basic physiological needs at the base of the triangle (this is what he meant by 'hierarchy').

TRY THIS!

Maslow's hierarchy shows that an individual's need for esteem and belongingness has to be met before optimum cognitive development can be achieved. In other chapters in this book you have read about the link between emotional and social development and learning. The Curriculum Guidance for the Foundation Stage and Birth to Three Matters both emphasise the importance of social and emotional development. Look at both documents and identify the sections that relate to promoting social and emotional development in early years settings.

DEFINITIONS

Self-concept – according to Rogers, the self-concept involves both the 'I', which takes decisions and acts, and the 'me', which is liked, disliked or thought about in some way.

Self-worth – according to Rogers this refers to the idea that to be mentally healthy an adult's self-concept must include a view of 'me' that is positive and liked. To develop a sense of self-worth, the individual must be given unconditional positive regard.

Unconditional positive regard – a term used by Rogers to show how a positive sense of self-worth can be developed – by being accepted and loved without condition or reservation by those around.

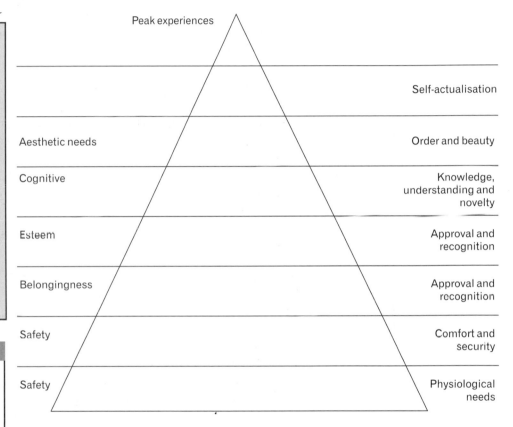

Maslow's hierarchy of needs

Maslow thought that we only work towards the higher order needs such as self-esteem or fulfilment when we have met our lower order needs. This means that someone who is hungry or cold (their physiological needs are not met) or afraid (their safety needs are not met) will not be able to self-actualise. There are exceptions – for example, some artists do starve – but in general Maslow thought that humans need to satisfy their lower order needs first.

Carl Rogers' views – esteem, belonging and self worth

Another very important theorist within the humanistic approach is Carl Rogers (1902–87). Rogers thought that a very important idea in self-actualisation is **self-concept**. The self-concept develops in early childhood and includes the idea of oneself as the 'I' that takes actions and makes decisions. Within the self-concept, according to Rogers, there is also the 'me' that is seen and thought about, liked or disliked. So 'I' take the decisions and also have a view of 'me' and both 'I' and 'me' are parts of my self-concept. Rogers felt that for an individual to be mentally healthy they need a solid sense of personal **self-worth** (which means having a positive self-concept, and liking the 'me'). To achieve self-worth, the child must be treated with unconditional positive regard. **Unconditional positive regard** means unconditionally loving without reservation, no matter what, and without conditions. From the humanistic point of view a child must be brought up with unconditional positive regard but this is not easy to do. It is not that the child cannot be criticised or corrected, as that is necessary on occasion. It is just that when a child is shown what is not acceptable, it is done in such a way as to show that the child is still loved, even though the child's behaviour at that time is not loved. Rogers thought people often do set conditions for their love (for example, if parents love a child when they are good, but only if they are good and do as they are told) and that when this happens children are likely to suppress some part of themselves in order to be loved. This suppression might make them doubt their self-worth.

Problems with the humanistic view

When looking at well-known figures that could be said to have self-actualised Maslow tended to point to Abraham Lincoln or Albert Einstein. One criticism here is that other influential figures like Hitler or Al Capone might also be said to have self-actualised but are not included because they are not considered 'good'. This is hard to follow through given the humanistic approach. Although it is thought that human nature is naturally good, so it is acceptable to give unconditional positive regard and still have a socialised and sensible kind human being, this may not be the case. This brings into question the idea of bringing a child up with unconditional positive regard, although the basic idea of loving others unconditionally to help them to develop a strong sense of self-worth seems in general a worthy idea.

Conclusions about the humanistic view

The humanistic view came about to challenge the ideas of both the behaviourists and those within the psychodynamic approach who took the view that humans have to overcome crises in order to develop successfully or are just shaped by their environment with no free will. Modern counselling techniques have arisen within the humanistic approach and the idea of listening using unconditional positive regard and allowing individuals to develop their own ideas of self-worth is a useful idea and one that appears to work. However, parenting using only those ideas might be difficult given that there are social rules that a child (and adult) must obey and also children need to be guided for other reasons, such as for their own and others' safety. The basic ideas of using unconditional positive regard are fairly similar to Erikson's ideas (outlined below) that children must be loved enough early on to develop basic trust, and must be given the freedom to act independently so that they can develop autonomy. The general idea of loving and encouraging a child being more useful than correcting them or punishing them seems to hold true for many different approaches, including Erikson's and the behaviourists. Erikson's ideas are outlined in the next section.

Erikson's psychosocial theory

The main psychodynamic theorist you will have come across so far in this book is Freud, and his views were outlined in reasonable detail in Chapter 7 when moral and gender development were considered. The psychodynamic approach represents Freud's ideas, the main ones being his three aspects of the personality (id, ego and superego) and his five psychosexual stages (oral, anal, phallic, latent and genital). Another psychodynamic theorist you have looked at is Bowlby, who focused more on parent–child interactions and how loss and separation from an attachment figure can affect development, leading to possible depression or even affectionless psychopathy. Psychodynamic theory has a general theme of some innate need, some social influences and individuals balancing their needs and their experiences and developing accordingly. Therefore, poor social experiences can lead to problems in personality development. Erikson is another psychodynamic theorist, who focuses quite clearly on social experiences and how they affect personality development.

TRY THIS!

Observe some interactions between adults and children in your setting and note down examples of where unconditional positive regard is given. It is hard to find examples where positive reinforcement is unconditional? You might find that it is – usually we give conditional praise and rewards. Think about how someone could give a child unconditional positive regard. Do you think this would be successful?

Erikson (1902–94) moved away from the emphasis Freud placed on psychosexual development and focused on psychosocial development. He emphasised social and cultural factors more than Freud did, and expanded on these influences, regarding them as being not just parents but everyone with whom the child came into contact. Freud thought that if there were problems at a stage then this would lead to fixations, whereas Erikson thought that people could, at any time, overcome setbacks that had occurred in their stages of development. This is a more positive view. Finally, Erikson thought that the whole of people's lifespan is important in their development, whereas Freud gave great importance to the first five or six years of a person's life. For these reasons many people find Erikson's ideas useful and interesting. Erikson considered that we continue to develop throughout our lives and that we can put right things that have gone wrong. This is reassuring perhaps.

Erikson's eight stages

Erikson suggested that we develop through eight stages, and these eight stages are outlined in Table 9.1.

Table 9.1 Erikson's eight stages of psychosocial development

Approximate time	Stage	Explanation	Freud's stage
Infancy	Basic trust **v** mistrust	The child develops basic trust if parents maintain a supportive, nurturing and loving environment	Oral
1-3 years	Autonomy **v** shame or doubt	Children develop a healthy attitude towards becoming independent and self sufficient, as they develop bowel and bladder control. If they are made to feel independence is wrong, they may develop shame and self-doubt instead of autonomy	Anal
3 5 years	Initiative **v** guilt	If children can discover ways to initiate actions themselves, and such attempts are acceptable, then they avoid feeling guilt	Phallic
5 to 12 years	Industry **v** inferiority	Children need to feel competent especially with peers or they can develop feelings of inferiority	Latency
Adolescence	Identity **v** role confusion	A sense of role identity is needed, especially in terms of future career and vocation	Genital
Early adult	Intimacy **v** isolation	There is need for close friendships and adult sexual relationships to form so that development is healthy	
Middle adulthood	Generativity **v** stagnation	For adults to develop a useful life they must help and guide children and those without children must be involved in helping children in some way. They must be contributing to the next generation.	
Late adulthood	Ego integrity **v** despair	The adult reviews their life and a life well spent results in a sense of wellbeing and integrity	

DEFINITION

Autonomy – where individuals have control and power over their own actions and are not acting on the orders of someone else or as somebody else's agent.

Each of the eight stages involves a conflict that must be resolved and successful resolution leads to successful development. At each stage there is a clear role for others and for social interactions. In the first stage the child must develop a sense of trust, for example, and for this to happen parents must build a healthy relationship with the child. Then **autonomy** develops, where children take responsibility for their actions. As children gain trust and autonomy, at around the age of

5 years, they can start to initiate their own activities. They need to be able to do this without fear of criticism. Of course parents will need to curb some of their activities but this should be done in a way that does not make them feel guilty – for instance, guide them gently, rather than shout at them. As long as children are not left feeling that everything they initiate is wrong, they can be guided appropriately. It is also important that the child is not made to feel **inferior**, for example, when compared with their peers – they must develop their activities and have at least some measure of success. They don't have to win at everything, of course. Adolescents who have a **basic trust** in their family can be autonomous, can initiate activities and do not have a strong sense of inferiority and will then be ready to discover their own **identity**. The next stage, in early adulthood, is for **intimacy** to be experienced rather than isolation. This is not only intimacy between lovers but also social intimacy and the development of close bonds with family, friends and colleagues too. In middle adulthood there is a need for **generativity**, which means that the individual's love and concerns must be focused not only on their own family and friends but also on future generations and society in general. They must be giving something to society in some way in order not to stagnate. If all the stages are successful the older adult will be able to look back on their life with a sense of accomplishment. If not, then they are likely to feel a sense of **despair**. Remember, that Erikson believed that early stages could be worked through at a later point if necessary, so that at least gives some hope to those who already feel they are heading for despair!

There is not much evidence for Erikson's ideas

It may seem that, in Erikson's stages, you either achieve what is needed (for example, basic trust) or you do not but this is not really the case. Most individuals in each stage are likely to be somewhere in between. For example, adolescents are likely to be somewhere towards gaining their own identity but still have some role confusion. So some level of despair when reaching older adulthood is healthy really – Erikson would not expect everyone to resolve their conflicts at each stage perfectly. There are bound to be things about someone's life or about the human condition that they would like to change. It is hard to find evidence for Erikson's claims, but they have been found useful by many therapists and individuals. Some of the principles make a great deal of sense. For example, if babies develop mistrust because they do not have strong, stable relationships with their parents, then this is likely to cause later problems. Bowlby did offer some evidence about this, suggesting that poor early relationships mean that a person does not have a good model for successful later relationships. Erikson's views do fit in well with what you have learnt so far about child development, even if there is not a great deal of evidence to support his claims about the eight stages.

EMOTIONAL DEVELOPMENT

Emotional development and social development are hard to separate. One feeds the other. Babies use emotional cues, for example, to interpret what is required of them in a social setting. There might be an innate tendency to recognise emotions. Studies have shown that people are able to recognise particular emotions on faces and that this ability exists across cultures, so it seems to be an instinct and not learnt.

THINK ABOUT IT

Think about your own development. Do you think you have achieved what is required for normal development in each of the relevant stages? Relate Erikson's ideas to your own background and if appropriate consider ways of achieving any aspect of development that you think you need to focus on.

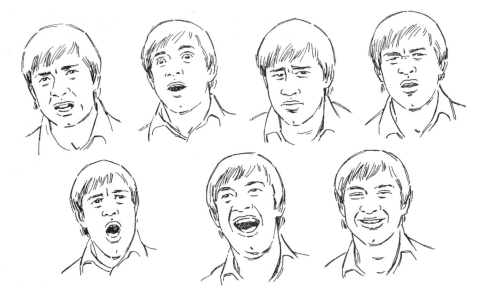

Pictures of facial emotions that we seem able to interpret without needing more information

It has been claimed that there are milestones in social emotional development and that these have the same sequence for each child. Greenspan (1985) looked at a lot of the research and came up with a sequence of six stages that he thought children passed through when developing over the first four years of their lives. It is not that each child reaches the same stage at the same age but that the stages are always in the same sequence for each child, even if they reach certain stages at different ages. Table 9.2 outlines Greenspan's six stages of social emotional development.

Table 9.2 Greenspan's six stages of social emotional development

Stage	Explanation
Stage 1: Self-regulation and interest in the world (birth to 3 months)	An infant is born into a world of stimulation and the first job is to deal with the shock of that after being in the womb for nine months. There are lots of sensations to deal with and the infant must learn to become calm and to sleep regularly. Infants show an interest when they see or hear something new and they like to be touched and moved about.
Stage 2: falling in love (2 to 7 months)	Infants begin to take a special interest in the people around them. They attach to individuals, who then become particularly enjoyable and attractive, so Greenspan calls this 'falling in love'. The infant's emotions are expressive.
Stage 3: Development of intentional communication (3 to 10 months)	The infant starts to want to communicate and to be communicated with. Turn taking takes place when the infant shows emotions to an attachment figure and wants emotions in response. The infant is likely to make sounds in response to a caregiver's sounds, for example, and they try to make the caregiver smile.
Stage 4: emergence of an organised sense of self (9 to 18 months)	Emotional interactions start to become more complex. The infant might no longer just cry when thirsty, to get the mother's attention, but now might lead the mother to a glass, for example. Children may indicate that they want to be picked up. Communication is more complex in this way, and a child might learn more about emotions, such as how to make people happy, and how to make them angry.

Stage	Explanation
Stage 5: creation of emotional ideas (18 to 36 months)	Children will have developed object permanence and can use their imagination and know that objects exist without having to be there. So they might become emotional because of imagined events (such as crying because they 'see' a monster). The child can pretend play and act out emotional thoughts. They learn that emotions can be used in communication, in a more complex way than just making their mother smile. They know that crying makes an adult pick them up (emotions motivate others) and that they enjoy something and stop crying (emotions go with particular situations).
Stage 6: emotional thinking – the basis for fantasy, reality and self-esteem (30 to 48 months)	Children learn through their own experiences about their own emotions and the emotions of others. They know which facial expressions go with which emotions. They learn to control their emotions too, and learn what is socially appropriate in the company of peers and adults. This can build their self-esteem.

Is all emotional understanding present at birth or does it develop?

Some researchers think that all emotions are present at birth, whereas some suggest that emotions develop as the infant develops. It does seem that babies can discriminate their mothers' different emotional states at only 10 weeks old, which does suggest that emotions and the ability to perceive emotions is an inbuilt ability but it is hard to get evidence for this. Infants do seem to develop the ability to use and understand emotions, as Greenspan suggests, but it is not clear whether this is because they can do this from birth (discrete emotions theory) but cannot demonstrate the ability, or whether they actually develop the ability (gradual development theory). Current research aims to look at physiological changes that happen during emotions to see whether they occur in infants (Fox, 1994). Physiological changes would include not only observable behaviour such as smiling and crying but biological changes such as heart and breathing rate. As with many aspects of child psychology we need to know more about this area.

Emotional intelligence

One area that has become very popular is the idea of **emotional intelligence**. It has captured people's imagination. For example, in the business field the idea of needing emotional intelligence – for example to be happy at work – has led to many publications on the subject and many training ideas. Theoretical research into emotional intelligence has not kept pace with its popularity, which means that claims are often not well researched. What is outlined here is a summary of the research situation, as well as an account of what emotional intelligence is and how the concept can be applied in childcare situations.

What is emotional intelligence?

The term 'emotional intelligence' was first coined in 1990, which makes it a very modern concept by psychology standards. However, the idea was around as early as 1920 when Thorndike talked about social intelligence. Also in 1983 Gardner discussed intrapersonal (between people) and interpersonal (within the same person) intelligences, and suggested that one form of 'intelligence' is being able to interact with others. So the idea of social intelligence – which refers to the ability to be social and to live in a social world with others – is not particularly new. John Mayer and Peter Salovey gave the first definition of what is called 'emotional intelligence' in 1990 and others built on the idea. One of the most well-known names in

> ### DEFINITIONS
>
> **Emotional intelligence** – a term that is hard to define but examples hopefully help. Someone with emotional intelligence would be good at managing their own stress, good at relationships with others, able to talk about their emotions, confident and successful. Someone with low emotional intelligence would find these sorts of interactions and strategies difficult.

TRY THIS!

Read through the list of what makes someone emotionally intelligent and then think about different people you know. Choose someone you consider successful and someone you think of as less successful in some way. Does the one you think of as successful have 'more' EI? Do you think you are 'emotionally intelligent'? Can you think of some children you work with who seem to have 'more' EI than others? Are they in some way more successful? Answering these questions will help you to see the points that are being made.

the field now is Goleman, who has written extensively about emotional intelligence (for example, Goleman 1995). There are different models of emotional intelligence (EI), which makes it difficult to summarise what it is, but they seem to have very similar components, and Table 9.3 lists some main ideas within the concept of EI. This should help to show what it is.

Table 9.3   Some main components of emotional intelligence, according to different models

Aspect of emotional intelligence	Explanation
Adaptability	Being willing to adapt to new conditions
Social competence	Excellent social skills and skills at mixing
Optimism	Looking on the bright side of life
Low impulsiveness	Unlikely to give in to urges
Self-esteem	Successful and confident
Self-motivation	Not likely to give up when things get tough
Emotional expression	Able to talk about their emotions with others
Assertiveness	Can stand up for their rights and what they believe in
Relationship skills	Able to have good personal relationships
Stress management	Able to avoid becoming stressed when pressured

People with EI would be good at managing their own stress, good at relationships with others, able to talk about their emotions, confident and successful. Someone with low EI would find these sorts of interactions and strategies difficult.

Research into EI

Research into EI has tended to use either self-report measures, where people make judgements about their own abilities and interests, or measures of a person's characteristics using tests. One problem is that saying what we are like ourselves (self-reporting) is not a very good measure. Using tests is a better measure but can be restrictive and might only uncover data within the areas tested, not outside them. An example of a self-report measure might be asking someone how good they are at social relationships, perhaps rating themselves on a scale. An example of a test is measuring more precisely, for example, how good individuals are at interpreting someone else's facial expression. If you measure EI using self-report techniques, then you are measuring what someone's personality is like – for example, how do they feel about themselves? If you measure EI using tests, then you are measuring cognitive ability – for example, how good someone is at judging another's emotional state. So for some EI is a personality trait and for some it is a cognitive ability. Consider how Freud and Erikson tend to look at how individuals develop their personalities, whereas Piaget looked at them developing their cognitive ability. These theorists take a very different approach and the approach to studying EI would also be different depending on what people think it is. The main point here is that although something like emotional intelligence can be discussed and studied as if it is 'something' there is no real agreement about what it is and so any evidence needs to be carefully evaluated. In Chapter 6 an argument is presented that 'intelligence' is not really a 'thing' and the same goes for EI. It seems as if it should be simple to consider something like EI (for example, relating well to others, having a strong sense of self-worth, and being clear about one's own feelings) but it is not an easy thing to measure, test or prove.

Emotional ability not necessarily intelligence

It is probably easier to think of EI as referring to emotional ability than referring to a kind of intelligence. Using the term 'intelligence' is not useful really. It implies that we are born with good or bad EI, and that if we do not have EI then we are not as 'good' as those with EI. None of this is helpful. when considering a child's development. The main aim of those working within the childcare field is to find out whether children can learn or be encouraged to develop EI and how this is important in the child's development. It is possible that the term 'intelligence' was used because it was thought that EI was a cognitive ability rather than a personality trait.

Emotional intelligence and educational progress

Some research has been done in schools with a view to linking EI to academic success although, as was mentioned above, not as much academic research has been carried out as might be supposed given the popularity of the concept. One problem is that measures of EI have not yet been found to be good measures. There are not really generally accepted tests. However, some research has been carried out and some findings suggest that those with low EI do not do as well in their school work, and this might be true in particular of vulnerable or disadvantaged children. Reiff and others (2001) found that college students with learning disabilities had lower EI scores than those without disabilities (reported in an article by Petrides *et al.*, 2004). Petrides *et al.* (2004) also found that those with low EI scores were more likely to truant and more likely to have been excluded from school for anti-social behaviour. Of course, this does not mean that having low EI causes the problems – just that the problems and low EI go together in some way.

Is it possible to improve EI in young children?

The question for those working in childcare services is whether EI can be improved. If EI is a characteristic (or group of characteristics) that is innate, then nothing can be done to improve it. If, however, it can be learnt, and if it improves or predicts academic performance, then it is useful to research this area and to find out how EI can be improved in children. There is not much research to show that EI can be improved – even though it is popularly thought that it can. Slaski and Cartwright (2003) think that EI can be improved although how this might be done or whether the effects last over time is not certain. Their study also involved business managers, not children. The development programme used by Slaski and Cartwright involved using short lectures, discussions, role playing and keeping a diary about emotions (based on Cherniss and Adler, 2000). These techniques are clearly not very useful for very young children, although they could be built upon. There is currently some interesting and thorough academic research being carried out in this area.

Is EI innate or learnt?

So far within this section on EI general views have been given about what EI is thought to be, how it can be tested, and what research there is to base the claims upon. It is thought that EI is about self-concept and ability to relate to others. There is a question about whether it is something we are born with – so we either have high EI or low EI, and cannot change it – or whether it is something we can develop with help. In general it is thought that we can develop it – but that is possibly because it is good business to think that, and it is a more positive way of looking at it. It is good business because training packages can be developed (and have been developed) and it is more positive because then we can all be seen as equal, and equally able to achieve. However, there is evidence to suggest that at least some part of EI is innate. Probably, as with other characteristics that have been mentioned in this book, there is an element of inheritance in EI and an element of learning. Goleman has written extensively about EI and has explained that we have an 'emotions' centre in our brain. This is the innate part of EI.

Goleman's views on EI

Goleman's views have been very influential in this field. He suggests that EI includes self-control, zeal and persistence, as well as the ability to motivate oneself.

Goleman did think that the skills involved in having EI could be taught. For example, he thought that impulses can be controlled by will and character and that it is important to encourage self-restraint and compassion. Emotional intelligence is a basic flair for living, according to Goleman. Temperament was discussed in Chapter 2 and is thought to be something we are born with. For example, some babies seem inherently 'difficult' and others are more placid. Goleman thought that EI is linked to temperament and we are born with it but he also thought that temperament (and also EI) can be affected by learning. He suggests that we focus on self-awareness, self-control, empathy, listening, resolving conflict and co-operation, and that these things can be encouraged in children and so learnt.

The innate part of EI is that it rests on the idea of our inborn emotional reactions. There is a part of the brain that controls our emotions – part of the brain stem. The site of this part of the brain strongly suggests that it was there before the reasoning or rational part of the brain developed. The limbic system sits at the top of the spinal column and is a ring around the brain stem. The hippocampus, which is very important in memory, and the amygdala, which is very important in emotions, are situated near the limbic ring. It is around these areas that the cortex and areas for higher order thinking are found. It is thought that there was an emotional brain before a rational one, which suggests that we should pay attention to our emotions because they guide us as well as our reasoning. It appears that the limbic system can in some intense moments completely take over our responses, and that the reasoning part of our brain does not have the chance to 'interrupt' – this emphasises again the importance of emotions in our development, lives and judgements.

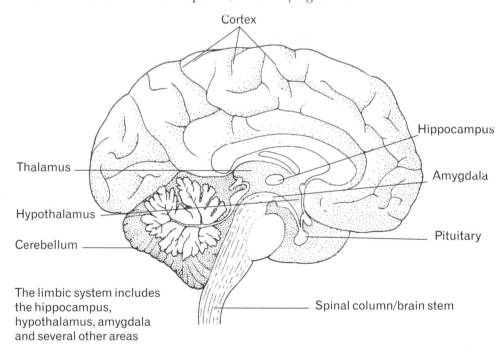

Basic diagram of the brain

It has become fashionable to attend to our emotions – and this is probably a good thing. It is sometimes suggested that we have three parts to our attitudes and decision-making processes. One part is behavioural (what we do), one is cognitive (what we think), and one is emotional (what we feel). The behaviourists focused on what we do and the other approaches tended to focus on what we think. The psychodynamic and humanistic approaches focused more on what we feel but not by looking much at actual emotions. So perhaps the idea of emotional intelligence has gained so much popularity so quickly because there was a need for emotional development to be considered.

SOCIAL INFLUENCES

From the start we have other people around us. They influence us, just as we are influencing them. This is the point of the social constructionist view. We cannot see ourselves or other people as separate from our social and cultural background. From the start infants are brought up in a social setting, to obey social rules and to fit in with others around them – they are **socialised**.

Identity

Our 'identity' is an important part of who we are. There are different ways of looking at this. There are many different theories looking at the idea of 'self'. Some ideas about what 'self-concept' is and what 'self-worth' means have already been given in this chapter. Theorists use different terms but the basic ideas are the same – that what we think about ourselves is very important and that self-esteem is an important part of being a healthy individual. This applies to children as well as to adults. Our identity is also affected by other factors such as our age, class, race, gender, culture and whether we experience prejudice and labelling. Some research into these areas is outlined below. All these areas have been researched extensively, not only within psychology but within sociology too and only a brief outline of the issues is presented here.

Self-recognition

One aspect of identity that has been investigated is how we recognize ourselves. This is an area of interest because it has been found that only humans from between 18 and 24 months old and apes (chimpanzees, orang-utans and some gorillas) recognize themselves in a mirror. This is called self- awareness and it is thought that this marks an important difference between humans and apes on one hand and other species. It is said that to know that our own face is our own requires a knowledge of self. It is thought that some disorders, including schizophrenia and autism, might include a difficulty with self-awareness so knowledge of it might be used to help in such disorders. Autism is discussed in Chapter 10. Recent research has suggested that if one half of the brain is turned off by anaesthetising it then self-recognition can be turned off. Self-awareness seems to be a process of the right hemisphere (right half) of the brain – the right frontal cortex. Human infants quite quickly develop self-awareness. The usual procedure is to put a blob of rouge on the face of a human child or ape and to let them look at themselves in a mirror. If they touch the rouge as if they know it is on their own face and should not be there, then it is thought that this means that they know their own face and they recognize themselves.

The humanistic view about identity and self-worth

The humanistic view is that individuals have to aim to self-actualise and their identity can depend on how far they achieve this. Rogers talks about self-worth and the self-concept, and these are outlined earlier in this chapter. Our identity depends on others, in that we have a greater feeling of self-worth if we are accepted by those around us and are free to self-actualise.

The psychodynamic view about identity and self-worth

For Freud, identity comes from balancing our innate desires (the id) with social demands and pressures (the superego), and the ego has the job of maintaining this balance. The superego includes an idea of our ego ideal, which is an image of the sort of person we think we should be, given to us by our parents and those we meet socially. If the ego maintains a balance then our self-concept should be good and anxieties kept to a minimum. Chapter 10 outlines how the psychodynamic view sees anxiety as being either neurotic (in that we feel we must repress our innate desires otherwise we might express those innate desires) or moral (in that we feel anxious because we think we might be punished for not doing what is right). Maintaining a balance between the demands of the id and the control of the

DEFINITIONS

Self-esteem – refers to whether we think we are worthwhile and achieving what we want to achieve. Self-esteem refers to feelings about oneself and evaluations about oneself. If these feelings and evaluations are positive, then we have high self-esteem and if they are negative then we don't think much of ourselves and have low self-esteem.

Social identity theory (SIT) – a theory that suggests we take our identity from the group we are part of, which is the 'in group'. Other groups become 'out groups' and if we become proud of our in group this enhances our self-esteem. Thus we take a social identity from in groups.

In group – part of social identity theory and refers to a group we are part of and identify with. This enhances our self-esteem.

Out group – part of social identity theory and refers to any group of which we are not part.

TRY THIS!

Observe people in one particular group and then watch how they behave towards those not in their group. Read about groups in a newspaper, for example, football teams, and find examples in which they favour their in group and are hostile in some way towards the out group (the other team). Note how they show their group identity – for example, in the clothes they wear.

TRY THIS!

Watch the children in your setting and see if you can pick out particular groups. Do the children show in group behaviour and exclude others whom they perceive as being in the out group?

superego should allay any anxieties and improve self-esteem. Our feelings about our identity would then be good ones.

Within both the humanistic and the psychodynamic approaches it can be seen that our identity depends on how others perceive us and how others treat us. Erikson also thought this – for example, he thought that we can develop independence if others allow us to test things out for ourselves. It is clear that we develop our identity in a social setting and that social influences affect our identity and what we think of ourselves.

Self-esteem and social identity theory

A term that is useful when considering how well we think about ourselves is 'self-esteem'. **Self-esteem** refers to whether we think we are worthwhile and achieving what we want to achieve. Self-esteem refers to feelings about oneself and evaluations about oneself. If these feelings and evaluations are positive, then we have high self-esteem, and if they are negative then we don't think much of ourselves and have low self-esteem. Social factors can affect our self-esteem and one factor that has been shown to have an effect is the group that we are in. **Social identity theory** (see, for example, Tajfel *et al.,* 1971) suggests that we take our identity from the groups we belong to – sometimes called our 'in groups'. The **in group** is the group you are part of and so all other groups become **out groups**. Social identity comes from the group. First, individuals categorise themselves as part of the group (for example, they put themselves in the category of 'childcare student'). Then they compare that group with other groups (for example, set themselves apart from other students). They then join in with a shared self-definition of the terms of the group (for example, the group defines what is important for being a member of that group, which can refer to clothing worn or ideas held). This process can help individuals to decide who they are, what they like, how they dress and what ideas to have.

Children develop in social groups and similar ideas can apply to them. You can watch different groups develop, with their own rules and attitudes. Individuals tend to see their own group members as being good and capable, and out group people as not being as useful. Thus people 'build up' their own group and in that way build their own self-esteem. Self-categorisation theory emphasises the importance not so much of the group itself in forming someone's identity but of individual group members categorising themselves as part of the group. By categorising ourselves as part of a group we take on the behaviours and ideas of the others within the group and this is what affects our self-concept and image of our own identity.

Race, age, class, gender, culture

People often seem to belong to groups because of their race, age, class, gender and culture. These issues seem to be important and affect a person's identity and their self-esteem. We have an idea of what we are like, which comes from our experiences whilst developing, and we use that idea to categorise ourselves into suitable groups. For example, our society is set up in such a way that we emphasise gender, as shown in Chapter 7. We also group people according to age and children will be used to that, so are likely to form groups according to age when appropriate. Race differences are often apparent too, and children are likely to pick up on that. Similarly, children are usually brought up within a specific culture, which can match to race but can also focus more on religion. Class differences may be less apparent to young children, so may not form the basis of group categorisation for them, although class differences may be more noticeable as the individual develops. Children can form groups based on other features too, such as language, although that is likely to go with race, class and culture. Forming groups using categories such as race, age, class, gender and culture means stereotyping is taking place, as outlined later in this chapter. Prejudice can also arise, together with discrimination and labelling. These issues are considered in the sections that follow.

Stereotyping

One important aspect of interacting with others, including with children, is stereotyping. Most people realise that we can stereotype with regard to gender – for example, treating boys as stronger and more independent than girls. These issues are mentioned in Chapter 7. But there are other areas that are less well known. For example, we might stereotype according to attractiveness or according to name, and these types of stereotyping may have just as strong an effect on the individual. The effect tends to arise through labelling and the self-fulfilling prophecy and these issues are outlined later in this section. Here some studies are outlined to give evidence for claims that children are stereotyped according to characteristics such as name and physical attractiveness.

Categorising

Stereotyping is really categorising and there could be a good reason for this. Often we don't have time to find out everything about people before we have to make a judgement about them, so we use stereotyping. This could have survival value. It is easy to imagine that you have to quickly make a judgement about someone and decide whether they pose a threat – your survival could depend on the accuracy of your judgement and using stereotyping could help. You might decide that a woman dressed in black, with a hood on and carrying a stick was not going to do you any good, so you might run – unless you were going to a fancy dress party, in which case you might smile and join her. **Stereotypes** are highly simplified images, usually about those in an out group, and often based on clearly visible differences between people(s).

A study to look at stereotypes

One study that shows cultural differences in stereotypes and helps to show the importance of stereotypes was carried out by Linssen and Hagendoorn in 1994. They sent a questionnaire to 277 school pupils aged from 16 to 18 years old. They surveyed pupils in England, Denmark, The Netherlands, Belgium, Germany and France. The aim was to see what was thought about the national characteristics of the different nationalities. Those completing the questionnaires had to note down what percentage of each national group they thought had each of 22 characteristics. The characteristics tended to describe someone who was dominant (proud, aggressive, assertive), efficient (scientific, rich, industrious), emotional (enjoying life, religious) and empathic (helpful and friendly). So each person noted down what percentage of each national group (English, French, German, Danish and so on) they thought had each characteristic (pride, aggression, helpfulness) and then the results were scored and added up to see what they thought of each nation. The findings showed that those in the southern part of Europe were seen as more emotional and less efficient than the more northern European nations. This suggests that we do have general ideas and stereotypes about other nationalities. These are likely to guide our thinking about those with that nationality.

Physical attractiveness

We can judge people according to their physical attractiveness. There have been studies that show that physically attractive children (well, those perceived to be attractive because, of course, what people see as attractive varies between people and between cultures) are more popular. Physically attractive people can be judged as less guilty by a jury too. An attractive person is less likely to be judged as having mental health problems (Dion, 1972) and is more likely to do well in a job interview (Dipboye *et al.*, 1977). Essays are marked higher if the marker sees pictures of the writers and judges them attractive. Attractive people are judged as more successful and happier too (Dion *et al.*, 1972). The point about these studies – and there are others – is that we judge people by features such as perceived attractiveness and our judgements can affect them. It is useful to be aware of this so that unfairness can be balanced perhaps, and less attractive people might then suffer less discrimination. Children seem to be judged by attractiveness too, and this is likely to affect their development. It might be that we find symmetrical features attractive and that this has survival value. Rhodes and Tremewan (1996) carried out a study where people rated average faces as more attractive than distinctive faces. 'Average' was decided by the face being regular and symmetrical rather than distinctive, which was when a face had striking features. Infants also seem to prefer average faces. It might be that an average face is the most 'face like' in having regular features and infants that survived were those that preferred 'face like' objects as this aided the likelihood of attachments being formed. See Chapter 2 for more on this argument. If we give preferential treatment to what we see as attractive people then this has quite important consequences for the individual (and for less attractive ones) as shown below when the idea of a self-fulfilling prophecy is explored.

Attractive names

Not only has physical attractiveness been shown to be preferred but some names are preferred over others. This can have quite important consequences for the individual, as the discussion below about the self-fulfilling prophecy shows. Some names are seen as more 'attractive' than other names, although this can vary over different time periods. Names have different 'meanings' to individuals. A study was done that showed that if an essay was written by 'David' it gained more marks than if it was written by 'Bertha'. Presumably markers think that people with some names are going to be academically more able than those with other names. Again this can have important consequences for the individual.

Maintain a balance of similarities and differences

Stereotyping involves categorising both others and ourselves. There is a tendency to see the similarities between people in any out group and the differences between ourselves and those in an in group. This is possibly because we know more about the characteristics of the in group so are more likely to see differences amongst those characteristics. With an out group we might see all the members as 'the same' as we know less about them and also are less interested in them and their differences. Stereotyping involves seeing mainly similarities in others in groups we are not part of and categorising accordingly. However, we also perceive ourselves as a bit different from others in an in group so, although our self-esteem is affected by being members of the group, we can also maintain differences from the group.

The fundamental attribution error

This is a bit like another aspect of our behaviour that is interesting so included briefly here. When we are making judgements about others (this is called making attributions) we use similar processes to those we use when stereotyping, focusing on differences within ourselves and groups we are part of and similarities in others, outside our groups. One aspect of making judgements about others is called making a fundamental attribution error. The term **'fundamental attribution error'** describes a tendency we have to say that others are responsible for their actions because of their personality, whereas where we are concerned we say the reasons for our behaviour are to do with the situation. For example, if someone is late for work because they missed the bus we tend to think of them as lazy, and we think they should have planned to be at the bus stop earlier. If we are late for work and miss the bus, then we tend to blame the bus for being early, or we blame the alarm clock for not being loud enough. When we think about the actions of other people we blame them (this is called dispositional attribution, because it involves blaming their disposition or personality). When we think about our own actions we blame the situation (this is called situational attribution) probably because we want to protect our self-concept, but also because we are more aware of the situation and the issues. Stereotyping can happen because we are not aware of the issues and we simply focus on what we see (which would be the character of the individuals and their visible characteristics, not individual differences or specific circumstances).

Guarding against making judgements unfairly

The above brief discussion about stereotyping and the fundamental attribution error should alert us to how we deal with others and to possibly unfairness in our judgements. We could be careful, for example, to find out more about a situation before making judgements, and we could find out more about out group members so that we make judgements about them based on real information rather than on vague categorisations because of their apparent group membership. Stereotyping is probably necessary in many situations, where we do not have enough information to do otherwise, however, it can be damaging in some situations, as further explored below.

Prejudice and discrimination

Prejudice involves stereotyping and pre-judging people. Prejudice can involve a cognitive (thinking) component, a behaving (action) component and a feeling (affective) component. **Prejudice** is usually taken to mean holding a negative attitude towards a person or a group, but in theory we could pre-judge someone in a positive way. For example, we might like a certain sort of person to work with, or think of others in that way based on some outward sign (such as their names), and so be prejudiced towards them. However, positive prejudice is not likely to be seen as very important in child psychology, and usually it is the negative aspects of prejudice that are considered, as they are likely to be damaging for the individual. **Discrimination** is the act of being prejudiced. If an employer is prejudiced against women, then a female applicant for a job is not likely to get the job – then she is discriminated against.

We do not always behave in accordance with our prejudiced views

You would think perhaps that if someone is prejudiced they would discriminate too – that is, they would behave according to their prejudices. This is not always the case. This means that we cannot necessarily predict our behaviour, or the behaviour of others, according to their views. A study by Lapiere as early as 1934 showed this. A young Chinese American couple travelled around America with Lapiere and visited 250 hotels and restaurants to see if they were served. They were only refused in one of the places (0.4%). However, when 128 of the places were contacted and asked if they would accept members of the Chinese race, 92% said they would not. So 92% said they would not serve someone with a Chinese background yet 99.6% served the couple in reality. It seemed from the telephone survey that there was a great deal of prejudice, yet from the visits there seemed to be very little. This shows the important of how data are collected and also strongly suggests that we might hold prejudiced views but might not act accordingly. It is probably something to do with being face-to-face with individuals that makes us act differently. Or it could be something to do with stereotyping an out group (in this case 'someone from the Chinese race') and looking at individuals when in the in group (in this case 'someone visiting your establishment'). There is a very large amount of research looking at prejudice and discrimination, and little room to expand here. For example, the Linssen and Hagendoorn (1994) study discussed above shows stereotyping of different nationalities, and prejudice against certain nationalities has been found.

Labelling

Labelling is the term used for stereotyping and categorising someone as being in a particular group and then attaching a shorthand label to denote that group and its characteristics. People can also be labelled because of their own characteristics – for example, if they are short, thin or tall. We categorise people, and when we categorise we give them a label. That label tends to have connotations, within certain cultures or subcultures at least, and those connotations become 'attached' to the individual. An example is useful. Within a city a certain area can be 'known' for deviant behaviour. If someone comes from that area, they can quite easily be labelled as 'deviant', without someone knowing anything else about them. It is more likely that the 'deviant' label would go with certain other characteristics besides area, such as age, gender and race. So if someone is from a certain ('bad') area, is young, male and black, then that person is likely to be labelled as 'bad'. Another area could be known as being 'posh'. If someone is known to come from that area they might be labelled as 'stuck up', in the same way. Labelling can lead to people adopting certain behaviours and the concept of the self-fulfilling prophecy has been used to explain the importance of labelling.

Self fulfilling prophecy

The **self-fulfilling prophecy** is another useful explanation for the way in which we treat others having made judgements about them. It is an important explanation as it underlines the impact of another's judgements and actions, and how they affect someone's self-concept and self-esteem – as well as affecting their actual behaviour and what they become.

Rosenthal and Jacobson's (1968) study

Rosenthal and Jacobson (1968) carried out an important study that helps to show what the self-fulfilling prophecy is. It looked at the effect of teachers' expectations on pupil performance. First, the researchers carried out an IQ test on some primary school aged children. Then they told the teachers that the test would reliably predict which children would 'bloom' in the near future. By 'bloom' they meant show rapid intellectual development. Twenty children were chosen randomly to be 'bloomers' – it is important to note that the IQ tests did not predict that these children would be any different to the others. So the teachers had children in the class who were 'non-bloomers' and children who were 'bloomers'. The question was whether those children would be treated any differently. Indeed, they were treated differently, and from the start. The 'non-bloomers' were rated as less curious, less interested and less happy – remember the 'bloomers' were randomly chosen so there should have been no consistent differences between the 'bloomers' and the 'non-bloomers'. It seemed that the teachers developed stereotypes of what they thought a 'bloomer' and a 'non-bloomer' would be like – for example, 'non-bloomers' were thought of as less interested in class. The researchers measured the IQ of the children at the end of the first year, and then again at the start and the end of the second year. In both measures the 'bloomers' had a greater IQ gain than the 'non-bloomers'. It has been concluded that the IQ differences came about because of the way the children were treated by the teachers. The teachers expected the 'non-bloomers' to act in certain ways, in some way looked for that behaviour, which they then saw, and so their expectations were confirmed. Not only that but the children must have been treated differently too because, somehow, the 'bloomers' did better in class. There was a self-fulfilling prophecy, in that the way the children were treated affected their behaviour and their 'destiny' was fulfilled – they became what was expected of them.

> ### CASE STUDY
>
> Linda is an early years practitioner in a nursery class attached to a nursery school. She is looking at the list of children to be admitted the following term. She exclaims 'Oh dear, we're in for trouble, we've two boys from the travellers' camp coming. You know what they will be like!' What stereotype do you think Linda holds about these children? How may it negatively affect the care she can give to the children and their families? If you were her colleague and overheard her how would you react?

The self-fulfilling prophecy suggests that we become what others expect us to become. This is quite a powerful claim as it means that if we expect others to do badly then they will become poor performers. As our expectations can come from categorising, labelling and stereotyping, then they are not really on firm

DEFINITION

Self-fulfilling prophecy – refers to the way we tend to act in accordance with the expectations of others and that these expectations can often rest on stereotypes. In this way we can fulfil expectations and become what others expect us to become. This can be a negative process – for example, if others expect us to be deviant.

foundations, and it means that people can become as 'bad' as others think they are. Jussim and Fleming (1996) carried out a review of studies looking into this area and concluded that there is evidence that we act in accordance with how others expect from their stereotypes. However, this might not be true of all stereotypes in that the evidence did suggest we act according to our gender stereotypes. However, there is not so much evidence regarding race and ethnicity and there seems to be little evidence that we act according to class stereotypes. It seems to be the case that we use stereotypes and act according to how others stereotype us more in group situations than when interacting with individuals. Probably regarding individuals we use our knowledge of them as people to guide us more than our stereotypes.

Personal space

Personal space is an area with both 'biological' and social aspects. This is because we seem to have an inbuilt instinct to desire there to be a distance between others and us and because this distance can both affect how we react to others and can affect how they react to us. Everyone has personal space – the distance they feel comfortable with between them and others. This 'distance' varies – for example, there can be gender differences in personal space preferences. We have a **body buffer zone**, which is a term for the area that we feel comfortable with, up to which people can approach, and beyond which we don't want them to go. Our body buffer zone will differ depending on the individual approaching. We feel very comfortable when those we are intimate with come very close but we feel very uncomfortable when those we hardly know come within even a metre of us.

Hall's (1966) zones of personal space

Hall (1966) did some work on this and suggested distances at which most people feel comfortable set against how much they know the person approaching. Table 9.4 outlines Hall's zone of personal space.

Table 9.4   Hall's four zones of personal space

Zone of personal space	Approximate distance	Description
Intimate distance	Up to 0.5 metres	People are comfortable being quite close to one another and there can be physical contact.
Personal distance	0.5 metres to 1.25 metres	This is an everyday distance, between family and friends. Touching is still possible.
Social distance	1.25 metres to 4 metres	This is a distance for casual interactions where people do not know one another very well, and also for business interactions. Furniture is usually arranged at this distance too.
Public distance	4 metres to 8 metres	This is the distance common for lecturers and public speakers. Courtrooms use this distance too. It is hard to read cues at this distance (for example, smell and touch).

Personal space can be used to open or close communication channels, as someone can move nearer to initiate a conversation and the other person can move further away to signal that they do not want to communicate. Personal space is linked to privacy too. We guard our personal space around our homes, for example, and even around our cars. It is possible that road rage occurs when one driver invades the personal space of another driver by driving too closely. When people invade our personal space then we seem to have an instinctive and strong negative reaction.

Children and personal space

Although it seems to be the case that we have an instinctive desire to maintain our privacy by having a personal space around us, which we do not want invaded, there seems to be an element of learning about personal space. It is thought that the idea is an instinct as everyone, in all cultures, seems to have a body buffer zone. However, children do seem to learn about space requirements according to Hall (1966). Girls seem to develop stable boundaries earlier than boys at first, but by the age of about 16 years there are no gender differences. It is interesting that those with schizophrenia and other mental health problems seem to have different personal space requirements on different occasions – their personal space varies, unlike most others who have fixed preferences. Those in prison with high aggressive responses have larger body buffer zones. There are cultural differences in personal space. It does seem to be the case that personal space preferences vary depending on behaviour patterns of the people around, although studies do not agree on this. It is useful to know the preferences of a particular group because if the personal space 'rules' are not known and people's space is inadvertently invaded, then this can cause offence.

FURTHER READING

Goleman, D. (1995) *Emotional Intelligence: Why It Can Matter More than IQ*, Bloomsbury, London.

DfEE (2000) *The Curriculum Guidance for the Foundation Stage*, QCA Publications Sudbury.
> This is the curriculum guidance used for children from 3 years to the end of reception class in schools. It has a good section on promoting personal, social and emotional development in early years settings.

Dowling, M. (2000) *Young Children's Personal, Social and Emotional Development*. Paul Chapman Publishing, London.
> This is a very practical book suitable for students and practitioners studying at Level 3 and above.

Goleman D. (1995) *Emotional Intelligence. Why it Can Matter More than IQ* Bloomsbury. London.
> This is an interesting read and recommended for students on Level 3 courses and above.

Manning-Morton, J. and Thorpe, M. (2003) *Key Times for Play*, Open University Press, Buckingham.
> This book is suitable for students studying at Level 3 and above. It gives very good practical suggestions for promoting social and emotional development in the under threes.

Roberts, R. (2002) *Self Esteem and Early Learning 2nd edition*, Paul Chapman Publishing, London.
> An easy read for students and practitioners studying at all levels.

Siraj-Blatchford, I. and Clarke, P. (2000) *Supporting Identity, Diversity and Language in the Early Years*. Open University Press, Buckingham.
> This book is full of practical suggestions for promoting social and emotional development within early years settings and is suitable for students studying at Level 3 and above.

Smith, P. and Hart, C. (Eds) (2002) *Handbook of Childhood Social Development*, Blackwell, London.
> This is an advanced book that is suitable for students studying at degree level and for tutors who wish to keep up to date.

Sure Start (2002) *Birth to Three Matters: A Framework to Support Children in their Earliest Years*, DfES Publications, Nottingham.
> This is the suggested curriculum framework for the under threes and gives suggestions for promoting social and emotional development. It is suitable for students on Level 3 courses and above.

http://www.surestart.gov.uk/surestartservices/health/socialandemotionaldev/
> This is a very useful website which gives information on promoting social and emotional development in children. It is suitable for students on all early years courses.

Abnormality in development

INTRODUCTION

This chapter will only consider some kinds of 'abnormality' in development. It will focus on autistic spectrum disorders (ASD), including autism and Asperger's syndrome, on Down's syndrome, profound visual impairment, and dyslexia. Other issues that are addressed include how to manage difficult behaviour, dealing with anxieties, barriers to language development, dysphasia, aphasia, aggression and effects of child abuse. Attention deficit hyperactivity disorder (ADHD) is also examined. For most of these disorders symptoms are considered, together with causes and treatments. The exact cause of many of these disorders is not clear, and because of this there may be a number of alternative approaches to treatment

As has been shown throughout this book, if we understand children's developmental processes we should be in a better position to help them to develop as positive, happy and thriving people. For example, if we know that young children find it difficult to understand another person's point of view we will not become angry with them for seeming selfish (Chapter 5). Similarly, if we understand that children copy adults' behaviour we will be less inclined to punish them in an aggressive way and will use positive behaviour techniques such as rewarding appropriate behaviour and ignoring inappropriate behaviour instead.

When children show abnormality in development in some way it may be even more important to understand that abnormality, so that they can be helped to achieve their potential. Looking at abnormal development can also help to shed light on 'normal' development. In this final chapter there is no real attempt to define what is 'normal' and what is 'abnormal' as that is not an easy task. What is 'normal' varies between cultures. For example, hearing voices in one culture may lead to a diagnosis of schizophrenia, whereas in another country it may be seen as having magical or mystical powers. 'Abnormality' in development, in this chapter, means having certain symptoms or disabilities not usually seen in children of a similar age. Only some of these are explored here.

There are many different ways of being 'abnormal'. Probably in the future certain characteristics that are now thought of as normal might be defined as abnormal. Similarly, in the past, children that might have been seen as 'abnormal' because of their behaviour may now be less likely to have problems because of scientific advancement. For example, a condition called 'phenylketonuria' (PKU) is a genetic disorder that can lead to mental retardation in the first year of life, although the infant is 'normal' at birth. It is now known that if these infants are given a special diet they will develop normally. So such an infant might have become 'abnormal' at one time, before certain scientific advances, but the child is now 'normal'. In the UK every child is tested for PKU at birth (although the incidence of PKU is quite rare – one case in every 14,000).

When considering any aspect of abnormal development it is important to have in mind explanations for normal development. It will also be important to remember the main theories or approaches that have been outlined throughout this textbook. Table 10.1 suggests how these approaches are linked to specific examples of abnormal development.

Table 10.1   Linking theories to understanding abnormal development

Example of abnormal development	Approach
Autism	a) Cognitive developmental approach – which suggests that normal development is in stages and ability to use mental operations increases. Perhaps that ability is limited in some children. b) Biological approach – which suggests that there might be some biological difference involved. c) Social approach – which looks at how a child with autism finds it hard (if not impossible) to develop normal relationships with others. d) Behavioural approach – which suggests ways of helping a child with autism, for example, in speech where shaping processes can be used.
Down's Syndrome	a) Biological approach – which explains how a genetic difference gives a child with Down's Syndrome specific characteristics.
Difficult behaviour	a) Behavioural approach – which is often used to improve difficult behaviour by rewarding desired behaviour and ignoring (or punishing) undesired behaviour. b) Social approach – which considers factors such as position of the child in the family (older children might have more confidence, for example) and issues such as self-esteem. c) Biological approach – which might suggest biological causes such as genes or nutrition, and might suggest biological 'cures' such as use of drugs.
Aggression (specifically)	a) Behavioural approach – which suggests that children learn aggression through modelling and imitation so suggests role models avoid being aggressive. This approach might also suggest ways of reducing aggressive behaviour through shaping, for example. b) Biological approach – which might consider biological bases for aggression such as inherited factors or dietary ones. This approach might also suggest drug treatments.
Visual impairment, dyslexia, dysphasia, aphasia, deafness	a) Biological approach – which tends to give some explanations for the types of behaviour and issues that will affect children with these developmental features.

AUTISM

Autism is an autistic spectrum disorder. The National Autistic Society gives a very good definition:

An autistic spectrum disorder is a complex developmental disability that affects the way a person communicates and relates to people around them. The term autistic spectrum is often used because the condition varies from person to person; some people may also have accompanying specific learning difficulties, while others are much more able with average or above average intelligence. Asperger syndrome is a condition at the more able end of the spectrum. At the 'less able' end of the spectrum is Kanner syndrome, sometimes referred to as 'classic autism'. Despite all of the wide ranging differences, everyone with the condition has difficulty with social interaction, social communication and imagination. (National Autistic Society, 2004)

Kanner (1943) defined autism as an inability to relate in an ordinary way to people and situations.

A 4 year old might seem not to hear other people even though the child might not be deaf. People could come into a room where the child was playing and would not be noticed or acknowledged. The child's attention would not be attracted by calling its name, and if a room was rearranged the child might react with a temper tantrum, because autistic children like order. The child would not start any conversations and might play, perhaps with one toy, with great intensity for much longer than would be expected, and using repetitive movements.

Babies with autism do not seem to need their mothers and are indifferent to being held. The baby would tend to be undemanding and unlikely to smile, babble or interact with others. At 6 months the child would not be affectionate and is likely either to under-react to situations (not be interested) or over-react (show a temper tantrum, for example). Sometimes babies appear to be developing normally and start to show autistic symptoms later.

Links to cognitive development

Autism has already been briefly mentioned in Chapter 5, which examined cognitive development, where theory of mind was outlined. It was claimed that autistic children do not have a theory of mind and that this is a fundamental difference between a child with autism and a child without autism. Such issues are examined in this section to see how that knowledge helps to understand both autism and normal development.

The incidence of autism is about 2 (0.0002%) or 3 (0.0003%) people per 10,000 of the population although it does seem to be increasing. There is often a problem in deciding whether there is really an increase in something because as more is known, more can be seen – just a greater recording of incidence. This can be the case with features such as autism and anorexia nervosa. When people (such as parents, and those in schools and nurseries) become familiar with symptoms and characteristics of such features of development, then it is more likely that a child will be diagnosed, and so it might seem that such a feature of development is increasing in incidence. Even so, it is generally thought that there is an increase in the number of children with autism.

The increase in the numbers of children with autism has been recognised by the government in its new strategy for Special Educational Needs 'Removing Barriers to Achievement' (2004) where the rise in the number of children with the condition was noted as placing growing demands upon schools.

It is suggested that the incidence of autism is three or four times higher in boys than in girls. It is estimated that one child in six has a disability of some sort, so the comparatively low rate of autism may make you wonder why so much emphasis seems to be placed on it as a disorder. This interest seems to be because the behaviour patterns of a child with autism are very distinctive and open to observation. It is interesting that, in China, one study (Kuo-tai, 1987) found only five cases from nearly 1200 cases of children with psychiatric disorders over 26 years, which is a low rate, and other studies have also found a low rate of autism in China compared with other countries. Japan, however, has a high rate of autism and one study found 0.16% (16 in 10 000, compared with two or three in 10 000 in Britain) (Tanoue *et al.*, 1988). So there seems to be a difference in rates of autism between different countries. This might be explained by saying that autism is at least partly caused by social and cultural factors (because they are different in the different countries) but it might be explained by differences in diagnosis and in detecting autism.

What is autism?

Wing in 1976 talked about a **triad of impairments** in autistic children. There are three areas of difficulty. These are difficulties with social behaviour, difficulties with communication, and difficulties with repetitive behaviour. Also most children with autism have learning difficulties and over half have an IQ of below 50 (see Chapter 6 for a discussion of intelligence and IQ – an IQ of 100 is the norm). Not all children with autism have learning difficulties, however, so it seems that autism is something separate from learning difficulties. Many researchers focus on more able children with autism, to separate the disorder from learning difficulties, in order to learn more about autism itself. There is no single explanation for autism, partly because although certain characteristics in a child are used to diagnose autism, the behaviour and abilities of each child with autism do differ and so it is not easy to find one single cause – if, indeed, there is one single cause.

Problems with diagnosis

The term 'autistic spectrum disorder' is used because there are so many different and seemingly unrelated symptoms in autism. With the knowledge we have at the moment, individuals with these types of symptom are put in one category. However, this does not allow us to assume that every one with an autistic spectrum disorder has the same cause for their illness. 'Autism', therefore, may be a term used for a number of different symptoms – main symptoms or features being loosely 'difficulty in social interactions' or 'compulsive behaviour'. It is important to be aware that having a word or label does not mean something exists. Consider 'intelligence' – there seem to be different kinds of 'intelligence' (see Chapter 6 for a discussion about this) and there may not be a 'thing' called intelligence.

There are very real difficulties in diagnosis and in investigating causes of autism because it has different symptoms and features and not all individuals with the condition show all of the symptoms.

Particular characteristics of autism

Social aloofness

Autism tends to be diagnosed around the age of 2 or 3 years although looking back (retrospectively) parents will often say they noticed differences in their child earlier than that (at around 9 to 12 months old) according to Baranek (1999). There is now a screening device available for detecting autism in infants (see, for example, Charman *et al.*, 2000). Early indicators include an infant not lifting their arms up to their parents, or not pointing to draw attention to something. Problems in interacting with others are referred to as **social aloofness**. Some children with autism do interact with others but their interactions are often seen as different in some way. They may, for example, not show real interest. Children with autism also seem to concentrate on one activity for a much longer time than usual, seeming not to notice anyone around them whilst they are preoccupied with one task. They may, for example, just rock backwards and forwards, or fiddle with a small object repeatedly. Many children with autism do not recognise familiar people (according to a study done by Bourcher *et al.* in 1998) and they do not respond appropriately to someone else's emotions (for example, when someone is upset they smile).

Communication problems

People with autism tend not to communicate meaningfully with others – and this includes verbal as well as non-verbal communication. Around half of those with autism do not manage useful speech at all. Faces often show no expression either. Children with autism find it hard to indicate what they want – even though they may cry or scream they do not show what it is they want – although some will guide a parent's hand to something they want. Remember there are many different features to autism and children show them in different ways. Usually, however, communication is impaired and is in some way 'different'. Children with autism who use language tend to have delayed speech. Indeed, delayed speech is often the

DEFINITION

Echolation – is the term used when a child with autism repeats a phrase over and over again, apparently without any understanding. Children with autism tend to use repetitive behaviour, and this is an example of that.

first sign that something is wrong. Children who do speak often find it hard to take turns in conversations (see Chapter 3 and Chapter 6 for a discussion of turn taking). Children with autism might only use speech in a repetitive way, copying some phrase they have heard and saying it over and over again apparently without any understanding. This is known as **echolation**. Even children with autism whose speech is quite good still do not seem to grasp that communication is a two-way process. They can talk non-stop about their own interests, for example. They tend to take everything literally and have problems with metaphor and irony according to Happé (1993).

For instance if you say that someone has laughed their socks off, a child with autism may think that the socks had really come off.

Repetitive behaviour

Echolalia is repetitive behaviour (repeating a heard phrase over and over) as is repeatedly twiddling with an object, or rocking. Children with autism tend to be fascinated by patterns and systematic arrangements and can become very upset if patterns they have built are disturbed. They rarely play spontaneously.

Savant skills – special abilities

DEFINITION

Islets of ability – sometimes called 'savant skills', refer to a special ability that around 10% of children with autism seem to have, such as an ability in art, music or mathematics.

Some children with autism show very special abilities – this is by no means true of all of them, however, even though this feature tends to be well known. Children with autism can be very good at visual/spatial tasks such as doing a jigsaw. Visual/spatial tasks are tasks that involve hand and eye co-ordination and judging elements of space and distance. Some children with autism are very gifted artistically or in some special way, such as showing musical ability, though they can still have a very low IQ. These skills are sometimes called **savant skills** or **islets of ability**. It is thought that around 10% of those with autism have such skills. They may have very good rote learning skills, for example.

A scene from Rainman, *a film that featured a person with autism who had unusual numerical abilities*

Causes of autism

We tend to look for one cause for one disorder even though the human body is complex and a particular behaviour, characteristic, feature or symptom may well have different causes. There are different theories put forward to explain autism and currently no single explanation is accepted. Perhaps it is not simply that the theories contradict one another and compete for the position of being 'the' correct

DEFINITIONS

Theory of mind – when older children understand that others' beliefs are different, they are said to have theory of mind. Younger children do not appear to have this.

explanation – they might all explain some part of what seems to be autism. Theories go in and out of fashion too. It used to be thought that parenting caused autism, and that the caregiver was cold and unloving, but this is now no longer thought to be the case. It also used to be thought that inappropriate reward and punishment caused autism. This theory too is now no longer thought to be the explanation. Blame is now no longer placed on parents and upbringing, and causes are thought to be to do with differences in development, possibly caused by biological differences that are as yet unknown.

In 1998 the *Lancet* medical journal published a report by Dr Andrew Wakefield and others from the Royal Free Hospital in London outlining a link between the MMR (measles, mumps and rubella) vaccination and the onset of autism. The press took this up and many parents have become fearful about having their children vaccinated. Some parents remain convinced that the immunisation is harmful. There now seems to be a rise in the number of children contracting measles.

Lack of theory of mind as an explanation of autism

One difficulty that children with autism seem to have is understanding that the beliefs that they have may not be the same as the beliefs of others (see, for example, Baron-Cohen *et al.*, 1985). When children understand that others do not share their beliefs, this is called a **theory of mind**. Chapter 5 describes theory of mind, as it is an important indicator of cognitive development.

Method to study theory of mind

There is a well known method used to test theory of mind, which is also outlined in Chapter 5. This method pretends that two dolls are 'people', one called 'Anne' and one called 'Sally'. Sally and Anne are in a 'room' and there is a basket, a box and a marble involved in the study. Sally hides the marble in the basket and then leaves the room. Sally is out of the room, and Anne takes the marble out of the basket and puts it into the box. Sally then returns. The child has watched all this. The child is then asked where Sally will look for the marble. Sally will have the false belief that the marble is in the basket, because Sally was out of the room when Anne moved the marble. The child knows that the marble is in the box, not the basket. Children of over 4 years old realise that Sally has the false belief and they will say that Sally will look (wrongly) in the basket. Most children with autism, and children under 4 years old, will say that Sally will look in the box. They will not understand that Sally has a belief that is different from their own belief.

Studies using various methods to test theory of mind – the understanding that others can have different beliefs – have strongly suggested that those with autism have difficulty with understanding minds. If people have a difficulty with understanding that someone else is thinking differently from themselves, then this could explain problems with social behaviour and problems with communication, both of which are features of autism. If a child with autism is not able to understand someone else's beliefs, thoughts and feelings, then they will find it hard to communicate with them and to interact with them. So it could be said that one explanation for autism is that children with autism have not developed cognitively as other children do – they have not developed theory of mind.

Weak central coherence as an added explanation to lack of theory of mind

There are a few issues to think about though. One issue is that not having theory of mind could be a feature of autism but might not help as an explanation as it is necessary to know why such children do not develop theory of mind. The second issue is that some children with autism do have theory of mind, especially children that develop good language skills – so not having theory of mind cannot be a complete explanation of autism. Children with autism who develop theory of mind do tend to develop it later than usual, but the ability still does develop. Third, the idea that children with autism do not have theory of mind is an insufficient explanation for autism as it does not explain the third main feature of autism according to Wing's triad (difficulties with communication, social behaviour and stereotyped behaviour). Stereotyped behaviour is not explained by a child not developing theory of mind. It is said that a child with autism has no theory of mind and also has difficulty drawing together information to construct an overall understanding. This would mean that a child with autism focuses on parts of information without easily putting parts together to make a complete understanding. This has been called **weak central coherence** (see, for example, Frith, 1989). This would mean that children with autism pay attention to parts of information, not to the whole, which can explain repetitive behaviour, and if their understanding is partial then they are perhaps more likely to engage in what we would see as meaningless repetitive behaviour.

An inability to stop inappropriate behaviour to obtain a desired response

Another feature of autism is that children with autism find it almost impossible to stop an inappropriate behaviour, even though this behaviour will not get them what they want. Children without autism quite quickly develop the ability to change a behaviour when they realise they need to in order to obtain a certain response. For example, if there are two boxes and one has chocolate and one does not, and children want the chocolate, they will point to the one with chocolate. If a task is devised where they only get the chocolate if they point to the empty box, they soon learn to do so. Children with autism still point to the box with the chocolate and do not learn to change their response and point to the empty box. This links to the idea of theory of mind. When asked where Sally will look for the marble in the test above, children with autism point to the box as they are pointing to where the marble is (in the box). They might be able to understand that Sally does not know the marble is in the box, but it might be that they cannot do other than to point to where they know the marble is. It is thought that children with autism cannot control their behaviour enough to change plan and work out that changing plan might achieve their goal. This is a type of fixed behaviour. This explanation can account for communication problems, difficulties with social behaviour, and the repetitive behaviour that is found in children with autism. The explanation might be that they have a difficulty in changing and controlling their responses – once a response is fixed, they do not have the necessary control to change it. One problem is that other children find it very hard to change fixed behaviours, as outlined above, yet they do not have autism. Pennington and Ozonoff (1996) suggest that children with damage to the frontal lobes demonstrate such behaviour. However, they do not have the other features of autism, so the explanation of lack of control does not seem to explain autism completely.

A biological explanation

Biological differences

It has been claimed that there is a biological impairment in children with autism, in that they are unable to engage in social interactions. This inability leads to lack of practice and so the later difficulty in developing theory of mind comes from lack of early social interaction and lack of opportunity to understand that other people have minds. Evidence for this is that children with profound visual impairment may not be able to interact with others much, and children where this occurs do develop behaviours that are similar to those in children with autism. Since these children's behaviour stems from their visual impairment (it is assumed) then this is evidence that biological impairment can cause such behaviour. A possibility is that there is a

DEFINITIONS

Weak central coherence – refers to the difficulty a child with autism has in putting together bits of information to make a whole understanding.

disorder in the central nervous system and some studies (such as Dawson *et al.*, 1983) suggest that there is reduced activity in the left hemisphere of the brain, which is the area for communication.

Genetic differences

Some researchers have considered whether there are genetic factors involved in autism, but it does not seem to be the case that autism runs in families. In any case the number of cases is low so there is not likely to be a high rate amongst relatives and it is hard to draw conclusions about a genetic cause. One study carried out by Folstein and Rutter in 1978 looked at 21 pairs of same-sex twins where one had autism. They looked at identical (MZ) and non-identical (DZ) twins (Chapter 2 explains more about identical and non-identical twins and genes). Monozygotic twins are identical and share their genetic make up whereas DZ twins are not identical, do not come from the same egg, and only share 50% of their genes as do other brothers and sisters. The study found that in 36% of the cases of autism in MZ twins both had autism whereas none of the DZ twins both had autism. This is fairly strong evidence for a genetic factor involved in autism. It was quite interesting that the 36% involved children with very clear diagnosis of autism. If the figures included children who did not 'strongly' have autism but who did have cognitive and language problems, then 82% of the MZ twins both had these difficulties (either autism or some problems) and 10% of the DZ twins also matched for these difficulties. Some researchers (such as Rubenstein *et al.*, 1990) suggest that there might be a type of autism that is inherited, and so there might be different forms of autism.

Disease factors

Another biological cause for autism could be that it comes after a disease. One suggestion is that children with congenital rubella (measles at birth) can be born with a number of abnormalities, and there might be a prenatal disease that leads to autism. Some researchers suggest that around 10% or more children with rubella have autism (see, for example, Chess, 1977) but these days it is not thought that disease is a cause for autism.

Conclusions about causes of autism

It is now generally thought that autism is a cognitive and social disorder with biological causes that occur between conception and birth, but more is not really known about these. Children with autism are born biologically different but environmental factors also affect how the disorder develops.

Treatments for autism

Children with autism who have some language ability seem to do better, as might be expected. However, only a few live independent lives. Intervention programmes can help to improve communication and social interactions. Treatments tend to follow from what is thought to be the cause. When it was thought that upbringing caused autism, then taking children away from parents and bringing them up differently was thought to help, but this is now longer the case. Some believe that medication can help although there is little evidence that stimulants, antidepressants or other medication has been of benefit (see, for example, Campbell, 1988). Around one-third of children with autism show high levels of blood serotonin so there were trials to see whether a medication that reduces serotonin would be of benefit. At first this was thought to be working but not all studies have found the same results. Treatments now tend to use behaviour modification techniques from the learning approaches. It might not be that the cause is problem reinforcements, but treatments to encourage certain behaviours by using reward techniques do seem to work to an extent.

TRY THIS!

Children with autism have a special educational need.

1 Find out who is the special educational needs co-ordinator (SENCO) in your early years setting. Ask the SENCO if there are any children with autism or suspected autism in your workplace.

2 Find out how the staff team would support an autistic child and his/her parents.

3 Read the fact sheet for professionals in education that can be found on the website for the National Autistic Society (NAS). (See further reading for details.)

TRY THIS!

Carry out research into the various approaches to helping children with autism. The NAS website is very helpful.

TRY THIS!

Look at the NAS website and find the information sheet 'A school's guide to Asperger syndrome'. Discuss this with the early years team with which you work. How much of this information can be applied in your setting?

ASPERGER'S SYNDROME

According to the National Autistic Society,

> Asperger syndrome is a form of autism, a condition that affects the way a person communicates and relates to others. A number of traits of autism are common to Asperger syndrome including difficulty in social relationships, difficulty in communicating, limitations in imagination and creative play.

Asperger's syndrome is generally considered a milder disorder than autism, although 'mild' does not mean unimportant or any less difficult for the individual. There are those with Asperger's syndrome who find it harder to cope with than others and it could be said that some have a milder version. As with many disorders, some have many of the symptoms strongly, whereas others have fewer symptoms, and not so strongly. Asperger's syndrome tends to be diagnosed when a child or adult has some features of autism but not all of them, and the picture is slightly different. The diagnosis of Asperger's syndrome is more likely to be made these days but until recently it is possible that those that would now be diagnosed were thought of as eccentric, absent minded, socially inept or awkward. The use of language should not be a problem but those with Asperger's syndrome are likely to use language differently in some way. For example, a child might have an excellent use of language but lack understanding in some way.

Asperger's syndrome is not treated here in as much depth as autism here because it is not quite as debilitating (some might say). Treatment could include helping individuals with social skills, for example, or helping them to learn appropriate responses to specific situations. However, it is important for diagnoses to be made because this enables the affected individuals to be understood and helped.

Diagnosing Asperger's disorder

There are five categories to consider when diagnosing Asperger's disorder according to the Diagnostic and Statistical Manual of Mental Disorders, fourth edition (DSM-IV). These are listed in Table 10.2.

Table 10.2   Diagnostic criteria for Asperger's disorder (DSM-IV)

Symptoms if Asperger's disorder is present

A	Impairment of social interaction – including two of the following: a) Problems in the use of eye-to-eye gaze, body postures and use of gestures to communicate b) Failing to develop appropriate relationships with peers c) Not spontaneously seeking to share interests and enjoyment with others d) Not responding socially and emotionally to others in response to their interactions
B	Repetitive and stereotyped behaviour – including at least one of the following: a) A preoccupation with an abnormal pattern of interest, strongly and unnaturally focused b) Inflexible routines c) Repetitive movements d) Preoccupation with parts of objects
C	Not being able to function in some social way or at work
D	The usual developmental stages regarding language should be present – there should be no language impairment
E	There is no delay in cognitive development or self-help skills – the only delay should be in social interaction

Most diagnostic lists about Asperger's syndrome include very similar factors, but other diagnostic lists have suggested that language problems are likely to be present such as the use of superficially perfect language or formal language. As with other abnormal behaviours it is not easy to give a precise list of the symptoms that would be present in anyone diagnosed as having Asperger's disorder. There are clusters of symptoms, as outlined in Tables 10.3, 10.4 and 10.5, and individuals can differ in their symptoms.

Any list of such behaviours is quite long because those with Asperger's syndrome do not have a set list of characteristics but, rather, a collection of likely behaviours. Some examples, however, are given below.

Likely social characteristics of someone with Asperger's syndrome

Some likely social characteristics are listed in Table 10.3 and include behaviours ranging from shyness and naïve trust in others to excessive talking and being perceived as 'being in their own world'.

Table 10.3   Some likely social characteristics in someone with Asperger's syndrome

Characteristics	
Difficulty in accepting criticism	Difficulty in giving criticism sensitively
Shyness	Naïve trust in others
Flash temper and tantrums	Excessive talk
Scrupulous honesty	Quick to react to being manipulated
Difficulty in hiding real feelings in a social setting	Abrupt and strong expression of likes and dislikes
Single minded	Social isolation and need for privacy
Limited clothing preference and discomfort with formal clothing such as uniforms	Intensely pursued interests
	Rigidly sticking to rules and social conventions
Often seen as 'being in their own world'	Bizarre or no sense of humour
Finds it hard to relax and take 'time out'	

Likely behavioural characteristics of someone with Asperger's syndrome

There is no list of characteristics that someone with Asperger's syndrome would have, but that there is a list of the sorts of behaviour that would be expected. A person with Asperger's syndrome would tend to have some of the characteristics listed in Table 10.4 – and this list does not include all likely characteristics.

Table 10.4   Some likely behavioural characteristics in someone with Asperger's syndrome

Characteristics	
Clumsiness	Strong sensory sensitivity
Balance difficulties	Difficulty in judging distances, height and depth
Verbosity	Difficulty in face recognition (prosopagnosia)
Anxiety	Self-injury
Sleep difficulties	Nail biting
Low apparent sexual interest	Unusual posture or stance
Depression	Rigid eating behaviours
Difficulty in expressing anger	Strong food preferences and aversions
Flat vocal expression	Unusual personal hygiene
Difficulty with eye contact	Raising voice when stressed

Some cognitive characteristics

Table 10.5 outlines some cognitive characteristics someone with Asperger's syndrome might exhibit.

Table 10.5   Some likely cognitive characteristics in someone with Asperger's syndrome

Characteristics	
Can be distracted	Difficulty in expressing emotions
Failing to respond to talk therapy	General confusion when stressed
Interrupting and dominating during conversations	Not good at rules of conversation
Insensitive to the verbal cues of others (such as their facial expressions)	Mental shutdown when faced with multitasking or conflicting demands
A lot of hidden anger and resentment	Interpreting literally (not reading between the lines)
Not producing results in an orthodox manner	Using step-by-step learning techniques
Attention to detail	Concrete thinking (see Chapter 5)
Need to end one task before starting another	An apparent lack of common sense
Rigidly sticking to rules and routines	Unmatched verbal and performance results when tested
Can miss someone else's agenda	Out of scale reactions to losing
Liking for simple routines	

DOWN'S SYNDROME

Whereas autism is relatively rare, children with Down's syndrome make up the largest group of children with learning difficulties and there are around 16 children with Down's syndrome for every 10 000 births. There are physical features associated with Down's syndrome, though they are not always present. These include a smaller nose with a flattened bridge, almond-shaped eyes that slant upwards, short fingers and broad hands. The neck tends to be short and broad and muscle tone tends to be poor. Children can often be identified by these features very soon after birth. There can be low brain weight, reduced number of cells and short dendrites (according to Coyle *et al.*, 1986). Down's Syndrome is named after Langdon Down, a British doctor who first described it in 1866.

Causes of Down's syndrome

Down's syndrome, unlike autism, has an accepted explanation and arises from an unusual pattern of chromosomes. Around 97% of children with Down's syndrome have an extra number 21 chromosome (a triplet instead of a pair) and the other 3% have part of the number 21 chromosome fused with part of another chromosome. Down's syndrome is caused by this abnormality on number 21 chromosome and therefore has a biological cause. Chromosomal abnormality can be detected before birth by tests such as an **amniocentesis**, which is where a sample of the amniotic fluid that surrounds the foetus is removed and the chromosomal cells looked at. The age of the mother at birth has been shown to relate to the condition and risk of having a child with Down's syndrome increases with age. For mothers who are 20 years old the rate of occurrence is around 1 in 2000 births and for mothers aged 35 the rate is around 1 in 500. By the age of 45 the incidence is 1 in 20 according to Evans and Hammerton (1985). There is more recent but controversial evidence that the father's age is also important (see, for example, Hook *et al.*, 1990).

Delay in development

Children with Down's syndrome may have learning difficulties because their development, though similar to the development of other children, is slower, or because it is different. Research focuses on the issue of whether their development is slower

DEFINITIONS

Amniocentesis – is where a sample of the amniotic fluid that surrounds the foetus is removed and the chromosomal cells are examined. This test can identify children with Down's syndrome.

or different. It is very hard to know which is the case as the development of most children with Down's syndrome is delayed in that they reach milestones at a later age than usual. Milestones include muscular development, the acquisition of motor skills such as sitting without support, and finer motor developments such as building a tower of bricks. These sorts of abilities are delayed in children with Down's syndrome. They also tend to show delays in smiling, speaking, making eye contact, walking and reacting to their parent leaving the room. However, these milestones are reached later, it is not that children with Down's syndrome cannot do these things. It might be that they take longer to process information and this causes all the developmental delays. One area of development that can take up to two years longer to learn is **contingency**, which is when they learn that something they do (for example, reaching out for something) will lead to something that happens (for example, they can pick it up). This may be because these children take longer to process information.

Carr (1994) has suggested that the delays in cognitive development that are apparent in young children with Down's syndrome are even more marked as they grow older. Chapter 6 discussed the idea of IQ (intelligence quotient) and explained that this was a measure of a child's actual (chronological) age and their mental age. If children at a certain actual (chronological) age can do what children of that age are expected to do and can usually do, then their IQ is 100 (see Chapter 6 for more information on this). In the first year children with Down's syndrome can have an IQ of around 70 (on average) and this falls to just over 50 by the second year and to 40 by the time they are 11 years old (as a general example). This suggests that the children's mental age is advancing more slowly than their chronological age, so their IQ falls. It should be noted that not all children with Down's syndrome develop in the same way. Some can start walking at 13 months and some not until 48 months, for example, whereas typically children walk between 9 months and 17 months. Language development also differs quite a lot. Some children with Down's syndrome develop language at a fairly usual age and some develop spoken language very late compared with typical development. The IQ scores also vary between individuals. One important point is that children with Down's syndrome can differ in what they can do on different occasions, and Wishart and Duffy (1990) found, for example, that given the same developmental test 2 weeks apart children varied in the individual items that they passed. This shows a lack of consistency, which is important when considering findings of studies because results might come from a test on only one occasion.

Different development

It may not be that children with Down's Syndrome are delayed in their development as much as that they develop differently. Tests tend to be arranged with items in order from easier to the most difficult. Therefore, if children with Down's syndrome are failing on different items, not all of them at the end, and if they are failing on different items on different occasions, this suggests that any difficulties are not just about developmental delay. If delay was the only issue, children with Down's syndrome would fail more on the items at the end of the test, and would do so on each occasion. Wishart and Duffy's findings outlined above go against this explanation and suggest that development is not just delayed, but different. Children with Down's syndrome do not pass Piaget's sequence of object permanence as children typically do, and they may fail tests they have passed before, so this suggests again that they develop differently not just more slowly. (Chapter 5 discussed Piaget's ideas about object permanence.) Research into the development of reading of children with Down's syndrome also backs up the idea of them developing differently rather than slowly. In typical development, reading skills and skills of understanding sound (such as not confusing 'mat' and 'hat') go together and develop together. However, in children with Down's syndrome perhaps their

DEFINITIONS

Contingency – when children learn that something they do (such as reaching out) affects something in the environment (for example, picking something up). Children with Down's syndrome can be as far as 2 years behind in learning that their action can affect the environment in this way.

understanding of sound is not as good. It seems that children with Down's syndrome learn to read by linking word with meaning rather than word with sound, as would be 'normally' expected. Children without Down's syndrome tend to make sound errors when reading (such as muddling 'mat' and 'hat') whereas children with Down's syndrome tend to make errors of meaning (such as reading 'seat' for 'chair'). This sort of evidence suggests that development of children with Down's syndrome is different rather than 'just' delayed when compared to typically developing children.

PROFOUND VISUAL IMPAIRMENT

Children who cannot see anything more than shades of light and dark are described as having a profound visual impairment. This is not the same as severe visual impairment, where children do sometimes have some limited vision of shape and form. One difficulty of studying those with a profound visual impairment is that they may also have other learning difficulties, and then it is hard to see what the effects of having profound visual impairment are. So usually studies involve those who have had a profound visual impairment since birth and who do not have other learning difficulties. Even then such children all have different backgrounds, which will affect them in different ways, so it is very hard to draw definite conclusions about the effects of profound visual impairment.

One way of overcoming such difficulties is to study as large a number of children who have a profound visual impairment as possible. In this way it is hoped that general trends will emerge that can confidently be attributed to the condition rather than random environmental influences.

By looking at children with profound visual development it is possible to draw conclusions about how vision affects typical development. Around one in 10 000 children has severe visual impairment and only some of these have profound visual impairment. It is known that children with no sight from birth do develop differently from children who have sight (Fraiberg, 1977). Children with profound visual impairment are not often diagnosed straight away at birth because, in the early weeks, they behave in a similar way to other children. They may smile when they hear their parents, react to sound, and can be comforted when held.

One important difficulty for a partially sighted infant is learning that things are there when they cannot see them. The concept of object permanence has to be grasped without the infant being able to see that the object reappears (for an explanation of object permanence, see Chapters 1 and 5). An infant with profound visual impairment will experience the world differently from a child with sight. Babies who can see will usually reach out for a toy at around 4 months, whereas a baby with profound visual impairment will reach out for an object at nearer 10 months. Children with profound visual impairment are often older than typically developing children when they reach the stage of showing distress when their parent(s) leave the room. Chapter 3 gives a discussion of separation anxiety.

DYSLEXIA – SPECIFIC LEARNING DIFFICULTIES AND IMPAIRMENTS OF LANGUAGE

Language is a very important part of a child's development. Children can experience difficulties in all aspects of language. Some find speaking difficult and are said to have a language impairment, aphasia is an example of this. Other children may have dyslexia, which is a difficulty with the written aspects of language (literacy).

Dyslexia is a reading disorder and in the DSM-IV (Diagnostic and Statistical Manual of Mental Disorders, fourth edition) is called a specific learning disability.

Other specific learning difficulties in DSM-IV are dyscalculia, which is a mathematics disorder, and aphasia, which is a disorder of verbal expression, outlined below. It is thought that between 5% and 15% of the population have a specific learning disability (Taylor, 1989) and that more males than females are affected

Sometimes a learning disability is global, that is a child has difficulties in all areas of learning. Sometimes children have problems with just one area of learning, for instance a child may just have problems with literacy or numeracy. These are often referred to as specific learning difficulties. One way of diagnosing a specific leaning difficulty is to test a child's IQ and find that they are normal on many measures except a particular one. For example, a child would be normal in tests, except for reading ability, so might be diagnosed as dyslexic. Another way of diagnosing a problem is to find out that a child is not developing a particular ability (such as reading) at the normal age. One difficulty is that a different disorder, such as attention deficit hyperactivity disorder (ADHD), might lead children to be below their 'normal' ability level, and that could be the problem – not their actual reading ability. ADHD is discussed later in this chapter.

Dyslexia is a very important specific learning disability because reading is such a central part of learning. Not only is the ability to read essential to access knowledge from books and other written material but it has been shown that the process of learning to read helps children's overall intellectual development. Some symptoms of dyslexia are:

- reversals – where letters like 'b' and 'd' are confused or words are written in reverse such as 'tar' for 'rat' and 'now' for 'won';

- elisions – when someone reads or writes 'cat' instead of 'cart';

- non-fluent reading, word-by-word and losing one's place when reading;

- being able to sound out the letters of a word without being able to read the word correctly – the child sounds out 'c-a-t' then says 'cold' when the word is 'cat';

- reading the letters in the wrong order – reading 'left' instead of 'felt' or reading 'are there' instead of 'there are';

- spelling words as they sound – 'rite' not 'right';

- reading without understanding and not remember what has been read;

- poor or slow handwriting.

Possible causes for specific learning difficulties

As with other disorders outlined in this chapter, the causes of conditions such as dyslexia are not really known, although some are suggested by the evidence so far. There may be genetic factors, difficulties in brain function and cognitive difficulties, for example, and these causes are outlined below.

Genetic factors in specific learning difficulties

Smith *et al.* (1990) looked at genetic causes and found that children of parents with reading difficulties were more likely to have reading difficulties themselves than children of parents without reading difficulties. A problem here is that this suggests an inherited factor – but children are more likely to be like their parents because of environmental factors (they learn from them) so this sort of evidence is not proof that conditions such as reading difficulties run in families.

Specific learning difficulties coming from brain dysfunction

Brain dysfunction may be a cause of specific learning difficulties too because many of those with brain dysfunction, for example from a head injury, do have specific learning difficulties. Dyslexia in particular has been studied to see if it is a result of brain dysfunction. A problem, of course, is that it is impossible to study the living brain directly to find out what is dysfunctioning. Scanning has been used and there have been autopsies on deceased people who have had dyslexia, and some evidence has been found. There is no absolute proof that brain dysfunction causes dyslexia though. There has been some evidence to show that those with dyslexia have a difference in the size of nerve cells in the part of the brain that helps to process sounds (the left medial geniculate nucleus). However, studies tend to use small samples, so it is hard to draw very firm conclusions. Even if it were found that a person with dyslexia has brain differences of some sort, it cannot be shown whether such brain differences come from the dyslexia or are a cause of the dyslexia.

Cognitive explanations for specific learning difficulties

It could be that cognitive explanations are more useful. For example, they suggest that a child who does not succeed at a certain task then lacks motivation and will continue to fail at that task. Alternatively, perhaps children who have specific learning difficulties have difficulties with processing information, rather than problems with motivation. There is some evidence for this and problems can involve difficulties in paying attention and failing to use appropriate learning strategies. The idea that problems come from failing to attend to certain factors in a task does go with the claim that children with ADHD tend to have specific learning difficulties, as they also have difficulties in attending appropriately.

Treating specific learning difficulties

Specific learning difficulties are often thought to be caused by poor cognitive processing or poor problem-solving strategies, and treatments focus on those areas. For example, one study showed that a group of children with specific learning difficulties in reading improved their reading by using techniques to monitor their performance by asking themselves questions whilst reading (see, for example, Wong and Jones, 1982). A control group of children who were not taught the technique did not improve their reading skills.

APHASIA/DYSPHASIA – MAINLY IN ADULTS

Aphasia/dysphasia is a specific learning disability as is dyslexia, but it is different as the cause is more likely to be known. The cause of aphasia is almost always brain injury of some sort. Aphasia is a language impairment and the production of speech, comprehension of speech and reading and writing ability are all affected. It is commonly caused by a stroke, particularly in older people. However, infections and brain injuries can also cause aphasia. Aphasia can be quite mild, involving a problem in retrieving names of objects, for example. It can also be very severe and can make communication more or less impossible. There are different types of aphasia.

Symptoms of aphasia/dysphasia

Table 10.6 lists some symptoms of aphasia.

Disorders that can relate to aphasia – apraxia, dyspraxia and dysarthria

Other disorders can go with aphasia or can be confused with aphasia and are briefly outlined here. Apraxia is concerned with problems with movement. Dyspraxia is also concerned with physical movements, but apraxia itself covers all movement including using gestures that accompany speech. Those with aphasia might also find it hard to accompany their speech with appropriate gestures, so might have apraxia too. They may find it hard to wave goodbye as well, for example. They may find it hard to pick up an appropriate object. Dysarthria refers to speech disorders where the speech mechanism is damaged in some way. So aphasia is about cognitive issues and speech problems arising from brain damage and dysarthria is about actual speech production concerning the necessary mechanisms, such as articulating sounds. It is not really about language as such, but about producing the sounds.

Table 10.6   Symptoms of aphasia

Category	Symptoms
Understanding	*Problems with:* Discriminating between sounds Understanding the meaning of words Understanding long material Processing complex sentences
Reading	*Problems with:* Recognising and understanding letters or words Remembering and understanding long sentences Recalling details from long stories
Speaking	*Problems with:* Thinking of the correct word Saying the word properly Forming correct grammatical sentences Explaining things clearly Using appropriate language in the right situations
Writing	*Problems with:* Forming letters Spelling Thinking of the right word Sequencing ideas Organising information grammatically

Treating aphasia

Most of those with aphasia have it following a stroke and also around one third of those who have had a head injury develop aphasia. Aphasia can be temporary, as indicated earlier, and more than half of those with aphasia recover completely very early on after the stroke or head injury. There is no cure for aphasia unless the cause is a brain tumour that can be removed, for example. Speech therapy is widely used to help individuals to improve, depending on their specific difficulty. Useful strategies include communicating in a quiet and relaxed setting, encouraging the use of gestures and pointing to help communication, and not shouting at the person.

DYSPRAXIA

Dyspraxia, unlike dyslexia and aphasia, does not involve language development but is an impairment of movement. It seems that the brain processes information about movement in an immature manner and messages are not fully transmitted. 'Praxis' means 'doing or acting' and dyspraxia affects planning what to do and actually putting the plan into action. Dyspraxia is associated with difficulties of perception, language and thought too. It is thought that up to 10% of the population can be diagnosed with dyspraxia and 2% of the population have severe dyspraxia. It is a developmental co-ordination disorder, and symptoms involve mainly clumsiness, which is often quite easily visible. It used to be called 'clumsy child syndrome'.

ATTENTION-DEFICIT HYPERACTIVITY DISORDER (ADHD)

Many difficulties with children involve their behaviour, and these difficulties range from problems with managing specific behaviours through problems with aggressive behaviour to problems that have a diagnosis, such as ADHD. Some of these problems are considered here. As they are behavioural problems they mainly tend to be treated using behaviourist methods, such as focusing on reinforcing desired behaviour and ignoring or punishing undesired behaviour.

Hyperactivity refers to behaviour such as being constantly on the go, rash, impulsive and impetuous. When behaviour also involves difficulty in focusing or concentration, the child may be diagnosed as having ADHD. There are different types of behaviour under the heading 'ADHD', including ADHD predominantly inattentive type, ADHD predominantly hyperactive type; and ADHD combined type – all are diagnosed and could be separate disorders.

Diagnosing ADHD

Hyperactivity suggests movement activity or motor activity, but the disorder involves more than that. There are three features of ADHD. They are:

- developmentally inappropriate levels of inattention
- problems with impulsivity, and
- hyperactivity, occurring before seven years of age.

For a diagnosis of ADHD these problems should occur at school, at home and in other contexts too. Inattention means not listening and having a short attention span. The child is easily distracted. Impulsivity means acting without thought. This can involve interrupting others or speaking without thinking or not waiting one's turn to speak. Overactivity means fidgeting and being unable to sit still. Hyperactive children are on the go and cannot play quietly. Children with ADHD also find it hard to interact with peers and they can behave aggressively. Children with ADHD tend to show opposition to their parents and interactions between parents and children with ADHD tend to involve more parental commands and punishment than usual (Barkley, 1981). Attention-deficit hyperactivity disorder tends to go with other disorders and, according to Szatmari and others (1989) 44% have at least one other disorder. Barkley (1990) suggested that around 20% of children with ADHD also have specific learning difficulties. They may also show anxiety and depression.

More boys than girls are diagnosed with ADHD and girls with ADHD have different behaviour patterns, tending to be less aggressive and more withdrawn than boys with ADHD. Great Britain seems to have a low rate of ADHD according to Taylor (1994), whereas in China there is a high rate of hyperactivity (according to Luk and Leung, 1989). However, it is not easy to draw comparisons between cultures because diagnosis can be made differently in different cultures. There may also be different cultural expectations of children's behaviour.

All children can be said to have problems in attention and to be impulsive, and ADHD is only diagnosed if there is evidence that a particular child is showing those types of behaviour inappropriately for its age and level of development. With a child with ADHD the difficulties in attentiveness usually do not go away as the child gets older and in many cases problems are present in adolescence too (see, for example, Fisher *et al.*, 1991).

A study of ADHD – Barkley (1991)

One research team that has studied ADHD is headed by Russell Barkley at the University of Massachusetts Medical Centre. The team carried out a study in 1991 and looked at 160 children – some with ADHD and some 'normal' children who

DEFINITIONS

Longitudinal study – a study that follows particular individuals over a period of time and studies them at certain points to track changes and similarities.

were used as a control group. The ADHD children were studied when they were diagnosed and then again 8 years after having been diagnosed. When a study follows up on particular participants, it is called a **longitudinal study**, because it studies the same individuals over a period of time. The team looked at behaviour problems and family conflicts. They also observed the child's interactions with their mother both at the time of diagnosis and at the later date. The children with ADHD were rated by their mothers as having more family conflicts, and more often, than the 'normal' children. The interactions seemed to show more controlling and negative behaviours between the ADHD children and their mothers than between the 'normal' children and their mothers (whose interactions were more positive). If there was conflict in a family and it continued, then there seemed to be more 'bad' behaviour from the child. This does suggest that family interactions might be at least in some part a cause of ADHD (because the children where there was not extended family conflict showed less 'conduct disorder'). It was found in general that difficulties with attentiveness and hyperactivity did persist into adolescence.

There are some problems with the study. For example, observing how mothers and children interact together at a young age (around 6 years old, for example, when ADHD is diagnosed) is not the same as observing mother/child interaction in adolescence (for example, around 14 years old). At 6 years old mothers and children play together, and their interactions are different at the age of 14. The team did use different measures and thought they had captured interactions at both ages but the differences in method might be important. Overall it is thought that this study did produce reliable results and that using different measures (including the children's own ratings of their behaviour) it was found that children diagnosed with ADHD do still have problem behaviour with regard to areas such as attentiveness and hyperactivity when they are older.

For ADHD to be diagnosed the behaviour must begin before the age of 7 years and symptoms must be found in at least two situations and for at least 6 months. There must also be evidence of distress. Not all children displaying impulsive or uncontrolled behaviour are diagnosed as having ADHD. Table 10.7 outlines some behaviour that would be found in a child with ADHD.

Table 10.7   Diagnosing ADHD

Category	Some examples of behaviours
Inattention	• Often has difficulty in maintaining attention in play tasks • Often does not follow through on an instruction • Often has difficulty in organising tasks • Is easily distracted • Is often forgetful in daily activities
Hyperactivity	• Often fidgets with hands or feet, or when seated • Often runs about or climbs in inappropriate situations • Often leaves seat when is expected to stay seated • Often has difficulty in playing quietly
Impulsivity	• Often interrupts others • Often finds it hard to wait their turn • Often blurts out answers to questions before the question has been completed

Methods of identifying ADHD

There are different ways of identifying ADHD, including ratings of the child by teachers and parents. One example of using ratings is to use a Matching Familiar Figures test. Children can be asked to match a particular item by choosing from other items, one of which is the same. The extent to which they do tasks like this quickly and without a lot of thought can measure their impulsivity. Interviews with the child, their parents and teachers can be very useful and observations are also carried out. By using a wide range of data-gathering techniques a diagnosis is more likely to be valid and reliable.

Causes of ADHD

No single cause has been identified for ADHD. It is suggested that causes include genetic ones, brain damage, problems with diet and also environmental factors to do with upbringing and the family situation. It is possible that a range of these factors need to be present.

Genetic factors in ADHD

It is usually accepted that our genetic make up can affect our activity levels. Temperament was discussed in Chapter 2 and it was suggested that we are born with certain tendencies regarding our temperament, such as being inherently quiet or noisy, extravert or introvert. There is some evidence that behaviour linked with ADHD has a genetic basis – at least to an extent. For example, ADHD does tend to run in families – at least it is found more often in first degree relatives of someone with ADHD than in the rest of the population. Deutsch (1987) found that adopted children with ADHD did not tend to have parents with ADHD patterns of behaviour (only 4% did), whereas 25% of natural parents of ADHD children had a tendency to have shown ADHD behaviour when they were young. It has also been shown that parents of ADHD children are more often to have mood disorders, which is an interesting finding and suggests that mood disorders and ADHD behaviour might go together as well as being biologically given in some way. There is also some evidence (for example, McMahon, 1980) that identical (MZ) twins are more likely to both have ADHD than non-identical (DZ) twins. Chapter 2 explains how this finding suggests a biological cause for ADHD: MZ twins share their genes and DZ twins only share 50% of their genes, so if MZ twins are more similar regarding some characteristic it is thought that that characteristic has a genetic cause.

Problems in brain function

Another possible cause for ADHD is a problem in brain function or brain damage. Studies have not found particular evidence of brain damage in children with ADHD and children with brain damage do not develop ADHD. For example, computer axial tomography scans (CT scans), which can give pictures of the brain, do not show brain differences between ADHD children and children without ADHD (for example, Shaywitz *et al.*, 1983). Brain function might be impaired, though. For example, as shown above, tasks are performed differently by ADHD children, such as they show more impulsivity. There is some evidence using EEGs (electroencephalograms, which measure electrical activity in the brain) that there is decreased blood flow and decreased activity in the frontal lobes of the brain in ADHD children (see, for example, Lou *et al.*, 1989). This different brain activity might be that there is less maturity in the brain – it is taking longer to develop – rather than there being differences in the working of the brain.

Problems with diet

It has been suggested that problems with diet can cause behaviour associated with ADHD. Suggested problems include eating foods with artificial dyes and preservatives. Feingold (1975) suggested that problems in diet can cause ADHD and scientists then started testing to find out whether this was the case. In general results are not conclusive and it is now thought that problems with diet are not a cause of ADHD (see, for example, Swanson and Kinsbourne, 1980). Other factors, however, such as toxins, might cause ADHD. Lead poisoning does cause increased impulsivity and hyperactivity, for example (Loeber, 1990) and it may be that pollutants are a cause of ADHD. This is yet to be determined though.

Social and environmental factors

It has been suggested that one cause of ADHD is that children do not learn cognitive and behavioural skills. This might be because they observe inappropriate behaviour in others. Social learning theory can help to explain this (see Chapter 4). Children with ADHD may not have been rewarded for appropriate behaviour and may have been rewarded for inappropriate behaviour. Operant conditioning principles can help to explain this (see Chapter 4). There is some evidence that parents of ADHD children do use more direct commands than other parents but this could be a result of the behaviour rather than a cause of it, and there is little evidence to show that 'bad' learning causes ADHD. If a child's behaviour is controlled by medication, it is shown that mothers then show less control, which does suggest that their controlling parenting style results from the behaviour rather than causing it.

A summary of current thinking about the cause of ADHD

It is currently thought that there are many factors that lead to ADHD, and that these factors add together to cause the behaviour. There seems to be a biological predisposition to developing ADHD, and this involves brain function. If children have this tendency then they might develop ADHD because of environmental factors such as family stress. There is no agreement about there being one single cause for ADHD and this has implications for treatment, as without knowing the cause, it is hard to know what the treatment should be. Table 10.8 summarises possible causes of ADHD

Table 10.8   Possible causes of ADHD

Possible cause	Current conclusion
Genetic factors	Some evidence of this from adoption and twin studies. ADHD and similar behaviour does seem to run in families at least to an extent.
Brain damage	No evidence for this as CT scans do not show differences in ADHD children and children with brain damage do not show ADHD symptoms.
Brain function problems	Some evidence for this, showing decreased blood flow in frontal lobes in ADHD children.
Diet problems	Little evidence for this and studies have not found evidence for claims that diet causes ADHD.
Pollutants	This cannot be discounted and symptoms of lead poisoning are similar to ADHD symptoms. Environmental pollutants might be found to be a cause, but this is not shown by the evidence at the moment.
Social and and environmental factors	There is little evidence to say that children develop ADHD because they learn inappropriate behaviour. Their parents are likely to be more controlling but this is probably because of the ADHD rather than a cause of it.

Treatment for ADHD

Treatment for ADHD involves medication and teaching strategies aimed at improving and changing the child's behaviour. Strategies can include using behavioural principles such as rewarding appropriate behaviour whilst ignoring unwanted behaviour. Other strategies can include cognitive principles such as encouraging appropriate skills to do with paying attention and concentrating.

Drug treatments

Various drugs are used. These are stimulants that help the child to focus. Their effects tend to wear off after a few hours so they tend to be taken two or three times a day. One well-known drug is Ritalin (methylphenidate), another is Cylert (pemoline) and another is Dexedrine (dextroamphetamine). Such drugs help the child to pay attention, they decrease impulsiveness and improve performance on tasks that involve concentration. Studies have also shown that such drugs help a child to do better on cognitive tasks (Barkley, 1990). It may seem odd that stimulants have a quieting effect but they do – on all children, not only ADHD children. Currently there is a trend for prescribing drugs to treat ADHD.

A report in the *Daily Mail*, 20 October 2004, summarised some current information about using drugs to control the behaviour of children diagnosed as having ADHD. The article did not quote all its sources, and the facts would need to be proved, however, it clearly shows current concerns about using medication to treat ADHD. The article suggests that the number of prescriptions for Ritalin has grown 25% in one year and that 6000 such prescriptions are now written out in Britain every week. It is claimed that drugs are a 'chemical cosh', which means that they are used to keep ADHD children quiet rather than used as a cure. Such drugs have side effects too, and this should be taken into account. The article claims that the use of drugs such as Ritalin has doubled in four years as more and more children are diagnosed as having ADHD. It is claimed that 314 500 prescriptions for Ritalin-type drugs were written over the previous year at a cost of over £10 000 000. The article claims that one in twenty children have ADHD, which would mean there is the equivalent of up to three such children in each classroom. Although it is claimed that many parents say their children's behaviour is transformed by medication, the article also states that some studies on animals suggest that it can cause long-term brain damage.

Studies have suggested that around 75% of children with ADHD do improve with medication (stimulants) (Cantwell and Hanna, 1989). However, there are side effects to take into account. These include hair loss, anxiety, increase in blood pressure, weight loss and insomnia (Barkley et al., 1990).

Teaching appropriate behaviour using behavioural and cognitive strategies

The main aim is to reduce the unwanted behaviour, such as impulsivity and poor attention, so focus is on giving children the skills to improve in these areas. Behaviour management is used and parents are given training too. Barkley (1990) explains that many of the problems come from lack of control over the child's behaviour so parent training programmes focus on helping parents to understand children's behaviour and to control it (or to help children control themselves).

Parent training programmes

Parents learn to reward appropriate behaviour and to shape desired responses. Chapter 4 explains how shaping works, with the desired behaviour being gradually achieved by rewarding partial performance. Direct punishment is not used, but 'time out' is a strategy where children are ignored when they exhibit undesired behaviour and sometimes are made to sit in one place until they calm down, for example. It is generally thought that parent training increases parent's self-esteem, reduced their stress and does give improvements in the child's behaviour too (Anastopoulos *et al.*, 1993).

Classroom management programmes

In classroom management programmes the procedure is to reward wanted behaviour. Teachers plan goals for the children and they reward them as these goals are achieved. Teachers complete a checklist to see how far children have progressed towards the goals each day, and according to their score on the checklist they are rewarded or not. This does seem to be an effective strategy but only whilst it is being used. Afterwards there is a tendency for children to go back to their original behaviour (Kazdin, 1994).

Skills training for the child

Behavioural programmes such as those outlined above, where appropriate behaviour is rewarded, can be improved if children also receive training on self-control skills.

Learning self-control skills makes it more likely that behavioural programmes will have a lasting effect. Children are taught to give self-rewards and to self-evaluate. They are also taught how to focus their attention more appropriately, as well as learning problem solving skills. Studies do not, however, tend to show that these strategies work very well outside the immediate situation in which they are being used.

Drug treatment together with behaviour management programmes

It is generally thought at the moment that a combination of drug therapy and behaviour therapy is the best way to 'treat' ADHD because the three approaches all have something to offer. However, conclusions are by no means certain, which is perhaps not surprising given that the cause of ADHD (if there is one cause) is not known.

MANAGING BEHAVIOUR AND DEALING WITH AGGRESSION

Behaviour management techniques have been outlined above when discussing treatments for ADHD. It has been found that in the short-term at least using a system of rewards and punishment (time out) has helped to improve the behaviour of children with ADHD, although such improvements may not last once the behaviour management programme has ended. Such programmes are not limited to children with ADHD and can be used to improve any child's behaviour. Often behaviour that needs to be managed is aggressive behaviour.

Conduct disorders and oppositional defiant disorder

Aggressive behaviour can be associated with different disorders. Aggressive behaviour itself is seen as needing correction, although the aggressive behaviour might itself be part of another disorder. Conduct disorders are sometimes diagnosed and sometimes a diagnosis of oppositional defiant disorder is made, so these two disorders are very briefly outlined here before aggressive behaviour itself is discussed. There are various types of conduct disorders. A **conduct disorder** is one where there is repeated behaviour that violates the rights of others and is not appropriate for the age of the child. This often involves physical aggression and cruelty. Oppositional defiant disorder is like conduct disorder in that there is negative hostile and defiant behaviour. For either conduct disorder or oppositional defiant disorder to be diagnosed the behaviour must last for at least 6 months. A diagnosis of **oppositional defiant disorder** (ODD) requires at least four of the following behaviours to be present: losing temper, annoying others, blaming others for mistakes, being easily annoyed, being angry and resentful, and being spiteful and vindictive. It is likely that a conduct disorder is diagnosed first, as the behaviours associated with oppositional defiant disorder will also be present, and then, if the behaviours persist oppositional defiant disorder may be diagnosed.

Aggressive behaviour in general (not a specific disorder)

Children can exhibit aggressive behaviour without being diagnosed as having a disorder. It is interesting that children who are aggressive are also often aggressive when older. Aggressive behaviour in adolescents and adults rarely starts in adolescence or adulthood. Loeber (1990), for example, concluded that between 70% and 90% of violent offenders were violent when they were young.

A study to show that aggression is stable over time

Huesmann and others (1984) carried out a study over 22 years. This was a longitudinal study and is good evidence as the same people were studied each time so any

---

DEFINITIONS

Conduct disorder – is where there is repeated behaviour that violates the rights of others and is not appropriate for the age of the child. This often involves physical aggression and cruelty.

Oppositional defiant disorder (ODD) – requires at least four of the following behaviours to be present: losing temper, annoying others, blaming others for mistakes, being easily annoyed, being angry and resentful, and being spiteful and vindictive.

individual differences are present on all occasions. Around 900 school children were tested at around the age of 8 years, and then tested again 10 years later. Six hundred of them were found and tested again when they were 30 years old, so many of them were tested three times. The participants were tested by asking their friends, their parents and when appropriate their wives or husbands. Self-reports were also used, which means the individuals themselves were asked. It was found that those who were aggressive at the age of 8 were also more aggressive later on. This was especially true of males. The most aggressive children at the age of 8 were likely to have criminal convictions when adults, and to punish their children more. This suggests that aggression might have a biological basis because an aggressive person in childhood tends, according to the study, to remain an aggressive person in adulthood. It could, of course, be that once aggressive behaviour is learnt and reinforced in some way then it continues unless treated.

Causes of aggression

There is unlikely to be one cause for aggression. Aggression is a behaviour that can be a symptom of a specific disorder, as suggested above, or it can be a behaviour exhibited by a child without there being an actual diagnosis of a disorder. Taking evidence from studies that say that an aggressive child becomes an aggressive adult, it could be said that aggression is a biological trait. However, others claim that aggressive behaviour in a child can be successfully changed, and would take a behaviourist approach, claiming that aggression is learnt from the environment. From a psychodynamic point of view aggression could come from repressed feelings and might be released through some physical exercise such as sport, and so treated that way. There is some evidence that aggression is a genetic trait and can run in families. Probably aggressive behaviour can come from any one of these causes or any combination of them.

Genetic factors in aggression

Chapter 2 explains how twin studies can help to identify genetic traits in people. If identical (MZ) twins, who share 100% of their genes, have a similar characteristic, then it is likely to have some genetic basis, especially if non-identical (DZ) twins are less likely to share that characteristic. Regarding antisocial behaviour studies have been reviewed and it is generally thought that MZ twins have a 68% chance of each exhibiting aggressive behaviour compared with a 33% chance for DZ twins (Merikangas and Wiessman, 1986). One problem here though is that identical twins might be more likely to copy each other's behaviour than non-identical twins (Carey, 1992). So there is evidence that aggression is an inherited tendency but the evidence can also suggest that it is learnt. Adoption studies can help to resolve this problem. If children who live with adoptive parents are more aggressive than their adoptive parents but similar to their biological parents in their level of aggression then this is evidence for a biological basis for aggression. This has been found. When studying criminal records there is evidence that people are more similar to their biological parents regarding criminality than their adoptive parents.

It is currently thought that some part of aggressive behaviour is genetic but that environmental factors are also important. Some relatively recent research has looked at a specific chromosome – the X chromosome. Brunner *et al.* (1993) in the Netherlands have studied a family where there is very noticeable and strong male violence. The research team looked for a genetic defect and found one, linked with low levels of serotonin.

Biological factors in aggression

Impulsivity and aggression have been linked to low levels of the neurotransmitter serotonin. For example, it has been found that violent suicide attempts in depressed people are linked with low levels of serotonin (see, for example, Coccaro *et al.*, 1989). Similarly, when studying marines who were discharged as being unfit because of excessive violence it was found that they had low serotonin activity (see, for example, Brown *et al.*, 1982). It is thought that impulsive aggression in particular, in other words aggression that is not planned, is linked to low levels of serotonin. It was claimed above that one genetic defect found in a family that exhibited excessive male violence was linked with low serotonin levels. Neurotransmitters such as serotonin are found in the brain and are involved in all our thinking processes, as well as many of our emotional responses. So there is evidence of some biological difference in those with aggression – in particular non-planned aggression.

Another biological cause for aggression is the male hormone testosterone. The evidence is not very clear though. Some studies have been reviewed and it has been found that there are associations between hormone levels and aggressiveness in prisoners – amongst rapists and weightlifters taking steroids (Carlson, 1994). It may not be the level of testosterone that gives aggression so much as sensitivity to the level of the hormone, and this might affect the developing brain of an infant according to Eichelman (1992). At the moment it is thought that testosterone plays a part in aggressive behaviour, but it is not known exactly how this happens or what this role is. Another biological cause could be a low level of emotional arousal, which makes the individual seeks arousal. This is then found in sensation seeking and dangerous experiences. This might make someone more aggressive.

Raine *et al.* (1990) carried out a study of 101 males aged 15 years. They took recordings of their heart rate and brain activity. Their skin conductance was also measured and this is a measure of sweating and stress. Then 9 years later they looked to see if any of them had criminal records. Seventeen of them did have criminal records and their physiological scores when they were 15 were compared with the scores of those that did not go on to have a criminal record. It was found that those with the criminal record did have lower levels of arousal on all the measures taken. This study suggests that low levels of arousal do link with criminality.

So there are three biological explanations for aggression outlined in this section. Some of the evidence has been presented but, of course, there is a lot more and nothing seems to be certain. One explanation is that aggression is caused by low levels of serotonin. Another suggestion is that the hormone testosterone has a role. The third explanation suggests that low levels of arousal cause aggression. These biological factors could be genetically given.

Aggression and learning from environmental factors

One explanation for aggression is that it is learnt. For example, a study of psychopaths showed that they found it hard to learn tasks when the wrong answers were punished with electric shocks but could learn quite well when correct answers were rewarded. It seemed that they did not fear the shocks, and it was concluded that they were not anxious and so did not learn as most learn (Lykken, 1957). Perhaps psychopaths cannot stop a response just because it may be punished, rather than due to lack of fear of the punishment. Different explanations have been put forward, but the main point is that psychopaths' behaviour may be due to problems with learning. It has also been claimed that all forms of aggression can come from inappropriate learning although it should be noted that psychopaths are a special case and, of course, not everyone who engages in aggressive behaviour is a psychopath! People can learn aggression by inappropriate patterns of reward and punishment. They may be rewarded for aggressive behaviour, if the only attention they get is when they misbehave, for example. So they find attention rewarding and become more and more aggressive to get their reward. Similarly, aggression can be learnt through social learning principles, where others in the family exhibit aggressive behaviour so the individual copies it and, therefore, becomes aggressive. An important area of study is violence on TV and in the media. Many studies have suggested that violence on television (and in computer games) can lead to more violence in society as such violence is likely to be imitated. Chapter 4 looks at social learning theory and explains how it is possible that aggression comes from role models including TV role models.

Dealing with aggressive behaviour

How aggressive behaviour is dealt with depends on whether it is part of another diagnosis, such as ADHD or a conduct disorder. In this section aggressive behaviour is dealt with by itself, rather than as part of another disorder. If it were part of a different diagnosis treatment may be different. Although here the disorders mentioned are conduct disorder and oppositional defiant disorder, note that there are other disorders characterised mainly by aggression such as antisocial personality disorder (APD). As with other disorders, aggression can be addressed by the use of drugs or by the use of behavioural and/or cognitive techniques. Aggression is a form of behaviour that can arise from different causes. If individuals are aggressive because they are frustrated about something in their life, then cognitive techniques can be useful as the individuals can look at their thinking and see if negative thoughts are making them dissatisfied. They can learn, for example, to use more positive thinking patterns. If, however, they are aggressive because of some personality disorder or because of some brain damage then perhaps cognitive techniques are not useful. Perhaps some form of psychopathology (drug treatment) would be more successful. If they are aggressive because that is how they have learnt to behave through copying their parents or because when they behave aggressively they get what they want, then behavioural techniques might be useful. You can see that the treatment depends on what is thought to be causing the aggression.

Cognitive techniques

Cognitive techniques are related to thinking patterns. It is thought that some problem behaviour can be helped if individuals learn to retrain themselves with regard to their thinking patterns. Self-instructional training can help them to change their thinking patterns. One way is to encourage them to make more positive statements about themselves and fewer negative statements. Self-instructional training can improve self-control so that they might be able to control their aggression better. Similarly, problem behaviour such as aggressive behaviour may arise from inappropriate interactions with others, and social skills training or anger management training can be useful. Cognitive behavioural therapy (CBT) can be useful, where a person's thinking habits and their behaviour are both considered. For example, offenders can meet victims to try to understand the effects of their behaviour, and they can learn when they get angry and so try to control their anger. These sorts of techniques tend to be called 'cognitive' because they involve a level of understanding and a depth of self-perception, and they can involve behavioural interventions too, because the person then aims to use more appropriate behaviour. **Anger management training** tends to involve more than one stage. The first stage is cognitive preparation when individuals analyse their anger patterns and try to find the triggers – what starts their aggressive behaviour. The second stage is skill acquisition, where they learn self-control and to manage their arousal. Social skills training can be useful too. The third stage is application practice, which is when stressful situations are created so that people can practise the techniques they have learnt. These techniques can work for those who can learn to identify the processes involved when they become aggressive but are not so useful for those who cannot do this. Children may be too young to use such techniques. Chapter 5 explains how children develop cognitively through stages and if they have not developed sufficiently to use such techniques then other methods need to be used.

Where children are treated using cognitive therapy they are taught to stop, to think and to use problem-solving techniques. It has been found that cognitive

DEFINITIONS

Anger management training – tends to involve more than one stage. The first stage is cognitive preparation when the people analyse their anger patterns and try to find the triggers – what starts their aggressive behaviour. The second stage is skill acquisition, where they learn self-control and to manage their arousal. Social skills training can be useful too. The third stage is application practice, which is when stressful situations are created so that people can practise the techniques they have learnt.

behavioural techniques have been successful in children. For example, when the behaviour of previously aggressive children is measured after cognitive behavioural treatment it is found that they participate more in social activities and engage more in co-operative play. They also progress better at school and show a reduced number of behaviour problems (for example, Lochman, 1992).

Drug treatment

It is unlikely that drug treatment would be used for aggressive behaviour without there being a diagnosis of some disorder, such as ADHD. Drugs have the effect of calming the individual and repressing impulsivity. Drugs are not really used 'just' for aggressive behaviour.

Behavioural techniques

Behavioural techniques involve the mechanisms of operant conditioning, and these are outlined in Chapter 4. The main mechanisms are positive and negative reinforcement, and punishment. Positive reinforcement involves giving someone something pleasant in return for desired behaviour – for example, a child can receive sweets or praise. Negative reinforcement involves avoiding something unpleasant in return for desired behaviour – for example, children could be allowed to avoid disliked homework if they do something good. Punishment involves individuals receiving something unpleasant when they do something wrong. In general it is thought that punishment is not very useful as it only shows children what is wrong and does not show the required behaviour. Punishment can also be seen as aggression and this can show a child that in some circumstances aggression is appropriate. Usually it is better to use positive rein- forcement whenever desired behaviour is shown and to ignore any unwanted behaviour. Some aggressive behaviour cannot be ignored, however, because it may involve harm. In that case sometimes 'time out' procedures are used, where children are removed from a situation and made to stay away until they have calmed down. This can be seen as punishment, but if it is done firmly, without shouting or aggression, it can be a successful strategy. When considering children and the use of behavioural therapies it is important to note that family therapy is used. An example is action-oriented family therapy where parents are taught skills for managing their children. Goals are set for wanted behaviour and the family is taught how to reward it. It has been found that such therapies can work quite well (for example, Patterson *et al.*, 1992) and following action- oriented family therapy the frequency of a target behaviour (which is a behaviour deliberately chosen to be reduced) drops to the level of that in other families.

Using positive behavioural techniques in early years settings.

Most early years settings have a behaviour management policy, which describes how settings will approach managing children's behaviour. When drawing up a policy there are several points to take into consideration:

- Who will contribute to the writing of the policy? It is always good practice to involve parents as well as staff and even very young children can be encouraged to give their views as well.
- Some policies include a simple code of behaviour for children. The younger the children the simpler the 'rules'. For example one nursery's code was 'be kind, be careful, be safe and you must not hurt anybody'.
- The policy will include a description of the behavioural techniques that will be used. For instance there may be a statement that inappropriate behaviour will be ignored as far as is possible and as far as it is safe, backed up by praise for appropriate behaviour.

- There should be a definite statement about what techniques will *not* be used – for instance humiliation and physical or verbal aggression.
- Publication of the policy needs to be discussed. For instance all parents should have a copy as well as staff.
- The successful implementation of the policy depends on consistency. All the staff team should be applying the same principles and parents should be encouraged to do the same when they are on nursery premises.

In addition to a consistently applied behaviour management policy, consideration should be given to managing the environment and resources in such a way as to discourage unwanted behaviour. Regular observations are very helpful in identifying problem areas. For instance one nursery discovered that it had unwittingly designed a race track for the children when it altered the layout of the room. Moving furniture and activity areas to prevent children running around soon solved the problem. Another setting discovered that there was often a dispute as to who was going to play with a certain piece of equipment. Buying duplicates resolved the area of conflict.

The value of well thought-out routines as a way of managing children's behaviour cannot be overstated. All children, not only those with worrying behaviour, feel secure if they can predict what will happen during the day. Very stressed children will need this even more than others. A degree of flexibility is needed, but children should be warned in advance of proposed changes.

DEALING WITH ANXIETIES

Children can be diagnosed as having anxiety disorders, for example, overanxious disorder (generalised anxiety disorder), avoidant disorder (social phobia) and **separation anxiety disorder**. Symptoms of an anxiety disorder include headaches, stomach aches, sweating, and feelings of choking. Such feelings can be due to **stress**, which is defined as when someone thinks that they do not have the abilities to cope with the demands of a situation. Separation anxiety disorder occurs only in children. Chapter 3 discusses attachments and explains that separation anxiety is part of normal development and comes from forming a normal attachment with one caregiver. It is usual for a young child to fear separation from that main caregiver. However, if this natural fear becomes excessive and if distress about being separated from the main caregiver is more than would be expected, then this can lead to a diagnosis of separation anxiety disorder. An example of separation anxiety is when a child refuses to sleep away from his or her main caregiver or refuses to part from that person, especially at times of stress such as when starting school. However, this anxiety can be seen as fairly normal. It is when there is an obsession, for example, about harm that might come to the main caregiver, that the disorder is diagnosed.

The diagnosis is usually made only in older children too – when fear about being separated seems inappropriate for their age. For example, 11 year olds who will not go to school as they fear something bad might happen to their mother whilst they are at school might be diagnosed as having the disorder. Even then other behaviours would be taken into account as well, such as having repeated nightmares about being separated or being reluctant to go out without the main caregiver at all.

Gender or race differences in anxiety disorders

Usually anxiety disorders are found more in adolescents than in young children, but young children are sometimes diagnosed as suffering from anxiety. Girls in adolescence tend to report more fears than boys (see, for example, Ollendick and King, 1991) although in childhood there are no real gender differences noted, which is interesting. That tends to suggest that there are social and environmental factors that lead to such fears because if there were biological causes it would be expected that there would be gender differences from the start. There seem to be few differences between different cultures where children are concerned. African American young people and white young people have showed similarities in the situations that they were afraid of (Neal *et al.*, 1993).

Causes of and treatments for anxiety disorders

Causes of anxiety disorders seem to include genetic predispositions (disorders can run in families), early trauma, the learning experiences of the child and family interactions. It is likely that such disorders come from a mixture of these factors, rather than one of the factors causing a disorder.

Anxieties such as phobias may be learnt

Phobias are discussed in Chapter 4 and are specific fears, unlike other types of generalised anxiety. Phobias can arise from classical conditioning and can be treated using classical conditioning principles, which are outlined in Chapter 4. Basically it is suggested that a phobia arises from associating something with a fear response. Treatment involves teaching the person to associate that something with a different response – a relaxation response. For example, if you have learnt to associate spiders with fear, then you can learn (with help) to associate spiders with relaxation, and thus the phobia can be removed. Table 10.9 lists some phobias.

Table 10.9 Some phobias

Label	Phobia
Pyrophobia	Fire
Xenophobia	Strangers
Astraphobia	Storms, thunder and lightning
Acrophobia	Heights
Arachnophobia	Spiders
Claustrophobia	Closed spaces and confinement
Hematophobia	Blood
Ophidiophobia	Snakes
Ailurophobia	Cats
Autophobia	Oneself
Hydrophobia	Water
Thanatophobia	Death

There may be a genetic basis to phobias

You would think that if phobias are learnt from associations in the environment then we could develop a phobia of just about anything. However, this is not really the case. Many phobias are of large animals, snakes, heights, spiders and closed spaces. It has been suggested that humans are prepared biologically to have certain fears (see, for example Seligman, 1971). It may be that ancestors that feared heights, for example, were more likely to survive, and so that fear has been genetically transmitted to some of us. Similarly, other common phobias could be genetically given. Cook and Mineka (1989) found that monkeys could be conditioned to fear snakes by watching other monkeys showing fear of snakes, but when the same process is tried with artificial flowers, the monkeys that watched did not show fear. Research seems to indicate that, although some individuals can develop phobias to everyday objects, such as buttons, most phobias have a survival value in evolutionary terms.

Anxiety disorders may be present at birth

Studies have demonstrated that it is possible to breed animals with anxious personalities (see Plomin and Daniels, 1985). This suggests that some people might have a tendency to anxiety – although remember that findings from studies on animals might not be true of humans. Jerome Kagan (1988) in the United States has observed children between 0 and 2 years old and found that some seem to interact less with others. When such children are followed up and observed again, it is found that this trait of not interacting much with others (social inhibition) is still there. This suggests that such a trait is biologically given. It occurs early in the child's life and is still there some years later, whereas you would expect different experiences to have made a difference to the way a child interacts with others.

More evidence that anxiety disorders could be biologically given is that children of parents with anxiety disorders are more likely to show anxious behaviour themselves (Biederman *et al.*, 1990). Children with other relatives with anxiety disorders are also more likely to show anxious behaviour (Last *et al.*, 1991). You might say that if parents have an anxiety disorder then children would copy their behaviour but when the findings extend to relatives too then it is thought that it is more likely that there is a biological cause. Panic disorder, which is a specific anxiety disorder, was found in around a quarter of close relatives of those with panic disorder, whereas panic disorder is normally only found in around 2% of the population (Crowe *et al.*, 1983). Again this is evidence for at least some genetic factors in causing anxiety disorders. Perhaps some individuals are born with a genetic predisposition for an anxiety disorder, which will only develop if there are environmental triggers. Kendler *et al.* (1992) suggested that around 30% of the likelihood of developing generalised anxiety disorder (GAD) is genetic. There is also some evidence that agoraphobia (fear of open spaces) has a high genetic component whereas simple phobias are less likely to have a genetic component and social phobia has some genetic basis. This suggests that agoraphobia is more likely to run in families, social phobia does to an extent, but simple phobias seem to come from circumstances not genes. There is still the problem that if a characteristic runs in families, it may not be genetically given, but may be learnt within the family.

Biological factors

There might be a connection between anxiety disorders and lack of certain neurotransmitters (chemicals) in the brain, but there needs to be more evidence of a definite link. Benzodiazepines are commonly used for treating anxiety disorders. It is thought that these drugs help relieve anxiety by increasing the action of a neurotransmitter in the brain called gamma amino butyric acid (GABA). Neurotransmitters are used to pass signals from one brain cell to another. Gamma amino butyric acid is a neurotransmitter that inhibits, or slows down, the passing of signals, which is helpful if one is overanxious. This is an area of research that might lead to more firm conclusions about chemicals in the brain and how some lack of these, or mismatch in combinations, could lead to anxiety. Obsessive compulsive disorder (OCD) seems to be quite successfully treated by using medication that blocks a chemical (serotonin) from being reused in the brain. Fluoxetine (Prozac) and clomipramine (Anafranil) act in this way, and this suggests that excess serotonin is a cause of OCD.

Psychodynamic explanations

Psychodynamic explanations focus around Freud's views and were outlined earlier on in the book. Such explanations can be used to explain abnormal behaviour of adults. Freud was a medical doctor and his whole theory revolves around an attempt to explain disorders and an attempt to 'cure' mental health problems by using psychoanalysis. Adults can undergo psychoanalysis, as they can understand a therapist's analysis, but children are not treated using psychoanalysis because they have neither the language skills nor levels of understanding needed for analysis. A form of psychoanalysis for children is play therapy, outlined in Chapter 8.

Psychodynamic theory might be useful in explaining anxiety disorders. It is suggested that there are **objective anxieties** that are given by events in the outside world, such as when someone points a loaded gun at you (this is fear). But there is also moral anxiety and neurotic anxiety. **Moral anxiety** refers to situations in which people are anxious about being punished for disobeying social rules or for going against what they ought to be doing. **Neurotic anxiety** refers to situations in which people are afraid that they will obey an uncontrollable urge and do something that might be harmful to society. Recall Freud's idea of the personality, which involves an id, a superego and an ego. The id is present at birth and represents our impulses and desires. The superego develops around the age of 3 years. It represents social rules and inhibits our impulses. The ego is the part of the personality that tries to balance the urges of the id against the controlling rules of the superego. Moral anxiety is linked to the superego and neurotic anxiety is linked to the id. Freud thought that in order for us to protect ourselves from moral and neurotic anxiety we have defence mechanisms such as repression. This occurs when we 'bury' painful emotions and feelings so that we cope. However, using defence mechanisms only suppresses the problems and can lead to other problems. Treatment is to unpack such defence mechanisms, to reveal any anxieties and thus deal with them. Modern psychodynamic theorists do not focus as much on the conflict between the id, ego and superego when explaining anxieties, but focus more on the mother–child relationship. Separation anxiety was discussed earlier in this section, and that is more representative of the sorts of anxiety that modern psychodynamic theorists research. Parent-child relationships might lead to later anxiety in some way.

DEFINITIONS

Objective anxieties – are given by events in the outside world, such as when someone points a loaded gun at you (this is fear). This is a psychodynamic concept.

Moral anxiety – refers to when someone is anxious about being punished for disobeying social rules or for going against what they ought to be doing. This is a psychodynamic concept.

Neurotic anxiety – when someone is afraid that they will obey an uncontrollable urge and do something that might be harmful to society. This is a psychodynamic concept.

Types of anxiety disorders

There are different types of anxiety disorders and some are outlined here. Around 15% of the population suffer from an anxiety disorder and anxiety disorders are the most common of all mental disorders. Anxiety disorders include generalised anxiety disorder (GAD), phobias, panic disorders, obsessive-compulsive disorders (OCD) and post-traumatic stress disorder. Much of what follows does tend to be about adults but is included here partly as it can apply to children, partly for your own interest, and partly because you will be dealing with families, not only children.

Generalised anxiety disorder (GAD)

When someone has persistent anxiety over many different issues then this is called generalised anxiety disorder (GAD). There is unrealistic and excessive anxiety and GAD is sometimes called 'free floating' because there is no single specific cause. Symptoms include being tense and nervous, waiting for something bad to happen. There are physical symptoms too, such as racing heart, shakiness and a sinking stomach. Sufferers can develop colitis, headaches and insomnia. The worry can prevent the person from focusing on tasks. For GAD to be diagnosed the excessive and unrealistic worry must last for 6 months, being present on many days within that time. There must also be at least three of the following symptoms – tiring easily, muscle tension, irritability, difficulty in concentrating, sleep disturbance and restlessness. Generalised anxiety disorder tends to be found more in women than in men and occurs in around 4% of the population. It has been suggested that GAD is caused by a desire to gain control. By worrying all the time sufferers may feel they are more likely to hold onto control, even though this might be a false sense of control.

Panic disorders

Another type of anxiety is panic disorder. Sufferers have panic attacks, where they experience fear and discomfort. Panic attacks are not predictable. A diagnosis of panic disorder is made when someone has recurrent unexpected panic attacks, with the attack leading the person to fear another attack and being worried about the implications of the attack. There must be at least four symptoms from the following list:

- sweating
- trembling
- chills
- numbness
- sickness
- chest pain
- feeling of choking
- shortness of breath
- fear of dying
- fear of losing control
- palpitations or pounding heart
- feeling dizzy or faint
- feeling of unreality

As with phobias (discussed earlier) and also anxiety disorders, twice as many women have panic disorder than men. One study found that out of 300 college students around 5% reported symptoms such as those found in panic disorder (Craske and Krueger, 1990). Another study found that homeless people had a higher rate – 8% of the residents in the same area (Koegel *et al.,* 1988).

Obsessive-compulsive disorder (OCD)

People are diagnosed as having obsessive-compulsive disorder when they feel compelled or driven to act in a certain way and when that drive does not seem natural to them. Real compulsions are avoidance behaviours as they seem to engage the person in actions they do not want to do, presumably to prevent them having to do other things. Some people have obsessional thoughts rather than obsessional actions, and they keep going over the same issues repeatedly even when there is no point in doing that. For example, they may be thinking about an important career choice and continue to go over and over the decisions even when it is too late to change job (for example, if another job is now no longer available). Obsessive-compulsive thinking means going over and over a decision, even one as seemingly trivial as washing hands. People with this disorder might wash their hands, check them, check again, then check again, ask themselves if they are sure they have washed them, and so on. Obsessions are persistent thoughts or ideas that a person does not want and the thoughts are annoying. Compulsions are repetitive rituals and are undertaken in order to put off doing something else. They are not done for their own sake. It is difficult to say how many people suffer from obsessions and compulsions, but it might be around 1% or 2% of the population. Obsessive-compulsive disorder tends to go with panic and phobias, as well as with depression. For example, Edelmann (1992) suggests that between 20% and 66% of patients with OCD also have depression. It is rare in childhood.

Post-traumatic stress disorder (PTSD)

Post-traumatic stress disorder occurs after a severe trauma. It involves a cluster of psychological symptoms. The traumatic event is likely to have given extreme fear and horror. Symptoms include reliving the event, avoiding reminders of the event, and experiencing a numbing of responsiveness. The symptoms must last for a month for PTSD to be diagnosed though acute stress disorder can be diagnosed if similar symptoms last for at least 2 days but less than 4 weeks. Children may suffer from PTSD.

Treatments for anxiety disorders

There are various treatments and as with other disorders treatments depend on the approach used and on the presumed cause for the anxiety. If a psychodynamic explanation is given, for example, that anxiety comes from not being able to express instincts (neurotic anxiety) then insight therapy can be used to help the person to bring their feelings into conscious awareness. Other treatments can be behavioural and cognitive-behavioural ones, similar to the techniques used to remove aggressive behaviour. Medication can also be used. Just a few ideas about treatments used are outlined in this section.

Behavioural and cognitive-behavioural therapies

Behavioural therapies use operant and classical conditioning principles, and these are outlined in Chapter 4. For example, phobias are treated using classical conditioning principles where an association that has led to a phobia can be changed when the individual learns to associate relaxation with the phobic object instead of fear. Operant conditioning principles use the idea of reward to encourage desired behaviour. For example, obsessional-compulsive disorder can be helped if the person is encouraged using shaping to stop their rituals. If people find it hard to touch something they see as dirty, for instance, then they can be encouraged, using a system of rewards, to approach that object and gradually touch it. Cognitive-behavioural therapies also use rewards to encourage desired behaviour but focus as well on the individual's thinking patterns. People can learn to focus on positive thinking rather than negative thoughts, for example, and this can make them less anxious. One form of cognitive-behavioural therapy is rational emotive therapy (RET).

Drug treatments

Medication is used to help those with anxiety disorders. Alcohol is a drug and can help people to relax, although it has side effects. Tranquillisers, which are used to treat anxiety, include barbiturates and benzodiazepine substances. Barbiturates are addictive and are also lethal if an overdose is taken. Other sedatives that are not barbiturates, such as meprobamate (Miltown) and barbiturates like diazepam (Valium) have fewer problems than barbiturates, although drugs do have side effects. Benzodiazepine drugs inhibit the central nervous system, reduce anxiety and calm people. Mellenger and Balter (1981) reported that around 9% to 10% of the population took benzodiazepines to reduce anxiety over a one-year period. Usually people use benzodiazepines for a short period although between 1% and 2% of the population use them regularly for a year or more (Salzman, 1991). In general it is thought that such drugs do work and do reduce anxiety. Benzodiazepines cause **tolerance**, which means that the individual gets used to the dose, which then has to be increased to get the same effect. They also cause **dependence**, which means that there will be **withdrawal symptoms** when the person stops using them. Withdrawal symptoms can include anxiety (!), irritability, tremor and insomnia. If the drugs are taken over a long period then withdrawal symptoms tend to be more severe.

CHILD ABUSE

The effects of child abuse are considered here because, although this is not really about abnormality in the sense of a disorder, it is about issues that affect a child's development. This is a painful subject. In your career you will, undoubtedly, come across children who have been abused. Some of you who are reading this may have

---

DEFINITIONS

Tolerance – is when people become accustomed to a drug they are taking and so have to take more to have the same effect.

Dependence – is when people rely on a drug and when they stop taking it they experience withdrawal symptoms.

Withdrawal symptoms – physical symptoms when someone stops taking a drug. These symptoms include tremors, anxiety, irritability and insomnia.

been victims yourself. This section of the book is only the briefest introductions. You will receive more detailed teaching on your course. If you are a practitioner and feel that your knowledge is insufficient it is advised that you undertake professional development in this area. Your local authority early years section will probably have courses you can attend.

It is generally accepted that there are four categories of child abuse:

- emotional abuse
- neglect
- physical abuse
- sexual abuse.

This chapter will concentrate on physical and sexual abuse but it must be recognised that all abuse carries with it a degree of emotional abuse.

Physical abuse of children

Physical abuse of children can occur within the context of what parents call discipline, and it could be thought that this is a private matter as a parent 'owns' their child. In some societies there have been practices that we would view as physical abuse of children, such as infanticide (killing) of female children, binding of girls' feet, and forced genital mutilation. There have been changes in what is seen as appropriate discipline, too, and currently there is discussion about whether parents should be allowed to smack their children. There is now thought to be a line between discipline and abuse. In legal terms whether discipline is abuse depends on what is intended, how much force is used and what sort of injury is sustained.

Abused children tend to show symptoms of depression, low intellectual functioning and emotional symptoms. There does not seem to be one single pattern of behaviour that characterises an abused child. Abused children can be more aggressive than non-abused children and case histories of violent criminal offenders often show that there was abuse in their background, so it is often concluded that the abused can become an abuser. Evidence is not very clear, though. For example, Widom (1989) followed up abused and neglected children and found that 26% did go on to commit juvenile offences, but 74% did not. It is possible, too, that males who are abused do turn to violence and crime when they are older, whereas women are more likely to become depressed and have psychiatric problems.

Sexual abuse

There are different forms of sexual abuse, which range in severity from full penetrative sex to allowing children access to material of an explicit nature (videos and so forth) which are inappropriate for young children to see. Most sexual abuse of children is carried out by someone close to the child, often a family member. Incest is the term used to describe abuse by a family member whereas the term paedophilia is used when a non-family member is the perpetrator. Girls are more likely to be abused than boys. Often the individual will believe that their actions are pleasurable for the child or educational – or even that the child was provocative in some way, so it is clear that the perpetrator suffers from distortions of reality. Some paedophiles do not seek out children by working in relevant areas, but others work in fields where they will interact with children.

One problem with research in this area is that studies tend to treat all child sexual abusers as being the same, whereas they are not all alike. In general they tend not to be very good at interacting in social situations, are passive and not aggressive, and are likely to have low intelligence. They tend to come from lower socioeconomic groups and have **dysfunctional families** (which means that there is a divorce in the family, parental mental illness, substance abuse or criminality, for example). Child sexual abusers are likely to have experienced physical abuse and

---

TRY THIS!

Either in your group at college, or among your colleagues in your early years setting, discuss how you were disciplined as a child. Would you continue using the same methods on your own children?

Early years practitioners would never use physical punishment to discipline children. It could be interpreted as an assault and research, as you have seen, indicates that it is an ineffective method of punishment. However you will meet parents who smack their children. What arguments against smacking would you use when discussing the topic with them?

DEFINITIONS

Dysfunctional families – are families where there is marital break down, substance abuse, criminality or perhaps parental mental illness.

neglect and 57% have been victims of sexual abuse themselves (according to Bard *et al.*, 1987). Around 23% of all sexual abuse of children occurs in the family (according to Siegel *et al.*, 1987). Father-daughter incest has been said to occur in around 1.5% of families (for example according to Finkelhor, 1980).

Why are abused children likely to be abusive parents?

Studies do tend to show that abuse runs in families. Studies in the 1980s showed that a high percentage of abused children come from families where parents had been victims themselves (Oliver, 1988). Oliver (1993) suggested that many abusive parents deny that they are abused too, which makes it hard to find the evidence. When interviewing abusive parents it may be found that they idealise their own parents and say that their childhood was very good, even if this is not true. This can be seen as even more of a problem because, in this case, abuse of a child could be seen as more likely. Parents who accept that they were abused and realise that the consequences might be that they become abusive are more likely to seek help and may be better equipped to change their own patterns of child rearing. One reason why abused children might become abusers is that children learn from the parents and environment and develop patterns of behaviour based on this learning. Consider social learning theory explanations of how we learn, outlined in Chapter 4; it is claimed that role models are used, and children copy the behaviour they witness. They may also learn to mistrust other people, and this can also mean they mistrust their own children and become poor parents. Another explanation comes from the psychodynamic approach, which suggests that the quality of a parent-infant bond acts as a guide for later relationships. If children do not have a good quality bond then they might not have a good model for their own later relationships. This can mean they have low self-esteem and also might mean any attachment with their own child is maladaptive. Chapter 3 looks more at attachment and the importance of parent-infant relationships.

Are abusive parents mentally ill?

Some abusive parents are mentally ill and may have personality disorders. However, most abusive parents are not diagnosed as being mentally ill. It has been found, however, that they find it hard to cope with stress and are not very socially competent. They also tend to have poor parenting skills and are not good at relationships. They also find it hard to control angry impulses. Abusive parents can be socially isolated and tend to be domineering. They can also have inappropriate expectations. For example, abusive mothers tend to say that their babies are difficult even when they do not seem to be any more difficult than average. Abusive parents are also more likely to think that behaviour is intentional and can misinterpret their children's behaviour – thinking something was done on purpose when another parent would not think that.

THE SPECIAL EDUCATIONAL NEEDS CODE OF PRACTICE

This chapter has described a variety of situations where children's development does not follow the expected pattern. Many of the conditions mean that children will have difficulties accessing the curriculum in the same way as their peers and will be defined as having special educational needs. In the UK the majority of children with special educational needs are educated in mainstream settings and early years settings, in particular, are in a strong position to offer inclusive education.

Each setting is required to appoint a special educational needs co-ordinator (SENCO) who has the responsibility of ensuring that the guidelines in the Special

> **GOOD PRACTICE**
>
> It is important that you know what to do if you have worries that a child in your care is being abused. It is not something that you should keep to yourself and you should discuss any concerns with your placement supervisor or line manager.
>
> All early years settings have a child protection policy. Make sure that you have read it and understand your role.

KEY TERMS

You need to know the meaning of the following words and phrases. Go back through the chapter to make sure you understand them:

Amniocentesis
Anger management training
Conduct disorder
Contingency
Dependence
Dysfunctional families
Echolation
Islets of ability
Longitudinal study
Moral anxiety
Neurotic anxiety
Objective anxieties
Oppositional defiant disorder (ODD)
Savant skills
Separation anxiety disorder
Social aloofness
Stress
Theory of mind
Tolerance
Triad of impairments
Weak central coherence
Withdrawal symptoms

Educational Needs Code of Practice (2001) are implemented. The code outlines procedures for the identification of children with special educational needs and the response that the setting is required to make to these needs. This may involve extra, targeted support for children using the resources that are already available, or may involve the child in a formal assessment of their needs and allocation of resources to meet these.

FURTHER READING

Afasic is the organization for children with speech and language impairments. The website contains useful information and links to other sites. www.afasic.org.uk/
British Dyslexia Association. This has a very useful information section with very helpful advice for early years educators: www.bda-dyslexia.org.uk/
British Dyslexics website www.dyslexia.uk.com/ is useful for its links to other publications.
Department for Education and Skills (DfES) (2001) *Special Educational Needs Code of Practice,* DfES, Nottingham.
All early years practitioners should have a copy of this. It is available free of charge from the DfES. It is the document that outlines responsibilities and procedures for identification and assessment of children who have, or may have, special educational needs.
Down's Syndrome Association. This UK organization has an excellent website which is a good place to start when researching into Down's syndrome: www.downs-syndrome.org.uk/
Hannah, L. (2001) *Teaching Young Children with Autistic Spectrum Disorders to Learn: A Practical Guide for Parents and Staff in Mainstream Schools and Nurseries,* The National Autistic Society, London.
This is an excellent, practical book, which will be invaluable for all early years practitioners and students at all levels.
Hobart, C. and Frankel, J. (1998) *Good Practice in Child Protection,* Nelson Thornes Ltd, Cheltenham.
This is a clear and accessible text for all students and practitioners.
Mukherji, P. and O'Dea, T. (2000) *Understanding Children's Language and Literacy,* Nelson Thornes Ltd, Cheltenham.
This is an easy read and suitable for students at all levels. Chapter 9 contains a section on language and communication problems, including language impairment, dyslexia, and autism, with a particular emphasis on practical guidelines for early years practitioners.
Mukherji, P. (2001) *Understanding Children's Challenging Behaviour,* Nelson Thornes Ltd, Cheltenham.
This is an accessible book that is written for early years practitioners and students of all levels. The book looks at behaviour management in early years settings as well as some of the conditions mentioned in this chapter, including autism, ADHD and dyspraxia.
National Austistic Society. This has an excellent website which will be a good place to start when researching into Autism www.nas.org.uk. Especially recommended is the fact sheet for Professionals in education.
Royal National Institute for the Blind (2001) *Focus on Foundation – Including Children with Sight Loss in Early Years Settings,* RNIB, London.
This text offers practical ideas for the inclusion of children with sight problems. It is recommended reading for all students and practitioners.

Tassoni, P. (2003) *Supporting Special Needs. Understanding Inclusion in the Early Years*, Heinemann Educational Publishers, Oxford.
This is an excellent book that will be useful for all practitioners and students on early years courses.

References

Abrams, R.M., Gerhardt, K.J. and Peters, A.J.M. (1995) Transmission of sound and vibration to the fetus. In: *Fetal Development: A Psychological Perspective* (eds LeCanuet J., Fifer, W., Krasnegor, N. and Smotherman, W.). Erlbaum, Hillsdale NJ, pp. 315–330.

Ainsworth, M.D.S., Bell, S.M. and Stayton, D.J. (1974) Infant-mother attachments and social development: Socialisation as a product of reciprocal responsiveness to signals. In M.P.M. Richards (Ed.) *The Introduction of the Child into a Social World*, Cambridge University Press, London.

Ainsworth, M.D.S., Blehar, M.C., Waters, E. and Wall, S. (1978) *Patterns of Attachment: Assessed in the Strange Situation and at Home,* Erlbaum, Hillsdale NJ.

Ainsworth, M.D.S. (1967) *Infancy in Uganda: Infant Care and the Growth of Love,* Johns Hopkins Press, Baltimore.

Anastopoulos, A.D., Shelton, T., DuPaul, G.J. and Gouvremont, D.C. (1993) Parent training for attention-deficit hyperactivity disorder: its impact on parent functioning. *Journal of Abnormal Child Psychology,* **21**, 581–596

Axline, V. (1971) *Dibs: In Search of Self*, Penguin, Harmdonsworth.

Baillergeon, R. (1993) The object concept revisited: new directions in the investigation of infants' physical knowledge. In: *Visual Perception and Cognition in Infancy. Carnegie Mellon Symposia on Cognition* (ed. Granrud, C.). Erlbaum, Hillsdale NJ.

Bandura, A. (1965) Influence of models' reinforcement contingencies on the acquisition of imitative responses. *Journal of Personality and Social Psychology,* **1**, 587–595.

Bandura, A., Ross, D. and Ross, S. (1961) Transmissions of aggression through imitation of aggressive models. *Journal of Abnormal and Social Psychology,* **63**(3), 575–582.

Baranek, G.T. (1999) Autism during infancy: a retrospective video analysis of sensory-motor and social behaviours at 9–12 months of age. *Journal of Autism and Development Disorders,* **29**, pp. 213–224.

Bard, L.A., Carter, D.L., Cerce, D.D., Knight, R.A., Rosenberg, R. and Schneider, B. (1987) A descriptive study of rapists and child molesters: developmental, clinical and criminal characteristics. *Behavioural Sciences and the Law,* **5**, 203–220.

Barkley, R.A.(1981) *Hyperactive Children: A Handbook for Diagnosis and Treatment,* Guilford Press, New York.

Barkley, R.A. (1990) *Attention Deficit Hyperactivity Disorder: A Handbook for Diagnosis and Treatment,* Guilford Press, New York.

Barkley, R.A., Fischer, M., Edelbrock, C., and Smallish, L. (1991) The adolescent outcome of hyperactive children diagnosed by research criteria – III. Mother-child interactions, family conflicts and maternal psychopathology, *Journal of Child Psychology and Psychiatry,* **32**, 233–255.

Barkley, R.A., McMurray, M.B., Edelbrock, C. and Robbins, K. (1990) Side effects of methylphenidate in children with attention-deficit hyperactivity disorder: a systematic, placebo-controlled evaluation. *Pediatrics,* **86**, 184–192

Baron-Cohen, S., Leslie, A.M. and Frith, U. (1985) Does the autistic child have a 'theory of mind'? *Cognition,* **21**, 37–46.

Bates, J. (1994) Introduction. In Bates, J.E. and Wachs, T.D. (Eds) *Individual Differences at the Interface of Biology and Behaviour*, American Psychological Association, Washington, DC.

Bates, J.E., (1987) Temperament in infancy. In *Handbook of Infant Development, 2nd Edn.* (ed. Osofsky, J.D.), John Wiley, New York, pp 1101–1149.

Bates, J.E., Marvinney, D., Kelly, T., Dodge, K.A., Bennett, D.S. and Pettit, G.S. (1994) Child-care history and kindergarten adjustment. *Developmental Psychology*, **30**, 690 – 700.

Bateson, M. (1975) Mother-infant exchanges: the epigenesis of conversational interactions. *Annals of the New York Academy of Sciences,* 263, pp 101-113

Belsky, J. (1988) Infant day care: a cause for concern. *Zero to Three*, **7**(1), 1–7.

Belsky, J. and Steinberg, L.D. (1978) The effects of day care: a critical review, *Child Development*, **49**, 929–49.

Bem, S.L. (1981) Gender schema theory: A cognitive account of sex typing. *Psychological Review*, **88**, 354–364.

Benoit, D. and Parker, K.C.H. (1994) Stability and transmission of attachment across three generations. *Child Development*, **65**, 1444–1456.

Bernstein, B. (1961) Social class and linguistic development. In: *Education, Economy and Society* (eds Halsey, A., Flaud, J. and Anderson, C.). Collier-Macmillan, London.

Biederman, J., Rosenbaum, J.F., Hirshfeld, D.R., Faraone, S.V., Boldue, E.A., Gersten, M., Meminger, S.R., Kagan, J., Snidman, N. and Reznick, S.(1990) Psychiatric correlates of behavioural inhibition in young children of parents with and without psychiatric disorders. *Archives of General Psychiatry*, **47**, 21–26.

Bigelow, B.J. and La Gaipa, J.J. (1980) The development of friendship values and choice. In: *Friendship and Social Relations in Children* (eds Foot, H.C., Chapman, A.J. and Smith, J.R.). Wiley, Chichester, pp. 15–44.

Binet, A. (1905) cited in Childs, D. (1999) *Psychology and the Teacher,* 6th edn. Cassell Education, London, pp. 248–249.

Bouchard, T. J., Jr., Lykken, D. T., McGue, M., Segal, N. L., and Tellegen, A. (1990) Sources of human psychological differences: the Minnesota study of twins reared apart. Science, **250**, 223–228.

Bourcher. J., Lewis, V. and Collis, G. (1998) Familiar face and voice matching and recognition in children with autism. *Journal of Child Psychology*, **39**, 171–181.

Bowlby, J. (1958) The nature of the child's tie to his mother. *International Journal of Psychoanalysis*, **41**, 350 – 373.

Bowlby, J. (1969) *Attachment and Loss: Vol. 1. Attachment,* Basic Books, New York.

Bowlby, J. (1980) *Attachment and loss, Vol. 3. Loss,* Hogarth Press, London.

Bronfenbrenner, U. (1979) *The Ecology of Human Development,* Harvard University Press, Cambridge MA.

Brown, G.L., Ebert, M.H., Goyer, P.F., Jimerson, D.C., Klein, W.J., Bunney, W.E. and Goodwin, F.K. (1982) Aggression, suicide, and serotonin: relationships to CSF amine metabolites. *American Journal of Psychiatry*, **139**, 741-746

Bruce, T (1987). *Early Childhood Education,* Hodder & Stoughton, London.

Bruner, J.S. and Kenney, H. (1966) *The Development of the Concepts of Order and Proportion in Children,* Wiley, New York.

Bruner, J.S. (1983) *Child's Talk: Learning to Use Language,* Oxford University Press, Oxford.

Brunner, H.G., Nelen, M., Breakefield, X.O., Ropers, H.H. and Van Oost, B.A.(1993) Abnormal behaviour associated with a point mutation in the structural gene for monoamine oxidase A. *Science*, **262**, 578–580.

Bushnell, I.W.R., Sai, F. and Mullin, J.T. (1989) Neonatal recognition of the mother's face. *British Journal of Developmental Psychology*, **7**, 3–15.

Butterworth, G. (1995) Origins of mind in perception and action. In: *Joint*

Attention: Its Origins and Role in Development (eds Moore, C. and Dunham, P.J.). Erlbaum: Hillsdale NJ.

Byrnes, J.P. and Takahira, S. (1993) Explaining gender differences on SAT-math items. *Developmental Psychology*, **29**, 805–810.

Campbell, M. (1988) Annotation. Fenfluramine treatment of autism, *Journal of Child Psychology and Psychiatry*, **29**, 1–10.

Cantwell, D.P. and Hanna, G.L. (1989) Attention deficit disorder. In: *Review of Psychiatry* (eds Tasman A., Hales R.E. and Francis A.J.) American Psychiatric Press, Washington, DC, pp.134–161.

Carey, G. (1992) cited in Kendall, P.C. and Hammen, C. (1995) *Abnormal Psychology,* Houghton Mifflin Company, Boston MA, p. 188.

Carlson, N.R. (1994) *Physiology of Behaviour,* Allyn & Bacon, Boston MA.

Carr, J. (1994) Long-term outcome for people with Down's syndrome. *Journal of Child Psychology and Psychiatry,* **35**, 425–439.

Caughy, M.O., DiPietro, J.A. and Strobino, D.M. (1994) Day-care participation as a protective factor in the cognitive development of low-income children. *Child Development,* **63**, 457–471.

Charman, T., Swettenham, J., Baron-Cohen, S., Cox, A., Baird, G. and Drew, A. (2000) An experimental investigation of social-cognitive abilities in infants with autism: clinical implications. In: *Infant Development: The Essential Readings* (eds Muir, D. and Slater, A.). Blackwell, Cambridge, MA and Oxford, pp. 343–363.

Cherness, C. and Adler, M. (2000) *Promoting Emotional Intelligence in Organisations*, American Society for Training and Development, Alexandria, VA.

Chess, S. (1977) Report on autism in congenital rubella. *Journal of Autism and Childhood Schizophrenia,* **7**, 68–81.

Chomsky, N. (1982) *Some Concepts and Consequences of the Theory of Government and Binding,* MIT Press, Cambridge MA.

Clark, A.H., Wyon, S.M. and Richards, M.P.M. (1969) Free-play in nursery school children. *Journal of Child Psychology and Psychiatry,* **10**, 205-216

Coccaro, E.F., Siever, L.J., Klar, H.M., Maurer, G., Cochrane, K., Cooper, T.B., Mohs, R.C. and Davis, K.I. (1989) Scrotonergic studies in patients with affective and personality disorders: correlates with suicidal and impulsive aggressive behaviour. *Archives of General Psychiatry,* **46**, 587–599.

Cohen, D. (2002) *How the Child's Mind Develops,* Routledge, Hove.

Coie, J.D. and Dodge, K.A. (1983) Continuities and changes in children's social status: A five-year longitudinal study, *Merrill-Palmer Quarterly*, **29**, 261–282.

Collaer, M.L. and Hines, M. (1995) Human behavioural sex differences: A role for gonadal hormones during early development? *Psychological Bulletin*, **118**, 55–107.

Cook, M. and Mineka, S. (1989) Observational conditioning of fear to fear-relevant versus fear-irrelevant stimuli in rhesus monkeys. *Journal of Abnormal Psychology,* **98**, 448–459.

Coyle, J.T., Oster-Granite, D. and Gearhart, L. (1986) The neurobiological consequences of Down's syndrome. *Brain Research Bulletin,* **16**, 773–787.

Craske, M.G. and Krueger, M.T. (1990) Prevalence of nocturnal panic in a college population. *Journal of Anxiety Disorders,* **4**, 125–139.

Crowe, R.R., Noyes, R., Pauls, D.L. and Slymen, D.J. (1983) A family study of panic disorder. *Archives of General Psychiatry,* **40**, 1065–1069.

Crusco, A.H. and Wetzel, C.G. (1984) The midas touch: the effects of interpersonal touch on restaurant tipping. *Personality and Social Psychology Bulletin,* **10**, 512–517.

Curtiss, S. (1977) *Genie: A Psychological Study of a Modern-day Wild Child,* Academic Press, New York.

Darwin, C. (1859/1958) *The Origin of Species,* Penguin, New York.

Davenport, G.C. (1994) *An Introduction to Child Development,* Collins Education, London.

David, T., Goouch, K., Powell,S. and Abbott, L. (2003) *Birth to Three Matters: A Review of the Literature Compiled to Inform the Framework to Support Children in their Earliest Years,* DfES, Nottingham.

Dawson, G., Warrenburg, S. and Fuller, P. (1983) Hemispheric functioning and motor imitation in autistic persons. *Brain and Cognition,* **2**, 346–354.

Department for Education and Skills (DfES) (2001) *Special Educational Needs Code of Practice,* DfES, Nottingham.

Deutsch, K. (1987) Genetic factors in Attention Deficit Disorders. Paper presented at symposium on Disorders of Brain and Development and Cognition, Boston, MA. As cited in Anastopoulos, A.D. and Barkley, R.A. (1988) Biological factors in attention-deficit hyperactivity disorder. *The Behaviour Therapist,* **11**, 47–53.

Dion, K. (1972) Physical attractiveness and evaluation of children's transgressions. *Journal of Personality and Social Psychology,* **24**, 207–213.

Dion, K., Berscheid, E. and Walster, E. (1972) What is beautiful is good. *Journal of Personality and Social Psychology,* **24**, 285–290.

Dipboye, R.L. (1977) Alternative approaches to deindividuation. *Psychological Bulletin,* **84**, 1057–1075.

Dodge, K.A., Pettit, G.S., McClaskey, C.L. and Brown, M.M. (1986) Social competence in children. *Monographs of the Society for Research in Child Development,* **51**(2).

Dodge, K.A., Schlundt, D.C., Shocken, I. and Delugach, J.D. (1983) Social competence and children's sociometric status: the role of peer group entry strategies. *Merrill-Palmer Quarterly,* **29**, 309–336.

Donaldson, M. (1978) *Children's Minds,* Fontana/Collins, Glasgow.

Dowling, M. (2001) *Young Children's Personal, Social and Emotional Development,* Paul Chapman, London.

Dunn, J. and Kendrick, C. (1982) *Siblings: Love, Envy and Understanding,* Blackwell, Oxford.

Edelmann, R.J. (1992) *Anxiety Theory, Research and Intervention in Clinical and Health Psychology,* Wiley, Chichester.

Eichelman, B. (1992) Aggressive behaviour: from laboratory to clinic. Quo vadit? *Archives of General Psychiatry,* **49**, 488–492.

Ekman, P., Friesen, W.V., O'Sullivan, M., Chan, A., Diacoyanni-Tarlatzis, I., Heider, K., Krause, R., Lecompte, W.A., Pitcairn, T., Riccibitti, P.E., Scherer, K., Tomita, M. and Tzavaras.A. (1987) Universals and cultural differences in the judgements of facial expressions of emotion. *Journal of Personality and Social Psychology,* **53**, 712–717.

Elfer, P., Goldschmied, E. and Selleck, D. (2003) *Key persons in the Nursery,* David Fulton, London.

Erikson, E.H. (1963) *Childhood and Society,* 2nd edn. W.W. Norton, New York.

Eron, L., Walder, L. and Lefkowitz, M. (1971) *Learning of Aggression in Children.* Little, Brown, Boston MA.

Evans, J.A. and Hammerton, J.L. (1985) Chromosomal anomalies. In A.M. Clarke, A.D.Clark and J.M. Berg (Eds) *Mental Deficiency: The Changing Outlook,* Free Press, New York.

Fagot, B.I. (1978) Reinforcing contingencies for sex role behaviours: Effect of experience with children, *Child Development,* 49, pp 30–36.

Farver, J. (1993) Cultural differences in scaffolding pretend play: a comparison of American and Mexican mother-child and sibling-child pairs. In: *Parent-child Play; Descriptions and Implications* (ed. MacDonald, K.). Albany, NY: SUNY Press.

Fawcett (2003) *Learning Through Child Observation,* Jessica Kingsley Publications, London.

Feingold, B.F. (1975) *Why your Child is Hyperactive,* Random House, New York.

Field, T.M. (1991b) Quality infant day-care and grade school behaviour and performance. *Child Development,* **62**, 863–870.

Fielder, A.R. and Moseley, M.J. (2000) Environmental light and the preterm infant. *Seminars in Perinatology,* **24**, 291–298.

Finkelhor, D. (1980) Sex among siblings: a survey on prevalence, variety and effects. *Archives of Sexual Behaviour,* **9**, 171–194.

Fischer, M., Barkley, R.A., Edelbrock, C. and Smallish L. (1991) The adolescent outcome of hyperactive children diagnosed by research criteria – III. Mother-child interactions, family conflicts and maternal psychopathology. *Journal of Child Psychology and Psychiatry,* **32**, 233–255.

Folstein, S. and Rutter, M. (1978) A twin study of individuals with infantile autism. In: *Autism: A Reappraisal of Concepts and Treatment* (eds Rutter, M. and Schopler, E.). New York: Plenum Press.

Fonzi, A., Schneider, B.H., Tani, F. and Tomada, G. (1997) Predicting children's friendship status from their dyadic interaction in structured situations of potential conflict. *Child Development,* **68**, 496–506.

Fox, N.A. (ed.) (1994) The development of emotion regulation. *Monographs of the Society for Research in Child Development,* **59**(240), nos 2–3.

Fraiberg, S.H. (1977) *Insights from the Blind,* Souvenir Press, London.

Fraiberg, S.H. (1974) Blind infants and their mothers: an examination of the sign system. In: *The Effect of the Infant on its Caregiver* (eds Lewis, M. and Rosenblum, L.). Wiley, New York.

Freud, S. (1930) Civilisation and its discontents. In: *The Standard Edition of the Complete Psychological Works of Sigmund Freud* (ed. and trans. Strachey, J.). W.W.Norton, New York.

Frith, U. (1989) *Autism: Explaining the Enigma,* Blackwell, Oxford.

Galton, F. (1879) Psychometric experiments. *Brain,* **2**, 149–162.

Gardner, H. (1992) *Multiple Intelligences,* Basic Books, New York.

Gardner, H. (1983) *Frames of Mind: The Theory of Multiple Intelligences,* Basic Books, New York.

Gessell, A. and Ames, L. (1940) The ontogenetic organisation of prone behaviour in human infancy. *Journal of Genetic Psychology,* **56**, 247–263.

Goldfarb, W. (1943) The effects of early institutional care on adolescent personality. *Journal of Experimental Education,* **12**, 106–129.

Goldschmied, E. and Jackson, S. (2004) *People Under Three. Young Children in Day Care,* 2nd edn. Routledge, London.

Goleman, D. (1995) *Emotional Intelligence: Why It Can Matter More than IQ,* Bloomsbury, London.

Golinkhoff, R.M. and Hirsh-Pasek, K. (1995) Reinterpreting children's sentence comprehension: Toward a new framework. In: *The Handbook of Child Language* (eds Fletcher, P. and MacWhinney, B.). Blackwell, Oxford, pp. 430 – 461.

Gopnik, A., Meltzoff, A. and Kuhl, P. (1999) *How Babies Think,* Weidenfeld & Nicolson, London.

Gottesman, I.I. (1991) *Schizophrenia Genesis: The Origins of Madness,* W.H. Freeman, New York.

Greenspan, S.I. and Greenspan, N.T. (1985) *First Feelings: Milestones in the Emotional Development of your Baby and Child,* Viking, New York.

Grossman, K.E., Grossman, K., Huber, F. and Wartner, U. (1981) German children's behaviour towards their mothers at 12 months and their fathers at 18 months in Ainsworth's strange situation. *International Journal of Behavioural Development,* **4**, 157–181.

Guilford, J.P. (1982) Cognitive psychology's ambiguities: some suggested remedies. *Psychological Review,* **89**, 48–59.

Haight, W.L. and Miller, P.J. (1993) *Pretending at Home: Early Development in a*

Sociocultural Context, SUNY Press, Albany NY.

Haight, W.L., Parke, R.D. and Black, J.E. (1997) Mothers' and fathers' beliefs about spontaneous participation in their toddlers' pretend play. *Merrill-Palmer Quarterly,* **43**(2), 271–290.

Haight, W.L., Wang, X., Fung, H., Williams, H. and Mintz, J. (1999) Universal, developmental, and variable aspects of young children's play; a cross-cultural comparison of pretending at home. *Child Development,* **70**(6), 1477–1488.

Hall, E.T. (1966) *The Hidden Dimension,* Doubleday, New York.

Hannah, L. (2001*) Teaching Young Children with Autistic Spectrum Disorders to Learn: A Practical Guide for Parents and Staff in Mainstream Schools and Nurseries,* The National Autistic Society, London.

Happé, F.G.E. (1993) Communicative competence and theory of mind in autism: a test of relevance theory. *Cognition,* **48**, 101–119.

Harlow, H. (1959) Love in infant monkeys. *Scientific American,* **200**(6), 68–74.

Hartup, W.W. (1996) The company they keep: Friendships and their development significance, *Child Development,* **67**, 1–13.

Hepper, P. (1992) Fetal psychology: an embryonic science. In: *Fetal Behaviour: Developmental and Perinatal Aspects* (ed. Nijhuis, J.). Oxford University Press, New York, pp. 129–156.

Hobart, C and Frankel, J (1998) *Good Practice in Child Protection,* Nelson Thornes Ltd, Cheltenham.

Hobart, C. and Frankel, J. (2004) *A Practical Guide to Child Observation,* 3rd edn, Nelson Thornes Ltd, Cheltenham.

Holland, P. (2001) *We Don't Play with Guns Here,* Open University Press, Buckingham.

Hook, E.B., Cross, P.K. and Regal, R.R. (1990) Factual, statistical and logical issues in the search for a paternal age effect for Down's syndrome. *Human Genetics,* **85**, 387–388.

Horn, J.M. (1983) The Texas Adoption Project: Adopted children and their intellectual resemblance to biological and adoptive parents. *Child Development,* **54**, 268–275.

Howes, C. (1990) Can the age of entry into child care and the quality of child care predict adjustment in kindergarten? *Developmental Psychology,* **26**, 292–303.

Howes, C., Phillips, D.A. and Whitebook, M. (1992) Thresholds of quality: implications for the social development of children in centre-based child care. *Child Development,* **63**, 449–460

Huesmann, L.R., Eron, L.D., Lefkowitz, M. and Walder, L. (1984) Stability of aggression over time and generation. *Developmental Psychology,* **20**, 1120 – 1134.

Humphreys, A. and Smith, P.K. (1987) Rough and tumble, friendship and dominance in school children: Evidence for continuity and change with age. *Child Development,* **58**, 201–212.

Huston, A.C., Donnerstein, E., Fairchild, H., Feshback, N.D., Katz, P.A., Murray, J.P., Rubinstein, E.A., Wilcox, B. and Zukerman, D. (1992) *Big Word Small Screen: The Role of Television in American Society,* University of Nebraska Press, Lincoln NE.

Ishi-Kuntz, M. (1994) Paternal involvement and perception towards fathers' roles: a comparison between Japan and the United States. *Journal of Family Issues,* **15**, 30 – 48.

Jarvis, M. and Chandler, E. (2001) *Angles on Child Psychology,* Nelson Thornes Ltd, Cheltenham.

Jensen, A.R. (1969) How much can we boost IQ and scholastic achievement? *Harvard Educational Review,* **39**, 1–123.

Jusczyk, P.W. (1997) *The Discovery of Spoken Language,* MIT Press, Cambridge, MA.

Jussim, L. and Fleming, C. (1996) Self-fulfilling prophecy and the maintenance of social stereotypes: The role of dyadic interactions and social forces. In:

Stereotypes and Stereotyping (eds McRae, C.M., Stangor, C. and Hewstone, M.). Guilford, New York, pp. 161–192.

Kagan, J., Reznick, J.S. and Snidman, N. (1988) Biological bases of childhood shyness. *Science*, **240**, 167–171.

Kanner, L. (1943) Autistic disturbances of affective contact. *Nervous Child*, **21**, 217–250.

Karen, R. (1998) *Becoming Attached. First Relationships and How they Shape Our Capacity to Love*, Oxford University Press, Oxford.

Karmiloff-Smith, A. (1995) *Baby it's You*, Ebury Press, London.

Kazdin, A.E. (1994) *Behaviour Modification in Applied Setting*, 5th edn. Brooks/Cole, Pacific Grove CA.

Kendler, K.S., Neale, M.C., Kessler, R.C., Heath, A.C. and Eaves, L.J. (1992a) Generalised anxiety disorder in women: a population-based twin study. *Archives of General Psychiatry* **49**, 267–272.

King, V. (1994) Nonresident father involvement and child well-being: can dads make a difference? *Journal of Family Issues*, **15**, 78–96.

Klaus, M.H. and Kennell, J.H. (1976) *Maternal-infant Bonding: The Impact of Early Separation or Loss on Family Development*, Mosby, St Louis MO.

Kleine, C.L., Bustos, A.A., Meeker, F.B., and Staniski, R.A. (1973) Effects of self-attributed and other-attributed gaze on interpersonal evaluations between males and females. *Journal of Experimental Social Psychology*, **9**, 154–163.

Koegel, P., Burnam, A. and Farr, R.K.(1988) The prevalence of specific psychiatric disorders among homeless individuals in the inner city of Los Angeles. *Archives of General Psychiatry*, **45**, 1085–1092.

Kohlberg, L. (1984) *The Psychology of Moral Development: The Nature and Validity of Moral Stages*. Harper & Row, San Francisco.

Köhler, W. (1925) *The Mentality of Apes*, Harcourt Brace Jovanovich, New York.

Koluchova, J. (1972) Severe deprivation in twins: a case study. *Journal of Child Psychology and Psychiatry*, **13**, 107–114.

Koluchova, J. (1976) A report on the further development of twins after severe and prolonged deprivation. In: *Early Experience: Myth and Evidence* (eds Clarke, A.M. and Clarke, A.D.B.). Open Books, London.

Krashen, S. (1985) *The Input Hypothesis: Issues and Implications*, Longman, London.

Kuo-tai, T. (1987) Infantile autism in China. *Journal of Autism and Developmental Disorders*, **17**, pp 289–296.

Ladd, G.W. (1983) Social networks of popular, average and rejected children in school settings. *Merrill Palmer Quarterly*, **29**, 283–307.

LaPiere, R.T. (1934) Attitudes vs actions. *Social Forces*, **13**, 230–237.

Last, C., Hersen, M., Kazdin, A., Orvaschel, H. and Perrin, S. (1991) Anxiety disorders in children and their families. *Archives of General Psychiatry*, **48**, 928–934.

Lee, V. and Das Gupta, P. (1998) *Children's Cognitive and Language Development*, Blackwell in association with The Open University, Oxford.

Lewis, M., Young, G., Brooks, J. and Michalson, L. (1975) The beginning of friendship. In: *Friendship and Peer Relations* (eds Lewis, M. and Rosenblum, L.). Wiley, New York, pp. 27–65.

Levy, G.D., Taylor, M.G. and Gelman, S.A. (1995) Traditional and evaluative aspects of flexibility in gender roles, social conventions, moral rules and physical laws, *Child Development*, **66**, 525–531.

Lieberman, A.F., Weston, D. and Pawl, J.H. (1991) Preventative intervention and outcome with anxiously attached dyads, *Child Development*, **62**, 199–209.

Light, P.H., Buckingham, N. and Robins, A.H. (1979) The conservation task in an interactional setting. *British Journal of Educational Psychology*, **49**, 304–310.

Lindon, J. (2000) *Helping Babies and Toddlers Learn: A Guide to Good Practice with Under Threes*, The National Early Years Network, London.

Lindon, J. (2001) *Understanding Children's Play,* Nelson Thornes Ltd, Cheltenham.

Linssen, H. and Hagendoorn, L. (1994) Social and geographical factors in the explanation of European nationality stereotypes. *British Journal of Social Psychology,* **23**, 165–182.

Lochman, J.E. (1992) Cognitive-behavioural intervention with aggressive boys: three-year follow-up and preventive effects. *Journal of Consulting and Clinical Psychology,* **60**, 426–432.

Locke, J. (1938) *Some Thoughts Concerning Education,* Churchill, London. (Original work published 1699.)

Loeber, R. (1990) Development and risk factors of juvenile antisocial behaviour and delinquency. *Clinical Psychology Review* **10**, 1–41.

Lorenz, K. (1935) Der kumpan in der umwelt des vogels, *Journal of Ornithology,* **83**, 137–213 (published in English (1937) The companion in a bird's world. *Auk,* **54**, 245–274.

Lou, H., Heriksen, L., Bruhn, P., Borner, H. and Nielsen, J. (1989) Striatal dysfunction in attention deficit and hyperkinetic disorder. *Archives of Neurology,* **46**, 48–52.

Luk, S. and Leung, P.W. (1989) Conners' teacher's rating scale: a validity study in Hong Kong. *Journal of Child Psychology and Psychiatry,* **30**, 785–794.

Lykken, D.T. (1957) A study of anxiety in the sociopathic personality. *Journal of Abnormal and Social Psychology,* **55**, 6–10.

Main, M. and Solomon, J. (1990) Procedures for identifying infants as disorganised/disoriented during the Ainsworth Strange Situation. In Greenberg, M.T., Cicchetti, D. and Cummings, E.M. (Eds) *Attachment in the Preschool Years,* University of Chicago Press, Chicago, pp 121–160.

Maratsos, M.P. (1999) Some aspects of innateness and complexity in grammatical acquisition. In: *The Development of Language* (ed. Barrett, M.). Psychology Press, Hove, pp. 191–228.

Maslow, A.H. (1970) *Motivation and Personality,* 2nd edn. Harper & Row, New York.

McGarrigle, J. and Donaldson, M. (1974) Conservation accidents. *Cognition,* **3**, 341–350.

McGraw, M. (1945) *Neuromuscular Maturation of the Human Infant,* Hafner, New York.

McLaughlin, S. (1998) *Introduction to Language Development,* Singular Publishing, San Diego CA.

McMahon, R.C. (1980) Genetic etiology in the hyperactive child syndrome. A critical review. *American Journal of Orthopsychiatry,* **50**, 145–150.

Mead, M. (1935) *Sex and Temperament.* William Morrow, New York.

Melhuish, E. (2004) *Child Benefits The Importance of Investing in Quality ChildCare,* Daycare Trust, London. Facing The Future Policy Paper No. 9.

Mellenger, G.D. and Balter, M.B. (1981) cited in Kendall, P.C. and Hammen, C. (1995) *Abnormal Psychology,* Houghton Mifflin Company, Boston, p. 188.

Meltzoff, A.N. and Moore, M.K. (1977) Imitation of facial and manual gestures by human neonates. *Science,* **198**: 75–78.

Merikangas, K.R. and Weissman, M.M. (1986) Epidemiology of DSM-III Axis II personality disorders. In: *The American Psychiatric Association Annual Review.* (eds Frances, A.J. and Hales, R.E.). Washington, DC: American Psychiatric Press.

Miyake, K., Chen, S. and Campos, J.J. (1985) Infant temperament, mother's mode of interaction, and attachment in Japan: an interim report. In: Growing points in attachment theory and research (eds Bretherton, I. and Waters, E.). *Monographs of the Society for Research and Child Development,* **50**(1-2, Serial No. 209), pp. 276–297.

Molina, J.C., Chotro, M.G. and Dominguez, H.D. (1995) Fetal alcohol learning resulting from contamination of the prenatal environment. In: *Fetal*

Development: A Psychobiological Perspective (eds LeDanuet, J., Fifer, W., Krasnegor, N. and Smotherton, W.). Hillsdale, NJ: Erlbaum, pp. 419–438.

Money, J. and Ehrhardt, A.A. (1972) *Man and Woman, Boy and Girl*, Johns Hopkins University Press, Baltimore.

Mukherji, P. (2001) *Understanding Children's Challenging Behaviour,* Nelson Thornes Ltd, Cheltenham.

Mukherji, P. and O'Dea, T. (2000) *Understanding Children's Language and Literacy,* Nelson Thornes Ltd, Cheltenham.

Neal, A.M., Lilly, R.S. and Zakis, S. (1993) What are African-American children afraid of: a preliminary study. *Journal of Anxiety Disorders,* **7**, 129–139.

Newcombe, N. and Dubas, J.S. (1992) A longitudinal study of predictors of spatial ability in adolescent females, *Child Development,* **63**, 37–46.

Oliver, J.E. (1993) Intergenerational transmission of child abuse; Rates, research and clinical implications, *American Journal of Psychiatry*, **150**, 1315–1324.

Oliver, J.E. (1988) Successive generations of child maltreatment: the children. *British Journal of Psychiatry,* **153**, 543–553.

Ollendick, T.H. and King, N. (1991) Origins of childhood fears. *Behaviour Research and Therapy,* **29**, 117–123.

Pan, B.A. and Snow, C.E. (1999) The development of conversational and discourse skills. In: *The Development of Language* (ed. Barrett, M.). Psychology Press, Hove, pp. 229–249.

Parker, J.G. and Asher, S.R. (1987) Peer relations and later personal adjustment: Are low-accepted children at risk? *Psychological Bulletin*, **102**, 357–389.

Parten, M.B. (1932) Social participation among preschool children. *Journal of Abnormal and Social Psychology*, **27**, 243–269.

Patterson, M.L. (1983) *Nonverbal Behaviour: A Functional Perspective,* Springer, New York.

Patterson, G.R., Chamberlain, P. and Reid, J.B. (1992) A comparative evaluation of a parent-training programme. *Behaviour Therapy,* **13**, 638–650.

Pavlov, I.P (1927) *Conditioned Reflexes,* Oxford University Press, Oxford.

Pellegrini, A.D. and Smith, P.K. (1998) Physical activity play: the nature and function of a neglected aspect of play. *Child Development,* **69**, 577–598.

Pennington, B.F. and Ozonoff, S. (1996) Executive functions and developmental psychopathology. *Journal of Child Psychology and Psychiatry,* **37**, 51–87.

Petrides, K.V., Furnham, A. and Frederickson, N. (2004) Emotional intelligence. *The Psychologist,* (October), 574–577.

Petrill, S.A., Johansson, B., Pedersen, N.L., Berg, S., Plomin R., Fran, A. and McClearn, G.E. (2001) Low cognitive functioning in nondemented 80+ year old twins is not heritable. *Intelligence,* **29**, 75–83.

Piaget, J. (1960) *The Child's Conception of the World*, Routledge, London.

Piaget, J. (1929/1979) *The Child's Conception of the World,* Harcourt Brace, New York.

Piaget, J. (1932) *The Moral Development of the Child,* Routledge, London.

Piaget, J and Inhelder, B. (1956) *A Child's Conception of Space,* Routledge & Kegan Paul, London.

Plomin,, R. and Daniels, D. (1985) Genetics and shyness. In: *Shyness: Perspectives on research and treatment* (eds Jones, W.H., Cheek, J.M. and Griggs, S.R.). Plenum Press: New York.

Plomin, R. and Neiderhiser, J.M. (1991) Quantitative genetics, molecular genetics, and intelligence. *Intelligence,* **15**, 369–387.

Raine, A., Venables, P.H., Williams, M. (1990) Relationships between central and autonomic measures of arousal at age 15 years and criminality at 24 years. *Archives of General Psychiatry,* **47**, 1003–1007.

Reiff, H.B., Hatzel, N.M., Bramel, M.H. and Gibbon, T. (2001) The relation of LD and gender with emotional intelligence in college students. *Journal of Learning Disabilities,* **34**, 66–78.

Rhodes, G. and Tremewan, T. (1996) Averageness, exaggeration and facial attractiveness. *Psychological Science, 2*, 105–110.

Robertson, J. and Robertson, J. (1968) Young children in brief separation: a fresh look. *Psychoanalytic Study of the Child, 26*, 264–315.

Rogers, C. (1951) *Client-centred Therapy*, Houghton Mifflin, Boston.

Rose, S.A. and Blank, M. (1974) The potency of context in childrens' cognition: an illustration through conservation. *Child Development, 45*, 499–502.

Rosen, K.S. and Rothbaum, F. (1993) Quality of parental caregiving and security of attachment. *Developmental Psychology, 29*, 358–367.

Rosenthal, R. and Jacobson, L.F. (1968) *Pygmalion in the Classroom,* Holt, Rinehart & Winston, New York.

Rothbart, M.K., Derryberry, D. and Posner, M.I. (1994) A psychobiological approach to the development of temperament. In: *Individual Differences at the Interface of Biology and Behaviour* (eds Bates, J.E. and Wachs, T.D.). American Psychological Association, Washington DC.

Royal National Institute for the Blind (2001) *Focus on Foundation – Including Children with Sight Loss in Early Years Settings,* RNIB, London.

Rubenstein. J.L.R., Lotspeich, L. and Ciaranello, R.D. (1990) The neurobiology of developmental disroders. In: *Advances in Clinical Child Psychology* (eds Lahey, B. and Kazdin, A.E.). Plenum Press, New York, volume 13.

Rubin, K.H., Watson, K.S. and Jambor, T.W. (1978) Free play behaviours in preschool and kindergarten children. *Child Development, 49*, 534–536.

Rutter, M. (1976) Maternal deprivation, 1972–1978: new findings, new concepts, new approaches. *Child Development, 50*, 283–305.

Sagi, A., Lewkowicz, K.S., Shoham, R., Dvir, R. and Estes, D. (1985) Security of infant-mother, father, metapelet attachments among kibbutz-reared Israeli children. In: Growing points in attachment theory and research (eds Bretherton, I. and Waters, E.). *Monographs of the Society for Research in Child Development, 50*(1–2, serial no. 209), pp. 257–275.

Salovey, P. and Mayer, J.D. (1990) *Emotional intelligence. Imagination, Cognition and Personality, 9*, 185–211.

Salzman, C. (1991) Why don't clinical trial results always correspond to clinical experience? *Neuropsychopharmacology, 4*, 265–267.

Sapir, E. (1920) The status of linguistics as a science. *Language, 5*, 207–214.

Scarr, S. and Weinberg, R.A. (1976) IQ test performance of black children adopted by white families. *American Psychologist, 31*, 726–739.

Schaefer, M. and Smith, P.K. (1996) Teachers' perceptions of play fighting and real fighting in primary school. *Educational Research, 38*, 173–181.

Schaffer, H.R. and Emerson, P.E. (1964) The development of social attachments in infancy. *Monographs of the Society for Research in Child Development, 29*, no.94.

Seligman, M.E.P. (1971) Phobias and preparedness. *Behaviour Research and Therapy, 2*, 307–320.

Selman, R.L. (2003) *The Promotion of Social Awareness: Powerful Lessons from the Partnership of Developmental Theory and Classroom Practice,* Harvard University Press, Cambridge MA.

Shaywitz, B.A., Shaywitz, S.E., Byrne, T., Cohen, D.J. and Rothman, S. (1983) Attention deficit disorder: Quantitative analysis of CT. *Neurology, 33*, 1500–1503.

Siegel, J.M., Sorenson, S.B., Golding, J.M., Burnam, M.A. and Stein, J.A. (1987) The prevalence of childhood sexual assault: The Los Angeles Epidemologic Catchment Area project. *American Journal of Epidemiology, 126*, 1141–1153.

Siraj-Blatchford, I. and Clarke, P. (2000) *Supporting Identity, Diversity and Language in the Early Years,* McGraw-Hill, Maidenhead.

Skeels, H.M. (1966) Adult status of children with contrasting early life experiences. *Monographs of the Society for Research in Child Development*, **31**(3, serial no. 105).

Skeels, H. and Dye, H.B. (1939) A study of the effects of differential stimulation on mentally retarded children, *Proceedings and Addresses of the American Association on Mental Deficiency*, **44**, 114–136.

Skinner, B.F. (1938) *The Behaviour of Organisms*, Appleton-Century-Crofts, New York.

Slater, A. and Bremner, G. (Eds), (2003) *An Introduction to Developmental Psychology*, Blackwell, Oxford.

Slaski, M. and Cartwright, S. (2003) Emotional intelligence training and its implications for stress, health and performance, *Stress and Health*, **19**, 233–239.

Smilansky, S. (1968) *The Effects of Sociodramatic Play on Disadvantaged Preschool Children*, Wiley, New York.

Smith, P.K. (1988) Children's play and its role in early development: A reevaluation of the 'play ethos'. In *Psychological Bases of Early Education* (ed. Pelligrini, A.D.). Wiley, Chichester, pp. 207–226.

Smith, S.D., Pennington, B.F., Kimberling, W.J. and Ing, P.(1990) Familial dyslexia: Use of genetic linkage data to define subtypes. *Journal of the American Academy of Child and Adolescent Psychiatry*, **29**, 204–213.

Snarey, J.R. (1994) Cross-cultural universality of social-moral development: a critical review of Kohlbergian research. In *New Research in Moral Development. Moral Development: A Compendium* (ed. Puka, B.). Garland, New York, vol. 5, pp. 268–298.

Spangler, G. and Grossman, K.E. (1993) Biobehavioural organisation in securely and insecurely attached infants, *Child Development*, **64**, 1439–1450.

Spence, M. and Freeman, M. (1996) Newborn infants prefer the maternal low-pass filtered voice, but not the maternal whispered voice. *Infant Behaviour and Development*, **19**(2), 199–212.

Stern, D.N. (1985) *The Interpersonal World of the Infant: A View from Psychoanalysis and Developmental Psychology*, Basic Books, New York.

Sternberg, R.J. (1984) *Beyond IQ: A Triarchic Theory of Human Intelligence*, Cambridge University Press, New York.

Suomi, S.J. and Harlow, H. (1972) Social rehabilitation of isolate-reared monkeys. *Developmental Psychology*, **6**, 487–496.

Sutton, J., Smith, P.K. and Swettenham, J. (1999) Social cognition and bullying: Social inadequacy or skilled manipulation? *British Journal of Developmental Psychology*, **17**, 434–450.

Swanson, J. and Kinsbourne, M. (1980) Artificial colour and hyperactive children. In *Treatment of Hyperactive and Learning Disabled Children,* (eds Knights, R.H. and Bakker, D.J.) University Park Press, Baltimore MA.

Szatmari, P., Offord, D.R. and Boyle, M.H. (1989) Ontario child health study: Prevalence of attention deficit disorder with hyperactivity. *Journal of Child Psychology and Psychiatry*, **30**, 219–230.

Tajfel, H., Billig, M., Bundy, R.P. and Flament, C. (1971) Social categorisation and intergroup behaviour. *European Journal of Social Psychology*, **1**, 149–177.

Tamis-LeMonda, C.S., Bornstein, M.H., Cyphers, L., Toda, S. and Ogino, M. (1992) Language and play at one year: a comparison of toddlers and mothers in the United States and Japan. *International Journal of Behavioural Development*, **15**, 19–42.

Tanoue, Y., Oda, S., Asano, F. and Kawashima, K. (1988) Epidemiology of infantile autism in Southern Ibaraki, Japan: Differences in prevalence rates in birth cohorts. *Journal of Autism and Developmental Disorders*, **18**, 155–166.

Tassoni, P. and Hucker, K. (2000) *Planning Play and the Early Years* (Professional Development Series), Heinemann Educational, London.

Tassoni, P (2003) *Supporting Special Needs. Understanding Inclusion in the Early Years*, Heinemann Educational, Oxford.

Taylor, H.G. (1989) Learning disabilities. In: *Treatment of Childhood Disorders* (eds Marsh, E.J. and Barkley, R.A.). Guilford Press, New York.

Taylor, E. (1994) Syndromes of attention deficit and overactivity. In: *Child and Adolescent Psychiatry* (eds Rutter, M., Taylor, E. and Hersov, L.), Blackwell Scientific Publications, Oxford.

Thelen, E. and Spencer, J.P. (1998) Postural control during reaching in young infants: a dynamic systems approach. *Neuroscience and Biobehavioural Reviews,* **22**, 507–514.

Thomas, A. and Chess, S. (1977) *Temperament and Development,* Brunner/Mazel, New York.

Thomas, A. and Chess, S. (1984) Genesis and evaluation of behavioural disorders: From infancy to early adult life. *American Journal of Psychiatry,* **141**, 1–9.

Thompson, S.K. (1975) Gender labels and early sex role development, *Child Development,* **51**, 943–963.

Thorndike, E.L. (1920) Intelligence and its uses. *Harper's Magazine,* 140, 227–235.

Thurstone, L.L. (1938) Primary mental abilities. *Psychometric Monographs,* no. 1.

Tincoff, R. and Jusczyk, P.W. (1999) Some beginnings of word comprehension in 6-month-olds. *Psychological Science,* **10**, 172–175.

Vygotsky, L.S. (1962) *Thought and Language,* MIT Press, Cambridge MA.

Watson, J.B. (1913) Psychology as a behaviourist views it. *Psychological Review,* **20**, 158–177.

Watson, J.B. (1970) *Behaviourism,* W.W. Norton, New York. (Original work published 1924.)

Watson, J.B. and Rayner, R. (1920) Conditioned emotional reactions. *Journal of Experimental Psychology,* **3**, 1–14.

Wentzel, K.R. and Asher, S.R. (1995) The academic lives of neglected, rejected, popular and controversial children. *Child Development,* **66**, 754–763.

Wertsch, et al. (1980) cited in Durkin, K. (1995) *Developmental Social Psychology: from Infancy to Old Age,* Blackwell, Oxford.

Whitehead, M. (1999) *Supporting Language and Literacy Development in the Early Years,* Open University Press, Buckingham.

Whiting, B.B. and Whiting, J.M.W. (1975) *Children of Six Cultures,* Harvard University Press, Cambridge MA.

Whorf, B.L. (1956) *Language, Thought and Reality,* MIT Press, Cambridge MA.

Widom, C.S. (1989a) Does violence beget violence? A critical examination of the literature. *Psychological Bulletin,* **106**, 3–28.

Widom, C.S. (1989b) The cycle of violence. *Science,* **244**, 160–166.

Wing, L. (1976) *Early Childhood Autism,* Pergamon Press, Oxford.

Wishart, J.G. and Duffy, L. (1990) Instability of performance on cognitive tests in infants and young children with Down's syndrome. *British Journal of Educational Psychology,* **60**, 10–20.

Wong, B.Y.L. and Jones, W. (1982) Increasing metacomprehension in learning disabled and normally achieving students through self-questioning training. *Learning Disabilities Quarterly,* **5**, 228–240.

www.afasic.org.uk/

www.daycaretrust.org.uk

www.Down's-syndrome.org.uk/

www.dyslexia.uk.com/

www.nas.org.uk/

www.zerotothree.org/brainwonders

www.bda-dyslexia.org.uk/

Index